Blood,

Ink,

and

Culture

BLOOD,

INK,

AND

CULTURE

Miseries and Splendors of

the Post-Mexican Condition

ROGER BARTRA

Translated by

Mark Alan Healey

DUKE UNIVERSITY PRESS   DURHAM AND LONDON 2002

© 2002

Duke University Press

All rights reserved

Printed in the

United States of America

on acid-free paper ∞

Typeset in Trump Mediaeval

by Wilsted & Taylor

Publishing Services

Library of Congress

Cataloging-in-Publication

Data appear on the last

printed page of this book.

Contents

Preface

There is a culture of blood and a culture of ink. These two cultures confront each other and intertwine with each other. I would like to say we are leaving an age of blood behind, to enter into an age of ink, but there is little basis for such optimism. At best, we might think that the space of ink has spread considerably. In fact, it seems to me that—with ideologies in crisis—we can see a return, and perhaps a strengthening, of this tragic duality.

The culture of blood exalts identity, religious fidelity, revolutionary struggle, and the defense of the fatherland. The culture of ink praises the multiplicity of writing and drives its arguments home on printed paper, not on the battlefield. The culture of blood is stained with the red color of life, but it is willing to trade that life in, for the good of the class or the homeland. It contrasts with the blackness that stains the minimal arguments of writers, although sometimes the culture of ink exchanges its ideas for a plate of beans. To strengthen these metaphors, we could turn to the ancient Nahua's images of black and red ink *(tlilli, tlapalli)* in a legendary land, the country of wisdom. But even there, in the inks that the wise used to paint the codices, this unsettling duality made its appearance, confronting the dangerous mysteries of the night with the bloody forces of life.[1]

Obviously, the essays in this book are the result of drinking ink, as Shakespeare put it, and eating paper. Many writers and intellectuals have abandoned the old activism of the political culture of blood, and our texts sprinkle ink over the history pages that others would print with tides of violence. We no longer

1. On Nahua uses of red and black ink in codices, see Elizabeth Hill Boone, *Stories in Red and Black: Pictorial Histories of the Aztecs and Mixtecs* (Austin: University of Texas Press, 2000). [Trans.]

live in the region of the open veins, not because exploitation and misery have come to an end, but because we believe that not everything in this world is rivers and swamps of blood.[2] We are no longer pleased by the invocations of a revolutionary Eucharist that transforms the bread and wine of daily life into martyred bodies and sublime hemorrhages. Yet with the collapse of political dogma, part of the Left has unfortunately drawn closer to religious symbolism, feeding the broken idols of traditional orthodoxy with the blood of the suffering.

Back in the eighties, we could still describe cultural battles as a confrontation between what I called, using the mythology dreamed up by Julio Cortázar, the *"cronopy* of the *famas"* and the *"famistics* of the *cronopios."*[3] The division was between epicurean exuberance and chronicles of barbarism (also known as magical realism) on the one side and a refined serenity of gothic souls and iron-bound structuralism on the other. This opposition could divide, to put it crudely and schematically, Gabriel García Márquez or Carlos Fuentes from Jorge Luis Borges or Octavio Paz. By contrast, at century's end what is more dominant, it seems to me, is the opposition between the cultures of blood and ink, although that earlier duality has not disappeared. A series of events has set a new dynamic in motion: the collapse of socialism and the rise of ethno-religious regional conflicts; the erosion of authoritarianism and the expansion of democracy and globalization; the wars in Iraq and the former Yugoslavia. In Mexico the end of the millennium is marked by the rupture of 1988, the appearance of Zapatista guerrillas in 1994, and the terminal crisis of the authoritarian political system in 2000.

The images of blood and ink were imposed on me by the course of events, especially the Zapatista uprising in Chiapas. The Zapatista army threatened to wash the country in blood, but what it actually produced was a vast ink stain: fortunately, more letters than bullets came out of Chiapas. Since then, the metaphors about the battle between blood and ink have showered down on us. Some seemed to take their unsettling exclamations from the Koran: "If your enemies attack you, wash them in their own blood." Some of us replied: "Let's wash ourselves in the enemy's ink." That is to say: let's listen to others' arguments, let's learn to read inks of various colors, and let's dip our pens in pessimistic inks before we plunge them into the sanguine optimism of coagulated identities.

2. This is a reference to the sixties leftist classic by Eduardo Galeano, *Open Veins of Latin America: Five Centuries of the Pillage of a Continent*, trans. Cedric Belfrage (New York: Monthly Review Press, 1973). [Trans.]

3. The terms are drawn from Julio Cortázar, *Cronopios and Famas*, trans. Paul Blackburn (New York: Pantheon Books, 1969). Roughly speaking, *cronopios* are intuitive, effusive, spontaneous, expansive, temperamental, and disorganized; *famas* are rigorous, restrained, prudent, scientific, dispassionate, and ordered. [Trans.]

Of course, the exaltation of ink has its risks. Next to the learned stand a legion of pen pushers; the unpleasant experts in friendly inks conceal disputes; and multicolored plurality is often diluted into halftones of opportunism and incoherence. Once one sets out to sweat ink, the arduous labor of putting ideas down on paper often ends up producing blank pages. But a blank page after nights of sterile sleeplessness is far better than the fire-eating verbiage of bloody-minded politicians ready to bleed civil society dry in the slaughterhouse of the fatherland. I prefer a useless ink sucker to a bloodsucker who lives off the consanguine loyalties of political mafias. And even worse are those leeches of ethnic identity who call for battle against neoliberal vampires: the result is the atrocious war that tears Balkanized societies apart. All this is done in the name of the blood with which borderlines are drawn between cultures and religions, tongues and nations.

These essays revolve around themes of identity, intellectuals, and the political culture of the Left. They form part of larger polemics, and they welcome debate. They open with an essay offering a critique of the Mexican calling—that nationalist will to define Mexicanness—and its worship of blood. Another essay is articulated around irony, referring to the Zapatista movement as "Tropical Kitsch," that cloying form of the art of politics which takes advantage of the popular taste for sensationalism and sentimentalism. Since this essay was cooked up over seven years (1994–2001), it is soaked through with the debates it provoked or responded to. In one way or another, the essays gathered in this book critique the culture of blood: they celebrate the post-Mexican condition, they reject the wailing wall some want to substitute for the fallen Berlin Wall, they criticize nationalism, and they praise the Left—but as a democratic luxury, not a historical necessity. And they include, as a guide for the perplexed Left, some thoughts on how to escape from the hermeneutic cage.

In closing, I should confess that I have spilled a few drops of blood into the inkpot I dip my pen into. I have noticed that without those drops, the ink never dries. They say the same happens with those who invoke blood rights: if they don't mix the life-giving fluid with ink, it evaporates without leaving any trace. This mix, and others, are what keep hope alive.

Blood,

Ink,

and

Culture

I

BLOOD

AND

INK

The Mexican Office: Miseries
and Splendors of Culture

To hide its nakedness in times of want, Mexican "official culture" has sent its jewels and treasures to New York, the metropolis of the north.[1] It dreams of flaunting the splendors of its art before the stunned eyes of savage millionaires, to warm the cold industrial heart of the United States. And as ever, it aims to affirm its identity by confronting Anglo-American culture, attempting to shore up the waning legitimacy of the Mexican political system.[2]

This essay was written for a conference entitled "Mexico: Here and There" at Columbia University, organized as a critical response to the Metropolitan Museum of Art's 1990 exhibition "Mexico: Splendors of Thirty Centuries." An earlier translation of this essay by Coco Fusco was published in *Third Text*.

1. This essay is built around the ironic use of the terms "office" and "official culture" in ways slightly unfamiliar to American readers, so a few definitions may be in order. As Merriam-Webster reminds us, "office" refers not only to a place of business but also, and more importantly for our purposes, to "a special duty, charge or position," to "the proper or customary action of something," to "a religious or social ceremonial observance" (a rite), and to "a prescribed form or service of worship," such as the Divine Office, the "office for the canonical hours of prayer that priests and religious say daily." Bartra's notion of the Mexican Office refers to all of these dimensions, to the sacralized ritual practice of cultural arbiters within the Mexican state—"official culture"—setting out the canonical forms and norms of Mexicanness. In this sense, the Mexican Office could be seen as a calling, a vocation in the Weberian sense. The essay is broken up according to the hours of the Divine Office and closes with references to the policing power of the Mexican Office, which recall those of the Holy Office, better known as the Inquisition. [Trans.]
2. Out of the political struggle of the revolution (1910–1920) there emerged a single political party that has come to dominate the Mexican political system. First formed in 1928, it has been known since 1946 as the Institutional Revolutionary Party (Partido Revolucionario Institucional, or PRI). The central concern of this book is the formation of a complex web of relationships

Mexican "official culture" is showing the world thirty centuries of splendor. I would like to take this opportunity to reflect on how "official culture" is generated. The concept can be understood from two angles. First, as an ethnographer, I can confirm that there is a culture that emanates from the offices of government and saturates the exercise of authority. This is an ensemble of habits and values that mark the behavior of the Mexican political and bureaucratic class: this swarm of *licenciados* and leaders share customs and folklore worthy of being carefully cataloged to be stored away in museum vaults. Painters have already begun this task: in his celebrated painting *The Bone*, Covarrubias portrayed the typical Mexican functionary with extraordinary irony.[3]

Second, we find that those very same government offices issue a seal of approval for artistic and literary production, in order to restructure it according to established canons. This peculiar reconstruction also makes up part of what I call "official culture," but it should be clearly understood that this does not mean that the writers and artists themselves are the official spokespeople of government culture (although that is the case for a few). Nonetheless there is a close relationship between the folkways of government offices and the form the official reconstruction of Mexican culture takes: together they can be seen as the practice of a Mexican Office.

Just as there is a Divine Office that marks off the hours of the canonical day with prayers, psalms, and hymns, so there is a Mexican Office that marks off the days of the nation according to officially established canons. There is a Mexican Office that sings and tells of the national splendors. That Mexican Office is the "official culture" that stamps its *nihil obstat* on the works of time.[4] That Mexican Office is what decrees that Mexico has been resplendent for Thirty Centuries.

---

between the PRI, national culture, civil society, and the democratic opposition, and the transformation of this web during the prolonged political and economic breakdown of the eighties and nineties. Two useful overviews of modern Mexican history are Héctor Aguilar Camín and Lorenzo Meyer, *In the Shadow of the Mexican Revolution: Contemporary Mexican History, 1910–1989*, trans. Luis Alberto Fierro (Austin: University of Texas Press, 1993); and Michael C. Meyer and William H. Beezley, eds., *The Oxford History of Mexico* (New York: Oxford University Press, 2000). [Trans.]

3. Miguel Covarrubias (1904–1957) was a painter and exceptionally astute caricaturist who worked extensively in Mexico and the United States. See Adriana Williams, *Covarrubias*, ed. Doris Ober (Austin: University of Texas Press, 1994). [Trans.]

4. *Nihil obstat* was the stamp that the Holy Office placed on books indicating that they were safe for the faithful's consumption. [Trans.]

Matins

At the dawn of history, the Olmecs raise their strange and enormous heads to look upon us. In the tradition of the old counterpoint Roger Fry noted at the beginning of this century, those first Mexicans are there to remind us that modernity is born stained with primitiveness.[5] Those faces of primeval art are there so that we, modern Mexicans, can recognize ourselves in them and see reflected in their otherness the buried and hidden part of our national being. This is an old and well-known theme in art history, but in Mexico it was made useful again by the frantic search for "Mexicanness" that accompanied the postwar modernizing boom.

So the origins of contemporary Mexican art should be found on the coast of the Gulf of Mexico, not in the Mediterranean or the Middle East. Contrary to appearances, it has been decreed that our roots lie more in the figures of pre-Columbian codices than in the verses of the Old Testament. This is a cultural decision that fully makes sense only if we read history against the flow of time: it is from our here and now—from the perspective of the present-day Mexican state—that the Thirty Centuries of Mexican art have a unified meaning. Reasons of state, when applied to culture, become naturalized. Nature is the first element that gives unity and continuity to cultural history. Geography is turned into an immense living frame for history. The earth becomes a fertile mother in whose body the deep roots of national culture grow. According to this idea of nature, volcanoes, forests, valleys, lakes, flora, and fauna are no longer part of geography but have metamorphosed to become the anatomy of the living body of culture. That is why José María Velasco and Doctor Atl are considered indispensable elements of Mexican art: they are at the same time witnesses and creators of the palpitating landscape that defines the outline of the nation-state.[6]

I do not mean to say that the awareness of a certain *origin* and a *landscape* is simply an ideological formation created by the Mexican state to trick a dominated population. Cultural processes have a legitimating, homogenizing, and unifying effect, but not because they are mere "instruments" of the ruling classes. Even "official culture"—which *does* have an instrumental character—

---

5. Roger Fry, *Vision and Design* (London: Chatto and Windus, 1920).

6. José María Velasco (1840–1912) painted idealized landscapes of the Mexican countryside. Dr. Atl (born Gerardo Murillo, 1875–1964) was best known for his series of volcano paintings and his aerial landscapes. He also was an important intellectual ally of the victorious group in the Mexican Revolution, led by Venustiano Carranza, as well as being the designer of a monument to Carranza after he was assassinated. [Trans.]

cannot be explained except as a function of the complex process that feeds it, and that process is the creation of an articulated ensemble of myths about Mexican identity.

Despite Weber's claims, modern society has not ceased to generate myths. One of those myths is precisely the myth of national character. In Mexico that myth has crystallized into what I have playfully called the *axolotl* canon. That canon orders and classifies the features of Mexican character according to a basic duality: Mexicans are amphibious beings who shift between the rural savagery of melancholy Indians and the artificial and playful aggressiveness of urban *pelados*. In my book *The Cage of Melancholy*, I carry out an anatomical dissection of that mythical amphibious creature, Mexican national identity. The results of the operation may surprise many sociologists, because it shows that the rationality inherent to the unification of the modern state requires a mythological structure to give it legitimacy. There is no such thing as a purely rational legitimacy produced by capitalist economic structures and modern bureaucracy. The legitimacy of modern political systems generates a mythology capable of creating the "subject" of the capitalist state. That mythology is developed around the notion of national culture and, more specifically, around the conception of a national character.

Lauds

We can praise the first twenty-five centuries of Mexican splendor that represent the solitary primeval otherness without which national culture apparently could not exist. But our praise cannot create a continuity that was broken by conquest and colonization; ancient artistic traditions were annihilated within a few years. Still, some insist on speaking of a cultural continuity that would span a bridge over the abyss opened by the conquest, between pre-Hispanic Mesoamerica and colonial and independent Mexico.

We can recognize an intense search by twentieth-century Mexican artists for formal or spiritual values in pre-Hispanic cultures. What they found undoubtedly enriched their creations, but it is doubtful that it contributed to filling the immense void left by the destruction of ancient societies. "Official culture" has also taken a great leap across the centuries to search for the foundations of the modern state in ancient Mesoamerica.[7]

7. The archaeological excavation of the Templo Mayor, in the center of Mexico City, is an example of the use of spectacles to connect the present with pre-Columbian history.

Many consider it useless to look to history for the formal or stylistic continuation of pre-Columbian art into colonial or modern Mexico. The only real continuity is not usually accepted anywhere but in ethnographic museums: the millions of marginalized indigenous peoples are the only battered bridge left. They are a symbolic referent to the past, but they are usually rejected as an active presence.[8] In his introductory essay to the exposition catalog, *Mexico: Splendors of Thirty Centuries*, Octavio Paz indicates how the continuity problem has been resolved: all across an incredible variety of forms, we find the persistence of a single *will*, the will to survive in and through form. An attentive and loving look can perceive a continuity that is not manifest in either style or ideas, but in something deeper, in a sensibility.[9] This will for form is nothing more than the transposition of reasons of state onto the Mesoamerican past, an artistic past where the figure, the form, reveals the metamorphoses of a single will.

This game of transformations, of transfigurations, perfectly exemplifies an intellectual process that has been used frequently by modern nationalism and in theology is called figural interpretation. Elsewhere, I have already pointed out this curious phenomenon, which goes beyond the imaginative metaphorical relationships artists establish between distant epochs and distinct cultural spheres.[10] We are facing a delicate and complex process that manages to establish in collective consciousness a structural relationship between two unrelated cultural dimensions. This structural link operates on two planes simultaneously: as *mimesis* on one, and as *catharsis* on the other. Mimesis finds a similarity between ancient cultural features, for instance of the Mexica or the Maya, and colonial or modern history. I am not going to go into depth on this issue, but I would like to mention some of the themes in which this metahistorical link is usually found: sacrifice, guilt, cyclical events, baroque exuberance, dualism, the worship of the Virgin, et cetera. We find a transposition of current themes and conflicts onto a more or less imaginary past, where a prefiguration of the modern scene is to be found. This transposition onto an imagined past is similar to the one that takes place in modern mythology's reconstruction of the *Homo*

8. For decades, the political actions of the National Indigenous Institute have been an example of the strange combination of an official policy of exalting "deep Mexico" with a governmental practice of burying the indigenous people progressively deeper in the mud of modern society.

9. Octavio Paz, "The Will for Form," in *Mexico: Splendors of Thirty Centuries* (New York: Metropolitan Museum, 1990), 4.

10. Roger Bartra, *The Cage of Melancholy: Identity and Metamorphosis in the Mexican Character*, trans. Christopher J. Hall (New Brunswick: Rutgers University Press, 1992).

mexicanus, an android whose anatomy must be examined because it will give us the keys to what I call the institutionalization of the national soul. A line reaches from the stooping Indian to the mestizo pelado, passing through the major points of articulation of the Mexican soul: *melancholy–idleness–fatalism–inferiority / violence–sentimentalism–resentment–escapism.* This line marks the voyage the Mexican must undertake to find himself, from the original Eden of nature to the industrial apocalypse.

Prime

The spectacle of this cultural simulacrum allows us to indicate the importance of the other plane, that of catharsis, in the link between real and imaginary dimensions. The stage set of national culture is a space where the feelings of the people can be released. That is where nationalism can achieve its greatest effectiveness, by managing to identify politics with culture.

Nationalism is the transfiguration of the supposed characteristics of national identity onto the terrain of ideology. Nationalism is a political tendency that establishes a structural relationship between the nature of culture and the peculiarities of the state. In our country the official expressions of nationalism tell us: If you are Mexican, you must vote for the institutionalized revolution. Those who do not either are traitors to their deepest essence or are not Mexican. Nationalism is, then, an ideology that disguises itself with culture to hide its intimate means of domination. But for this identification of politics with culture to be successful, a process of sedimentation must have taken place already, separating elements socially held to be national from those that are not specifically held to be so. This is a complex process that cannot be produced artificially. That is to say, neither the state nor the ruling class can direct this process from above. This is a global process shaped by the interplay of several factors, including the very formation of the national state. On the basis of this process, the ruling class may be able to establish its cultural hegemony by using a nationalist ideology. But this is not the only way in which a social class can gain hegemony. I would say that the nationalist path is one of the most dangerous ways for achieving it and can lead—as it has in Mexico—to the institutionalization of a pernicious authoritarian system. And this system is all the more pernicious when nationalism produces a collective catharsis, through which it legitimates one way of doing politics as the only way of being Mexican.

Terce

We live in the age of the collapse of great ideological blocs, and because of that, cultural critique becomes more important every day. There are different ways of conceiving of cultural critique. In Mexico it has been common to offer a critique from the perspective of nineteenth-century rationalism, that is, from the perspective of modernity, which says that it is crucial to "modernize" Mexican culture to adapt it to the needs of industrialization and mass society. This approach quickly leads to a dilemma: should we remake national culture along the lines of "true" popular culture, or should we accept the transnationalizing invasion of the new mass culture? But this dilemma is soon revealed to be a false one. It is false because our present-day national culture is precisely the amalgam of these two options, which are therefore complementary. With this I mean to say that the modernization of Mexican culture has already taken place. What I call the exercise of the Mexican Office is precisely the result of the modernization of national culture, and not some archaic and premodern leftover that must be redirected, or even destroyed, to open the way to modern culture.

What I am critiquing is precisely the modernity of national culture. It is its modernity that oppresses us, since that is where the authoritarianism that characterizes the Mexican system came from. Our choice at present is therefore not between a populist option or a transnational proposal: we need only turn on Mexican television to realize that hegemonic culture has already managed to overcome that contradiction, by imposing on us a deeply jingoistic culture that is aggressively aligned with U.S.-produced mass culture. By approaching these problems from the perspective of postmodernity, I am suggesting that the dividing lines have shifted and the contradictions have been displaced onto new terrain. We can no longer critique Mexican culture in the name of modernity, of a liberal-inspired modernity that raises up the banner of "progress." We have to critique modernity from the standpoint I call dismodernity, or better yet—taking a cue from *desmadre*, Mexican slang for disorder—*dismothernity*.[11]

Sext

These observations lead us to conclude that we should distinguish between three phenomena: national identity, political culture, and official cultural policy. In examining the relationship between these three, we see that this is a mat-

---

11. *Desmadre* is slang for excess, chaos, disorder, and *madre* means mother. [Trans.]

ter of the ties between the formation of a myth (identity), its insertion into institutional life (political culture), and the ideology that attempts to explain and
direct the process (official culture).

The myth of national identity is not a merely ideological phenomenon manipulated by the ruling class or the government. For the myth to be incorporated
into political culture in what we might call a "natural" and lasting way, several
conditions are necessary, which it would be excessive to explain fully here. Suffice it to say that this is a matter of the accumulation of a series of historical moments through which various elements are transfigured and transposed until
political culture becomes relatively homogeneous and coherent. For its part,
government cultural policy is an ideological practice that, in addition to many
other tasks, uses cultural expression to legitimate the system. An example: the
circulation of Mexican culture defines the officially national space, yet official
cultural policy only slightly modifies the constitution of Mexican political culture. *Fotonovelas*, commercial television, comics, commercial music, detective
novels, popular best-sellers, and romance or pornographic novels continue to exercise enormous influence. No matter how much they are denounced as "foreign," they still form an integral part of Mexican political culture. On the other
hand, the myth of the "Mexican soul" has managed not only to successfully survive the avalanche of "foreign" influences but to stake out a lasting place in political culture.[12]

The "Mexican soul" has held a stable place in political culture precisely because it appears as something non-Western. The myth of Mexican being has contributed to the legitimation of the political system, but it has taken on a mythical form hardly consistent with the Western capitalist development typical
of the twentieth century's end. Of course, if one wishes to see it this way, the
myth did correspond to the peculiarities of a backward, corrupt, and dependent
capitalism. Hence the contradictions contemporary Mexican culture is living
through: the myth of national identity is becoming dysfunctional. But this dysfunctionality comes in great measure from its "popular" and "anticapitalist"
origins. The myth stores up a good dose of protest, bitterness, revolt, and resistance: this circumstance explains the popularity of the stereotype of the
Mexican.

12. On mass culture in modern Mexico, see Eric Zolov, *Refried Elvis: The Rise of the Mexican
Counterculture* (Berkeley: University of California Press, 1999); and Anne Rubinstein, "Mass
Media and Popular Culture in the Postrevolutionary Era," in Meyer and Beezley, *The Oxford
History of Mexico*, 637–70. [Trans.]

None

The idea of the boundary, the tear, or the border is an important ingredient in the constitution of national identity. In Mexico this should be understood in at least two senses. First, as an inner tear or wound: Mexicanness split between the destroyed ancient autochthonous world and the colonial, Christian, and modern world. Second, as the great border dividing Mexico from the potentially hostile territory of Anglo-American culture. Without any doubt, confrontation with the northern Other has spurred the definition of Mexican identity. But here we come across a pious medieval Christian idea: one had to go to the land of the Moors, one had to undergo temptation and suffering, to reaffirm the faith. The border is a permanent danger. The border is a constant source of contamination and threats to Mexican nationality. The mere existence of the border is what permits nationalist passions to remain tense. It permits, we might say, a permanent state of alert against outside threats. Clearly this functions mostly on a symbolic level, since the demographic reality of the thousands of Mexicans who come and go across the border (more going than coming) generates a sociocultural process of *mestizaje* and symbiosis that no nationalist discourse could bring to an end.

Although this dialectic between Self and Other has been important, we should also recognize that the very long border has also been a wide space of interaction. From a cultural perspective, I do not think that we should be alarmed by what happens on the border. What is usually called the "Americanization" of border life is not a particularly damaging and threatening process. As an anthropologist, I cannot conceive of a border territory between two cultures in which transculturation processes do not take place. Any attempt to block this would be utopian at best. Some in the United States are also alarmed by the "Mexicanization" of border life: they have the same conservative and reactionary impulses as Mexican chauvinists.

This does not mean that there are no problems on the border. But for the most part, these are political problems of the relationship between two states. One is a very rich state headed by imperialist governments, and the other a very poor state monopolized by authoritarian governments. A mechanical transposition of political problems onto the territory of culture will only manage to deform our understanding of an extraordinarily complex situation.

Every Mexican (and Latin American) who has lived in the United States knows that Latin America does not end at the Río Bravo: the Latin continent has penetrated deeply into the Anglo-American sociocultural world. Within the United States, the "Hispanic" sector of society, economy, politics, and culture is enormous and exercises notable pressure on the American system. Mexican nationalism has traditionally refused to recognize this fact, since this "Mexicanization" of life in the United States is usually seen instead from a different perspective, as the "Americanization" of Mexicans. As they say, some see the glass half empty, some see it half full.

Vespers

On the eve of a new era that will lead us who knows where, Mexican culture is experiencing tensions that are tearing it apart.[13] The Thirty Centuries of Splendor fall on the heads of Mexican writers and artists like a bewildering avalanche. Yet all around us there is nothing to be seen but an eternal present, collapsed onto itself. It seems as if our cultural context was put up yesterday and is on the verge of falling down. In our everyday cultural landscape—as in our urban surroundings—the past barely exists, and we live in the fragility of a dream that ends each morning when we awaken to a miserable and backward reality. An armor-plated aesthetic of willful resplendence chases after cultural creators and hides from them the dark side of the myth. They are compelled to express an identity that is not theirs; they are forced into a millennial originality that they do not understand. Everyone must create bleeding from the same wound, aching from the same border, or from the same fracture. Everyone must be a native of one and the same landscape, and suffer in the same way from that geography.

On the eve of a drab financial battle that should open up to Mexico the doors of the mercantile paradise of the northern powers, official culture has adapted Napoleon's famous speech to the present day: Soldiers of culture, from the heights of these pyramids Thirty Centuries are watching you! This adaptation has ten centuries fewer than those that watched over Bonaparte in Egypt in 1798, since it did not seem wise to mention the barbarism of descendants who are all too close to Tepexpan man.[14] This triumphalist vision of Mexican cultural history seems to follow the old recipes of Orientalism, which often concentrated the entire history of non-Western peoples into great packages of shining exoticism. This is a service in praise of museum culture, composed of the cumulative sum of great blocks built into monuments of pyramidal splendor in which the

13. The "eves" at the opening of these two paragraphs are plays on the timing of vespers, prayed at evening each day, with the coming of dusk. [Trans.]

14. Napoleon had spoken of a distance of thirty centuries between the builders of the pyramids and his soldiers; the distance from Tepexpan man to present-day Mexico would be more like forty centuries.

nuances of individual creation are lost, smothered by the mass of symbols: jaguars, eagles, baroque angels, violently colored tropics, inflamed revolutionaries, and long-suffering women. In the cracks of these great granite symbols, living intellectuals are often smothered, intellectuals who inhabit a world whose new signs they have not yet learned to decode. So writers and artists run the risk of ending up trapped in the solitude of a dense jungle of national symbols or embarked on a war against words, in an effort to lead those words toward the triumphant splendor of the signs of identity like a flock of sheep.

Compline

The canonical hours of national identity are complete. The circle of immanence has closed, the Office has reached its end, and we have had our fill. Nationalism has invented a Mexican who is the very metaphor of permanent underdevelopment, the image of blocked progress. This devalued being only makes sense inside the networks of official political power. He or she is a being who lives on thanks to the state. This individual is seen as an incomplete larval being whose metamorphosis can take place only in the bosom of the revolutionary state.

But the revolutionary state is coming to an end, and this Mexican Office is becoming an office for the dead. It is not modernization that brings on its extinction, but postmodernity, that is to say, the tensions provoked by an excess of modernity in a context of weak modernization. Here I am making use, hopefully not in an abusive way, of the literary notion of modernism, translated into political theory. Modernity is a revolt against the rigidity of the old oligarchic order in search of political forms that are free although they are circumscribed and unified by national symbolic and imaginary structures. Thus modernity is a specific form adopted by civil society, a structure of cultural mediations that legitimates the political system. Modernization is, according to the usual sociological terminology, the capitalist transformation of society, based on industry, science, and secular institutions. Modernity is the imaginary country whose legitimating networks trap civil society. Modernization is the actual state of capitalist economic and social development.

In Mexico we have had an excess of modernity, so much that its weight has become unbearable: national identity in excess, exorbitant nationalism, revolution beyond measure, abuses of institutionality, a surplus of symbolism . . . We have put up with just sixty years of institutionalized modernity, but it seems like thirty centuries! By contrast, as the crisis that began in 1982 has revealed, our modernization is weak and flawed in many ways. The country is crammed full of modernity, but thirsty for modernization. This is the unpleasant paradox: behind the "Splendors of *Thirsty* Centuries" we discover the "Miseries of Thirty Centuries."

Even with all its bitterness, postmodernity has nonetheless brought us the hope of escaping these smothering metadiscourses. The experience of a fragmented Mexico—the Mexico of "Here and There"—and the constant transgression of all borders, political and cultural, is one of the most stimulating signs of recent years. Far from closing off the creative impulses of Mexican intelligence, this lived experience has on the contrary opened up new vistas. One the most refreshing effects of what Guillermo Gómez-Peña has called the "borderization" of the world is proof that it is possible, we could say, to be Mexican without being subject to a state and a territory.[15] That deterritorialization and destatification of intellectuals is beginning to shape the outlines of postmodern society. We don't know where this trail will lead, but let's hope the only possible future of cultural life is not on a pedestal under glass in a museum.

15. See Guillermo Gómez-Peña, *Warrior for Gringostroika: Essays, Performance Texts, and Poetry* (St. Paul, Minn.: Graywolf Press, 1993).

Tropical Kitsch in Blood and Ink

Mexico is living through a profound fin de siècle malaise, an unease that I think might appropriately be described as an attempt to escape from its cage of melancholy. The war in Chiapas and its dramatic results have shaken the Mexican cage with an intensity we had not seen in a quarter century.[1] Many things about these events are surprising, but I would like to linger over one aspect that I find especially revealing: why did only ten days of war so radically

This essay is the product of several years of reflections about the Zapatista uprising in Chiapas. The first section appeared in embryonic form in 1994 as an essay entitled "Kitsch tropical y elecciones"; a version of the second section was published in 1996 as "La tentación fundamentalista y el síndrome de Jezabel"; a version of the third section was published in 1997 as "Violencias indígenas"; all these sections and the fourth, "Moby-Dick in the Lacandon Jungle," were included in my 1999 book *La sangre y la tinta*. The postscript is published here for the first time.

1. Twenty-five years before, the Mexican cage was shaken by the emergence, suppression, and aftermath of the 1968 student movement. The crisis of 1994 began with the uprising by the Zapatista Army of National Liberation (Ejército Zapatista de Liberación Nacional, EZLN), was deepened by the assassination of two leading PRI officials—including the presidential candidate—and reached its culmination with the sudden devaluation that came shortly after President Salinas left office late in the year, erasing the economic "progress" made during his administration. For an overall account of the 1994 crisis written shortly afterward, see Jorge G. Castañeda, *The Mexican Shock: Its Meaning for the United States* (New York: New Press, 1995). The writings of the EZLN leader have been published as Subcomandante Marcos, *Our Word Is Our Weapon: Selected Writings*, ed. Juana Ponce de León (New York: Seven Stories Press, 2001). A wave of writings about the EZLN and Chiapas has appeared since the uprising; the two most useful and authoritative works in English are Neil Harvey, *The Chiapas Rebellion: The Struggle for Land and Democracy* (Durham: Duke University Press, 1998); and John Womack Jr., ed. and trans., *Rebellion in Chiapas: An Historical Reader* (New York: New Press, 1999). [Trans.]

change the rhythms of Mexican political culture? What powerful force compelled the government to open up toward a democratic transition? What managed to convince and captivate such a large part of civil society and intellectuals? What was it that filled Mexican society with dark humors and tensions?

Violence and Melancholy in Fin de Siècle Mexico

To answer these questions, even superficially, I find it suggestive to look at the problem as a medieval doctor would.[2] If Mexican culture has been struck by a melancholy fin de siècle malady, we might suspect that this curious postrevolutionary disease is a morbid condition of a society that, immersed in the drab coldness of the daily routine of building a modern economy that never quite manages to come together, mourns the loss of its wild primordial state. What I want to ask is this: Is Mexican melancholy a disease of the heart or a disturbance of the mind? Is this a cultural malady or a political ailment? Is this a matter of moral delirium or ideological disturbance? My answer is that we are looking at a malaise of the cultural heart of Mexican society that also has produced a fin de siècle political syndrome, that is to say, symptoms of the critical extinction of the authoritarian political system. If we look at the ideological and political dimensions of the problem, we notice that those dark humors looming on the cultural horizon have made themselves evident in a crisis of nationalism, a demand for democracy, and a search for new forms of identity, as well as in many other ways.

Mexico reaches the end of the century feeling a sharp moral discontent in the deepest strata of its culture. What I mean is that Mexico finds itself, along with other Third World nations, facing an intricate and tragic *problem of civilization*, not simply a *problem of development*. Besides being a political problem, Mexican melancholy is also, and above all, a sign of a sharp cultural crisis. The ailment affects Mexico's "heart of darkness" more than its mental machinery, so Joseph Conrad can light our way through this juncture better than Keynes or Marx. The heart of darkness is an excellent metaphor, for it points to the internal knot in Latin American societies that binds wild original solitude to the anxieties brought on by the ills of civilization and modernity. The heart of darkness that Conrad explored is a symbol of all those nonrational ingredients clustered around the cultural constitution of the Western world. I use the metaphor to re-

2. An early version of my ideas about Mexican maladies can be found in my 1991 essay "Mexican Heart of Darkness," in Elizabeth Sussman, ed., *El Corazón Sangrante = The Bleeding Heart* (Boston: Institute of Contemporary Art and University of Washington Press, 1991).

fer to the set of imaginary mediating networks that ensure the cohesion and identity of any social system. A deep discontent is running through that knot of networks. This critical situation has been exacerbated by the grand global transition begun in late 1989, which has brought the Cold War and bipolarity to an end and led us into an uncertain and unclear twenty-first century.

These considerations shed some light on the surprising reaction of Mexican society and government to the events in Chiapas. The uprising takes place in 1994, at the very heart of the melancholy Lacandon rain forest, and its protagonists are indigenous peasants possessed of a tenacious rancor at the longstanding wrongs they have suffered. On the early morning of 1 January, several hundred indigenous peasants, grouped in the Zapatista Army of National Liberation (EZLN, for its initials in Spanish), seize the city of San Cristóbal de las Casas and the county seats of Las Margaritas, Altamirano, and Ocosingo. Tourists, journalists, and passersby talk to the rebels. They take their pictures. The army makes no appearance in San Cristóbal. The conflicts are not very bloody: there are reports of one man wounded in San Cristóbal, and a few policemen killed or wounded in Ocosingo. To everyone's shock, the Chiapas rebels propose to march on Mexico City to overthrow the president of the republic.

A sudden cardiac arrest strikes the Mexican heart of darkness. That is why the indigenous rebels quickly win the sympathy of independent intellectuals and a large portion of national and international public opinion. "We are the product of five hundred years of struggle," they state in their "Declaration from the Lacandon Jungle." "Today we say: enough!" They lay claim to Article 39 of the Constitution, which guarantees the people's right to alter or modify the form of government. Based on this, they issue a "declaration of war" on the Mexican army and ask other powers of the nation to restore legality and stability "by deposing the dictator." They ask international organizations and the Red Cross to monitor combat. They declare themselves subject to "the Geneva Convention laws on war" and therefore declare themselves to be a "belligerent force."

From San Cristóbal, Subcomandante Marcos announces that the uprising is a response to the implementation of NAFTA, which is a "death certificate for the indigenous peoples of Mexico." And he warns that "this is not the classic guerrilla army that steals, kidnaps and deals spectacular blows . . . this is not the classic blow of guerrillas who strike and flee, but of those who strike and advance."

For its part, the government stutters and sputters. It grabs hold of the traditional explanation: "The region suffers from a serious historical setback which has not been completely compensated." It adopts a "prudent" attitude. On 2 January, by surprise, the rebels withdraw from San Cristóbal but attack the neighboring military barracks. That same day, the bishops of Chiapas warn that this is an "unprecedented" phenomenon and negotiation is necessary. During the following days, the army responds, combat is joined, and there is shelling on the outskirts of San Cristóbal. Independent intellectuals, the bishop of San Cristóbal, the leftist opposition, and various NGOs call for a cease-fire and amnesty.

After ten days of fighting, the government accepts these proposals. It realizes that this certainly is an unprecedented situation and that the movement, far from falling back, is advancing. After trying out its traditional response—repression—the government suddenly reverses position, decrees a cease-fire, and opens the door to negotiations. At that moment, the doctors of the system do not understand the nature of the illness, nor do they foresee the official reversal in time. They attack the disease with cures that are far from conciliatory. Octavio Paz denounces the presence of infiltrators. He forcefully declares that "the uprising is unreal and condemned to fail" and that military resolution will come quickly, since the army will promptly reestablish order in Chiapas. "The movement lacks an ideological foundation, and in military matters, strategic thinking," Paz says. He adds, "the archaic feel of their ideology is also noteworthy—these are the simplistic ideas of people who live in a different time from ours."[3] His disdain for the melancholy voices coming out of the primeval forest is evident. Indians might be useful when one wishes to spill ink about Mexican identity, but they are also archaic and dangerous beings who might cause blood to be spilled. A little while later, another modern doctor, an "expert" in agrarian and indigenous issues, sets out the ideological basis for repressive action. "This is not an indigenous movement," Arturo Warman concludes, "it is a politico-military project implanted among the Indians without representing them."[4] Along these same lines, others go so far as to assert that the problems of Chiapas are an extension and penetration of Central American conflicts into a modern, North American Mexico.

But Mexican civil society takes a different view, largely supported by the international public, forcing the government to undertake a process of democratic transition. So Secretary of Government Patrocinio González Garrido is relieved of his post, a cease-fire is declared, amnesty is proposed, and Manuel Camacho

3. "El nudo de Chiapas," *La Jornada,* 5 January 1994.

4. "Chiapas hoy," *La Jornada,* 16 January 1994. Ironically, Arturo Warman is best known for his sophisticated and sympathetic earlier study of the original Zapatistas (of the Mexican Revolution): *"We come to object": The Peasants of Morelos and the National State,* trans. Stephen K. Ault (Baltimore: Johns Hopkins University Press, 1980). This dramatic shift is symptomatic of the larger aporias of revolutionary nationalism, a movement founded by some of Zapata's killers that made him into a saint. [Trans.]

Solís is named peace commissioner. For its part, the EZLN makes known its conditions for opening a dialogue. The peace commissioner begins the task of pacification, declaring that he is looking for a truce and not extermination. A significant part of Mexican society is beginning to doubt whether revolutionary nationalism—for decades, the hegemonic official ideology—is still one of the bases of the Mexican system. The problem is not merely the cracking of the ideological foundations of the official party. Indeed, far from being damaging, that helps the democratic transition along. A much thornier problem is the breaking of the chains that tied the very existence of the Mexican state to the nationalist political culture that is now in crisis. If, in some way, much of the population came to be convinced that their Mexicanness was proved and reflected by the peculiarities of their system of government, then we should not be surprised that for many Mexicans the political crisis meant that national reality was falling apart.

The tensions of Chiapas affect the networks that define national identity. A group of indigenous peasants suddenly appear and throw the whole system in doubt: they wear masks, they lack names, and they can't speak Spanish well—but they know how to dialogue. They are flexible and intelligent, plus they are armed and seem willing to die. They are a strange detonating mix, a cocktail that sparks an explosion of tropical kitsch, placing the very assumptions of modernity in question.[5] They are an expression of our postmodernity. With their mix of revolutionary schlock and critical intelligence, of populist holiness and political creativity, they have defeated the pro-government rhetoric of the official intelligentsia, like Octavio Paz himself, who confessed that he was honestly moved by a letter from Subcomandante Marcos, the charismatic spokesman for the rebels, rejecting the government's offer of pardon.[6] The uprising produced extraordinary effects: it opened the way to a democratic transition. But that opening soon sparked violent reactions from the forces within the system that reject change—the most malign of which was the assassination of PRI presidential candidate Luis Donaldo Colosio.[7]

The immense and surprising consequences of the Chiapas uprising are largely explained by the fact that we are passing through a period of fundamentally cultural unease, although it is true that we are also experiencing an ideological cri-

---

5. I'm not using kitsch in a negative sense, although I'm certainly making use of its ironic charge. I like the attractive complexity of things kitsch described by Celeste Olalquiaga in her magnificent book, *The Artificial Kingdom: A Treasury of the Kitsch Experience* (New York: Pantheon, 1998).

6. "Chiapas ¿nudo ciego o tabla de salvación?" *La Jornada*, 23 January 1994.

7. For a general account of the 1994 crisis, see Castañeda, *The Mexican Shock*. [Trans.]

sis, a crisis of revolutionary nationalism. Nationalism is the transfiguration of the supposed characteristics of national identity onto the terrain of ideology. Nationalism is a political tendency that sets up a structural relationship between the nature of culture and the peculiarities of the state. In Mexico, the official voices of nationalism tell us: If you are Mexican, you must vote for the PRI. Whoever does not do so is either betraying his or her deepest nature or is not a Mexican at all. But it turns out that in Chiapas, according to official figures, the immense majority of the population does vote for the PRI. So the uprising must be explained by outside factors.

This explanation could not withstand the blows of an indigenous uprising that unexpectedly shook the foundations of national identity. The culture of mestizaje as the mediating solution for conflict has been shattered. In Mexico, mestizaje is presented not only as the union of races and cultures, of Indians and Europeans, but also as the blending of the rural world and the industrial world, of development and underdevelopment. But I must forcefully point out that however much we criticize it, mestizaje as a social ideal is vastly more democratic and developed than the model that governs ethnic and racial differences in the United States. In a multicultural society like the United States, the absence of any notion of mixture is a consequence of the widespread racism and exaggerated Anglo-centrism characteristic of the hegemonic culture.

The indigenous uprising in Chiapas touches the most sensitive nerves affected by the deep discontent in Mexican culture—to continue with the Freudian metaphor (of civilization and its discontents). It has brought a great mass of Mexicans face-to-face with the possibility of leaving their assigned role as domesticated barbarians behind. What is most surprising is that this cultural shock was provoked by the unexpected intervention of the very domesticated barbarians—the Maya Indians of Chiapas—who were not invited to the banquet of North American modernity. With their abrupt intervention, they made it evident that the culture of duality has come to an end: the theater of the institutional revolutionary or the semi-Oriental mestizo has openly gone bankrupt. Mexican political culture is passing through the traumatic but unavoidable experience of entering without duplicity into the world of Western democracy. In a certain way, we could say this is already a fait accompli: the conquest, the war for independence, and the revolution have already integrated the country into Western culture. Yet that integration produced a revolutionary nationalism that attempted to exalt Mexican culture but instead led it into an implicit acceptance of its semi-Western condition, stained by officious mixtures, doublings, and twists. What is bleeding out of this wound is the heart of darkness of Mexican culture: the mythical and primeval core whose beating is about to cease.

The Indians have showed up to give the cocky technocrats who were piloting the ship of Mexican authoritarianism a lesson in modernity (and even in post-modernity). They have placed national identity and the legitimacy of the political system in doubt. They have shown civil society that the myth of Mexicanness that helped to legitimate the postrevolutionary government was set up in a way hardly consistent with the Western capitalist development characteristic of the century's end. In other words, the myth has been effective at legitimating PRI power but ineffective at legitimating the rationality of factories and NAFTA. The myth is locked into a cage of melancholy, not the iron cage that Max Weber saw as the disenchantment of modern society.[8]

Democracy, the Left, and Zapatismo

The Zapatista rebellion poses an unsettling question: can democracy grow today in the vast spaces once inhabited by the socialist and communist Left? Or has that territory perhaps become so sterile that we cannot envision the development of democracy there in the near future? I won't make more than passing reference to the problem of building democratic systems in countries formerly controlled by communist parties. But without losing sight of that global background, I want to briefly reflect on the democratic challenges for Mexico, where the unusual combination of the neo-Zapatista revolutionary uprising in 1994 and the persistence of the authoritarian system of government has given much food for thought.

The combination is unusual but revealing. It shows us that the opposition between emerging capitalist democracy and decadent authoritarian socialism is a model that does not always correspond to reality. In Mexico the traditional administrators of capitalism are anything but democratic. And the forces of the Left suffer from many ills and lacks, but they harbor a persistent vocation for democracy. This inversion of the traditional canon—which is valid for describing the political spectrum in Russia or other formerly socialist countries—is one of the keys to understanding the great vitality of the Mexican Left, even during this dark period for socialism.[9] I think a similar inversion helps us to understand the

8. See my book *The Cage of Melancholy.*

9. A democratic challenge to the PRI emerged in 1988 from within the party itself, headed up by Cuauhtémoc Cárdenas (b. 1934), the former governor of Michoacán and son of former president Lázaro Cárdenas (1895–1970). Incorporating a broad swath of the independent Left along with dissident elements of the official party, the Cárdenas campaign posed the most serious threat to the PRI in a half century. Widespread fraud by the PRI machine secured the 6 July 1988 election

dynamism we can see in movements of the Left in Brazil or Italy (in contrast with what is happening in, say, Argentina or Spain).

One cannot help but admire and wonder at the extraordinary democratic tolerance of the organized Left in Mexico, which has paid for its oppositional calling with hundreds of assassinations. If the PRI government did not bring us to the verge of a broad, violent confrontation, that peaceful outcome was thanks not to government technocrats but rather to the leaders of the Left, and especially of the Democratic Revolutionary Party, who were able to resist the authoritarian temptation even at the cost of losing electoral ground to the skillful opportunism of the right-wing National Action Party (Partido Acción Nacional, or PAN).[10]

When I speak of the authoritarian temptation, I am referring, in this case, to the appeal of revolutionary and violent forms of struggle against established power. Even those who gave in to this temptation—the members of the EZLN —later proved not to be driven by a hard core of purist ideology. Surprisingly enough, they revealed a sophisticated openness to different options and a creative plasticity able to rapidly adapt itself to the great complexity of this political moment in Mexico. That is why, paradoxically, one of the first effects of the Chiapas uprising of 1 January 1994 was to write the democratic question into the political agenda with indelible ink.

I do not want to tell the history of the slow and troubled process of democratic transition here. What I want to point out are some less visible tendencies that also accelerated in 1994. I am referring to the emergence of fundamentalist options and what I have called the "Jezebel syndrome."

Despite the evident dynamism of the Mexican Left, the new situation at this moment in Chiapas has also spurred the emergence of fundamentalist tendencies. Staring into the abyss left behind by the collapse of the socialism in the former Soviet Union and Central Europe, many have felt vertigo and looked to old metadiscourses for a life raft, so as not to drown in the postmodern flood. One of

---

for the official candidate, Carlos Salinas de Gortari, but afterward the dissidents founded a new organization, the Democratic Revolutionary Party (Partido Revolucionario Democrático, or PRD). On the 1988 election and allegations of fraud, see Jorge G. Castañeda, *Perpetuating Power: How Mexican Presidents Were Chosen,* trans. Padraic Arthur Smithies (New York: New Press, 2000). On the founding of the PRD, see Kathleen Bruhn, *Taking on Goliath: The Emergence of a New Left Party and the Struggle for Democracy in Mexico* (University Park: Pennsylvania State University Press, 1997). [Trans.]

10. Both greatly expanded their influence in these years of more open elections, culminating in the PRD's winning the mayoralty of Mexico City in 1997—it had previously been an appointed position—and the PAN's winning the presidency of Mexico in 2000. [Trans.]

these old ideas is autonomy, or the possibility that communities or regions with a high percentage of indigenous inhabitants be ruled by their own forms of government, adapted to their own ethnic particularities. Dragged out of the dusty Soviet chest by the Left (even though the various levels of autonomy have been revealed to be one of the greatest fiascoes of the socialist regime), this notion has clearly received the blessing of various sectors of the government who understand that indigenist policies aimed at integration have reached a dead end. The creation of autonomous communities according to "customs and mores" is a patrimonialist solution—in the sense Weber gives to the word—that guarantees power to a specific segment of the population.

We should recognize that it was not only in the former Soviet Union that experiments in autonomy of a patrimonial bent were carried out. I would like to remind readers that in the United States, after the failure of the distribution of small landholdings on Indian reservations, legislation was passed in 1934 that promoted forms of self-government combining traditional mechanisms with modern legislative methods. In Mexico at the same time, the government of Lázaro Cárdenas followed a nationalist and integrationist policy and produced a radically different "solution" to the indigenous problem than that of the United States, oriented toward praising mestizaje and national unity. We know the defects and virtues of this model all too well. But in making the comparison, we run into a strange paradox: despite everything, the Mexican integrationist path is more in keeping with the requirements of representative democracy than the segregationist U.S. alternative, which has obstructed or paralyzed many channels of democratic expression through a corrupt system of protection and patronage. This system has been extended to the government's ties with all kinds of ethnic, religious, racial, and sexual minorities, and it is one of the most important components of postdemocratic forms of political legitimation.

I find it symptomatic that in Mexico there should be attempts to establish postdemocratic mechanisms of legitimation, trying to push political parties aside, when we have not even managed to make modern representative democratic processes function adequately. And it is tragic and paradoxical that this happens with the encouragement and enthusiastic blessing of the Left.

Fundamentalist impulses have also promoted the legitimation of rigid hierarchies of a clerical and military nature. This has brought back the dogmatic values proper to sacred spaces: instead of witnessing a secularization of civil society (and politics), we are in many cases seeing its sacralization. We cannot close our eyes to the situation in Chiapas: it is the expanding focal point of this revalorization of clerical and military authorities, both in their rebellious versions (the diocese of San Cristóbal and the EZLN) and in their institutional manifestations (the Catholic Church and the Federal Army). We should add the proliferation of non-Catholic religious organizations and the expansion of reactionary paramilitary groups. We can observe a certain complementarity, although not without contradictions, between marginal spaces and official ones in this process.

Something similar can be observed in another field, the expansion of violence and war into political spaces, which produces what I have called the Jezebel syndrome, after the female character from biblical mythology. I originally developed this idea, in opposition to the theories of Jean Baudrillard, in my book *The Imaginary Networks of Political Power*.[11] This syndrome has to do with the spectacular elevation of marginal groups to the stage of a guerrilla theater where revolutionary actions are so outrageous, overblown, and provocative that they produce wide-ranging symbolic effects. The government responds in a spectacular way with a strategy of simulation, but this action is cloaked by strange veils that suggest the existence of a cryptic, exotic, and mysterious world. In Europe this kind of situation traditionally ends with the bloody repression of the so-called terrorists and causes society to rally around the government threatened by revolutionaries. In Mexico both the government and the armed rebels have avoided this cruel outcome, thanks in part to the influence of a democratic civil society. The simulacrum has led to a new situation in which the war of spectacle has triumphed over real violence.

This complex moment is being used by the political establishment to implement a new model of postdemocratic hegemony, which in the long term might allow the system to survive the dangerous zigzags provoked by the electoral shifts and countershifts that democratic participation produces. But we cannot deny that the tendencies allowing this situation have largely emerged from the terrain of the postcommunist, metacommunist, or paracommunist Left. In this way, a peculiar link has been made between the ruins of socialism and the new needs of capitalism. There is much irony in the fact that the Mexican government in crisis is concerned with salvaging the ruins of a Left that has collapsed and has a need—as in postmodern societies—for Jurassic Parks where it can carry out experiments with species that are already extinct or well on their way. Even so, under certain conditions, mutations can occur that change the course of things: that is what happened in Chiapas, where the genetic crossing of species and subspecies in danger of extinction, such as Communist dinosaurs and

---

11. Roger Bartra, *The Imaginary Networks of Political Power*, trans. Claire Joysmith (New Brunswick: Rutgers University Press, 1992).

Indians, gave birth to new varieties, which are even visited by famous specialists in guerrilla paleontology.[12]

The problem for the Mexican Left is not only resisting the authoritarian temptation. Today it faces, better stated, a fundamentalist temptation. But the true danger is not that fundamentalism might take us back to a world that was already extinguished. I do not think that is a real danger today, not even in the countries where socialism collapsed. The danger does not lie simply in the possibility that extremist currents on the Left might dedicate themselves to restoring dogma and Stalinism.

The greatest danger to democracy comes from the way in which aggressive fundamentalist tendencies have linked up with new forms of postdemocratic legitimation. What is dangerous, we might say, is the cocktail that mixes neoliberalism with postcommunism, segregation with populism, or patrimonialism with autonomy. If we add a good dose of religion and militarism to this mixture, we produce situations as explosive as those of the Middle East, North Africa, or Bosnia.

One of the most serious problems with modern democracy is that it now has to function without the overall framework of the threat of Communist alternatives. Whether threatened by the specters of nuclear war, subversion, or the instability caused by radical movements and their parliamentary representatives, the fact is that before 1989 democracy seemed to be a territory under siege. Now the political siege has lifted, and with it, many of the legitimating processes that protected the governments of the so-called First World have crumbled. The threat of the Third World, of the Global South, could compensate for the loss, but on a very reduced scale. What is left is the temptation to encourage and manipulate cultural, ethnic, and religious fundamentalisms, or even renewed forms of the revolutionary spirit, to provide the political incentives that seem required to correct certain democratic systems' malfunctioning because of corruption, poisoning, or aging. Faced with these threats, democratic systems invent and construct strange political prostheses to protect themselves. But we will be poorly served by a democracy that, like those famous characters in science fiction literature and film, is sustained by cybernetic organs, has to be fed by artificial additives, depends on an iron lung, and finds itself surrounded by a zone of barbarians whose main function seems to be stimulating its defensive reflexes.

12. An ironic reference to the steady stream of well-known leftists and former guerrilla leaders who have visited the EZLN in the Lacandon jungle. [Trans.]

In conclusion, I could say that many Communists and post-Communists have today learned to live in democracy. But I fear that democracy, in legitimating itself, has not yet learned to live without the threat of Communism.

Savage Violences: Customs, Mores, and Civil Society

One of the most unsettling tendencies of contemporary thought is the curious revalorization of so-called primitive cultures, seen as spaces where peculiar forms of violence flourished that have now been overcome in modern societies by civilized forms of exercising legitimate force. In my judgment, these tendencies can be understood as a kind of medievalization of primeval, primitive, or savage societies. This is a mapping of European medieval characteristics onto the world of premodern primitive societies. One symptomatic example can be found in an essay by the French philosopher Gilles Lipovetsky, which establishes that in all savage societies, violence is not explained by ideological, economic, or utilitarian considerations, but is regulated by a code based on vengeance and honor.[13] The way Lipovetsky throws all the societies he calls "savage"—an archaic term that French culture has kept to refer to the non-European peoples modern ethnology calls "primitive"—into a single sack is bloodcurdling.[14] Lipovetsky rejects the interesting suggestion René Girard made in *Violence and the Sacred* that ritual sacrifice could be a form of breaking the circle of vengeance in order to protect the community.[15] For Lipovetsky, vengeance and violence designed to defend honor are values that savage society is obliged to defend, not to stop. It seems to me that we are facing a vision of primitive society derived more from reading novels of chivalry, or even Spanish baroque plays, than from knowledge of the societies termed "savage." Yet Lipovetsky's major source is a well-known essay in which anthropologist Pierre Clastres theorized his research experiences in the Paraguayan Chaco.[16] According to Clastres, the indigenous peoples of this region are characterized by a bellicose passion based on the desire for prestige and the zeal for glory. He describes an ethos whose es-

13. Gilles Lipovetsky, "Violences sauvages, violences modernes," in *L'ère du vide: Essais sur l'individualisme contemporain* (Paris: Gallimard, 1983).

14. Of course, "primitive" is itself a hardly satisfying term and is falling into disuse. See Adam Kuper, *The Invention of Primitive Society: Transformations of an Illusion* (London: Routledge, 1988).

15. René Girard, *Violence and the Sacred* (Baltimore: Johns Hopkins University Press, 1977).

16. Pierre Clastres, *Society against the State* (New York: Urizen Books, 1977).

sential norms lie in—perhaps we should say this in French—the *gloire* of the warrior, the *volonté* to kill, and the *mépris* of danger. The logic of glory, will, and contempt has nothing to do with economic interests or ideological discourses: it is the logic proper to undivided societies. Clastres's interpretation comes less from his field research than from the descriptions of eighteenth-century chroniclers and Jesuit missionaries and is inspired, as he admits, by Georges Dumézil's reflections on the mythical representation of the warrior in Indo-European tradition.[17] The bloody Chaco War between Bolivians and Paraguayans is barely mentioned in passing by Clastres, who obsessively concentrates on the task of elaborating a general theory of savage and primitive violence.[18] He does not even stop to think that the proverbial bellicosity of the Chaco Indians might in large measure come from the disintegration of indigenous societies as an effect of colonization and of pre-Columbian historic confrontations that might have provoked dramatic population displacements. It is known that contact between nomadic or seminomadic peoples and colonizer groups with a strong will to establish sedentary forms of exploitation invariably sparks violence and feeds the myth of the bloody and warlike savage.

One might suspect that the ideas of honor and glory as detonators of violence have a strong Eurocentric charge. What is interesting about Clastres's and Lipovetsky's interpretations is that their ethnocentrism maps elements of medieval and Renaissance history onto the primitive world, but maps a medieval image cleansed of the great feudal and ecclesiastic institutions. Savage society appears as a projection of the medieval town in which the peasants have adopted the values of knights and courtesans, without abandoning their traditionally holistic, undivided, and homogeneous world along the way. Some of the first chroniclers of the conquest of America saw indigenous societies in this way.

This mythology of primeval violence coexists, as is well known, with the myth of the noble savage and with the dream of a natural primitive society lacking the evils that modern civilization has brought. Of course, this condition is just as imaginary as that of the warlike savage and has served to concentrate all the blame for violence on urban industrial culture. Non-European societies, the so-called primitive societies, harbor extensive and varied forms of formal and in-

17. George Dumézil, *The Destiny of the Warrior* (Chicago: University of Chicago Press, 1970). The French title of Clastres's original essay, "Malheur du guerrier sauvage," is a direct reference to the French title of Dumézil's book, *Heur et malheur du guerrier.*

18. Between 1932 and 1935, Bolivia and Paraguay fought the Chaco War in areas near where Clastres's "savages" reside, leaving 100,000 dead. [Trans.]

formal violence. They in no way conform to the idyllic image of a golden primal peace.[19] This longing for an original savage Eden has caused many to spill tears over what I call tropical kitsch. Milan Kundera wrote: "Kitsch causes two tears to flow in rapid succession. The first tear says: how nice to see children running on the grass! The second tear says: how nice to be moved, together with all mankind, by children running on the grass! It is the second tear that makes kitsch kitsch."[20] The specialist in mythical savages could paraphrase this: "How lovely to see Indians fighting in the tropical jungle! How lovely to feel ourselves moved, along with all of humanity, by Indians fighting in the tropical jungle! The second tear, which falls from the eyes of progressives in the United States and Europe, tends to be the best substance around for embalming artificial Indians and savages."[21]

Of course, my point is not to debate which myth is closer to reality. What I want to stress is the paradoxical fact that certain medievalizing European traits have been added to accentuate or highlight primitivism. This is something that happens often in Mexico, where certain peculiarities with colonial roots have been used to define ethnic groups of pre-Columbian origin. On this point, I will only refer here to the normative systems that, expressed in certain customs and mores, govern violence and internal conflict in indigenous villages. The possible approval of these normative systems at a constitutional level has sparked a great debate, whose starting impulse was undoubtedly the violent eruption of the EZLN into Mexican politics on 1 January 1994. We should not be surprised that violence itself should have provoked a great discussion about how violence can legitimately be exercised to resolve conflicts; we already know that violence engenders more violence, although in this case the violence engendered has been more rhetorical than physical. In any case, what really matters is that the government, political forces, and many intellectuals are seriously contem-

19. On this point see the interesting book by Lawrence Keeley, *War before Civilization: The Myth of the Peaceful Savage* (Oxford: Oxford University Press, 1996). On the imagery of savages, see my books *The Artificial Savage: Modern Myths of the Wild Man*, trans. Christopher Follett (Ann Arbor: University of Michigan Press, 1997); and *Wild Men in the Looking Glass: The Mythic Origins of European Otherness*, trans. Carl T. Berrisford (Ann Arbor: University of Michigan Press, 1994).

20. Milan Kundera, *The Unbearable Lightness of Being*, trans. Michael Henry Heim (New York: Harper and Row, 1984), 251.

21. On kitsch, see the excellent reflections of Celeste Olalquiaga in chapter 3 of her *Megalopolis: Contemporary Cultural Sensibilities* (Minneapolis: University of Minnesota Press, 1992), as well as her more recent book, cited earlier.

plating the possibility of establishing, alongside republican mechanisms, new forms of government based on the autonomy of a so-called indigenous system of norms, customs, and mores that would (symbolically or actually) exercise legal violence to resolve internal conflicts.

In facing this, we can consider two aspects of the problem. First, we can investigate the concrete characteristics of the indigenous normative system.[22] Second, later on, it will be necessary to examine the consequences of setting up a plurality of mechanisms for political representation and control. Of course, it is important always to keep in mind that these normative systems form part of the broader context of what are usually called "indigenous cultures"—the collection of ethnic ruins that managed to survive after modernization destroyed and liquidated the best of indigenous traditions.

In taking up the topic of ethnic normative systems, I want to suggest that their "indigenous" character is in many cases the transposition (real or imagined) of colonial forms of domination. That is, certain traits of the Spanish colonial structure have been elevated to the category of indigenous normative elements (with pre-Columbian ethnic peculiarities). In many cases, these supposedly indigenous traits have been exaggerated enormously or have even existed only in the minds of certain officials, politicians, or intellectuals. We often witness the construction of colonialoid versions of Indian reality, just as exotic as the bloody Guaicurú equestrian warriors or the valiant screaming redskin of indigenist mythology.

The forms of government ethnologists have observed in various indigenous communities in postrevolutionary Mexico can be summarized by four characteristics. We should warn that in many communities, the four traits I describe below are in a process of extinction (or have already died out).

1. Supreme authority usually falls in the hands of a governor, *cacique*, chief, or head, whose functions of vigilance, control, and punishment are in some cases granted for life. This is frequently an elder who has the respect of the community—and is never a woman. His decisions cannot be appealed and are obeyed

22. One anthropologist who has angrily criticized my interpretation maintains that my calling indigenous political systems "normative systems" proves that I do not want to understand the internal dynamics of native peoples. But it turns out that this is precisely the concept used by the Commission for Concord and Pacification (COCOPA) in the initiative that led to the first agreements of San Andrés (between the government and the EZLN). I don't get the impression that their use of the term suggests any repugnance toward indigenous peoples on the part of the EZLN, which supported the COCOPA's initiative. See Miguel Angel Bartolomé, "El antropólogo y sus indios imaginarios," *Ojarasca*, October 1997.

without debate. In recent years the term *cacique,* which was common in southern Mexico among the Mixtec, Triques, and Zapotecs, has fallen into disuse because of the pejorative connotations it has acquired. The title of governor, used among ethnic groups in the North (Coras, Huicholes, Mayos, Pames, Pimas, Seris, Tarahumaras, Tepehuanos, and Yaquis), undoubtedly comes from the government official of the same name who in Golden Age Spain administered justice in the towns, and was also called a *corregidor.* One widespread symbol of authority among indigenous peoples is the use of a staff as a symbol of power. Among the Coras the transmission of rulership takes place in a ceremony of handing over the "staffs of rule"; similarly, among the Zapotecs there is a "presentation of staffs"; Mixtecs speak of a "presentation of the club"; the Chontales in Oaxaca name a "major of staffs" to keep order. In some communities of the Nahuatl-speaking zone of the Gulf Coast, a *tlaihtoani* is elected, and when the authorities of the council are replaced, there is a "changing of staffs" festival. Among the Tarahumaras and Triques there is also ritual use of the staff as a sign of authority.

I have cited these examples not to dwell on the folklore of forms of power but because they reveal the symptomatic presence of a single symbol in very different ethnic contexts. I suspect this is due to a common Spanish colonial origin: on the Iberian Peninsula, court magistrates, corregidores, judges, and bailiffs carried staffs as a sign of their representation of royal authority.

2. In many cases, the naming of governor, chief, or cacique is the work of a council of elders or of an assembly; at times they are elected by plebiscite. The council of elders is a residual form originating in pre-Columbian systems of communal government.[23] Its organization varies between peoples, and its power has managed to last even among people where traditional rulers are no longer named. There the elders name the municipal authorities.[24] The most famous examples of the survival of the power of councils of elders are found in southern Mexico, in the Tzeltal and Tzotzil regions, as well as among the Mixtecs and Zapotecs. In contrast, among the ethnic groups of the North, popular assemblies and at times plebiscites are the predominant means of electing authorities. It is interesting to note that it was the Spaniards who, from the sixteenth century on,

23. See Charles Gibson, *The Aztecs under Spanish Rule: A History of the Indians of the Valley of Mexico, 1519–1810* (Stanford: Stanford University Press, 1964).
24. Anthropologist Maurilio Muñoz offered some interesting reflections on councils of elders in *Mixteca Nahua-Tlapaneca,* Memoria del Instituto Nacional Indigenista 9 (Mexico: Instituto Nacional Indigenista, 1963). See also Roberto Ravicz, *Organización social de los mixtecos* (Mexico: Instituto Nacional Indigenista, 1965).

introduced collective systems of local government, in *cabildos* and councils, to counteract the power of caciques and heads.[25]

3. One distinctive trait of the forms of government of indigenous communities is their fusion of civil and religious powers. The administration of justice, the organization of worship, the maintenance of order, and the organization of religious festivals form an integral part of normative systems of government. These are rigidly hierarchical systems in which the posts connected to maintaining public order are intermingled with those related to Catholic ceremony. Stewards, *topiles*, staff majors, *rezanderos*, *chicoteros*, and chiefs form part of the same system. Anthropologist Alfonso Fabila went so far as to speak of a "theocratic Yaqui government."[26] Ethnologists have observed in various regions how confraternity ceremonies, the organization of collective labor, police functions, church maintenance, steward responsibilities, and the administration of whippings to those accused of adultery or robbery are fused into a single system. This fusion originated in the omnipresence of the colonial Catholic Church in all aspects of social life, although the sacred character of certain functions undoubtedly has pre-Columbian roots, as in the *piaroles* or *fiadores* of the Tzeltal-Tzotzil region.[27]

4. Indigenous forms of exercising power have an extremely authoritarian character and are often based on a hierarchical system with a military edge. In the Maya region of the Yucatan Peninsula, for example, traditional authorities use military nomenclature to refer to various functions and hierarchies: general, captain, commander, lieutenant, sergeant, corporal, and soldier. Generals name others to the lower posts as they wish and are treated with a courtesy that reaches the extreme of kissing their hand, bowing at their passing, and kneeling while speaking to them. The Yaqui name their governors or *cobanáhuacs*, and

---

25. See José Miranda and Silvio Zavala, "Instituciones indígenas en la colonia," in *Métodos y resultados de la política indigenista en México*, ed. Alfonso Caso (Mexico: Instituto Nacional Indigenista, 1954).

26. Alfonso Fabila, "Las tribus Yaquis de Sonora, su cultura y anhelada autodeterminación," in *Primer Congreso Indigenista Interamericano* (Mexico: Departamento de Asuntos Indígenas, 1940). On the nonseparation of religious functions from political ones, see Julio de la Fuente, *Relaciones interétnicas* (Mexico: Instituto Nacional Indigenista, 1965); and Eva Verbisky, "Análisis comparativo de cinco comunidades de los altos de Chiapas," in *Los Mayas del Sur y sus relaciones con los Nahuas Meridionales: VIII mesa redonda de la Sociedad Mexicana de Antropología* (San Cristobal de las Casas, Mexico: Sociedad Mexicana de Antropología, 1961).

27. See Gonzalo Aguirre Beltrán and Ricardo Pozas A., "Instituciones indígenas en el México actual," in *Métodos y resultados de la política indigenista en México*, ed. Alfonso Caso (Mexico: Instituto Nacional Indigenista, 1954).

they are helped by lesser officials with military ranks: ensign, drummer, captain, lieutenant, sergeant, and corporal. The Huichols name a colonel, subordinated to the governor, who is entrusted with enforcing justice. These examples reveal survivals from the dramatic history of uprisings and wars of indigenous peoples who rebelled for centuries against repression and exploitation. The military nomenclatures I have cited as examples—and the resulting forms of submissive respect for authority—are an inheritance of the long Caste War that began in 1847 in the Yucatan, and of the insurrections of the Yaqui, Ópata, and Mayo Indians that began in 1825 and lasted for more than a century. We could say that the authoritarian and even military peculiarities of the indigenous forms of government have their origins more in the constant state of siege and war that indigenous peoples have endured than in remote pre-Columbian traditions.

In synthesis, indigenous normative systems—or what is left of them—are colonial politico-religious forms of exercising authority, profoundly shaped by wars and repression, in which the survival of pre-Columbian elements can barely be glimpsed. These forms of government have been deeply infiltrated and astutely manipulated by mestizo or ladino interests and by the political bureaucracy of postrevolutionary governments in order to stabilize the national state's hegemony in indigenous communities. The ingredients we could classify as "democratic" are precarious; they are limited to the plebiscite and to the exercise of direct democracy in assemblies, where women and minority alternatives are usually excluded or squashed.

Luis Hernández Navarro has reproached me for not mentioning consensus as a democratic form for decision making in indigenous communities.[28] Another critic says the same thing: in communal assemblies "the decision-making mechanisms are generally based on 'consensus' and not on a majority."[29] In my judgment, they are misusing the notion of consensus, which is not a way for reaching agreement but a social and political situation—a "state of feeling," as my critic Antonio García de León would surely put it—of support for general principles, values, or ends. In contrast, reaching agreement by unanimity almost always indicates a lack of democracy and an authoritarianism hidden beneath a populist veil. If one does not govern through majority agreements, minorities are inevitably excluded: unanimity does not provide tolerant mechanisms for representing minorities. In indigenous communities, one of these critics ingenuously

28. Luis Hernández Navarro, "¿Violencias indígenas o derechos pendientes?" *La Jornada*, 9 September 1997.
29. Bartolomé, "El antropólogo y sus indios imaginarios."

says, "leaders are regulators but not directors of collective life, they take care that it transpires in keeping with tradition."[30] That is to say: their functions are essentially repressive and blockade any less "traditional" minority. Perhaps mechanisms of government by unanimity are proper to certain indigenous communities. But rather than giving off a pre-Columbian aroma, these arrangements undeniably reek of the PRI.

It is worth briefly touching on a theme the Zapatista armed uprising has brought to the table: the ethical or moral repercussions of the process of developing new forms of identity. The fact that indigenous political systems have a colonial origin does not seem to worry Luis Hernández Navarro too much, since what supposedly gives "the system of offices its indigenous character is that indigenous people recognize it as such."[31] For his part, Antonio García de León thinks that identity is principally "an option towards what has been inherited and what has been constructed."[32] I agree that identity is a complex process of creations and inventions. But that does not authorize us to put aside its temporal and historical dimension, which is where a community consensus sediments around certain symbols and values. I do not want to automatically exclude creations that were made only yesterday or were inspired by people recently arrived at new forms of identity.[33] Yet the absence of historical depth, or the artificial adoption of traits from other traditions in order to strengthen identities in extinction, makes such new processes more debatable, precisely because their moral and ethical content is more evident and close to the surface. It is more evident because it is connected to recent political decisions, which are still fresh. In contrast, the long history of certain identity traits has buried moral values beneath the dust of the centuries, and it has become very difficult to disinter them.

The fact that the moral dimension has now come to the fore does not always simplify things. In some cases, it is accompanied by a certain intolerance. In criticizing the curious customs of a community of the United States that is building its identity around a supposed visit by flying saucers fifty years ago, we

30. Ibid.

31. Hernández Navarro, "¿Violencias indígenas o derechos pendientes?"

32. Antonio García de León, "Identidades," *La Jornada Semanal* 133 (21 September 1997).

33. In "Identidades," García de León says that "a large portion of the promoters of the new consciousness of indigenous peoples . . . are not in reality indigenous." With a sharp African gaze, Anthony Appiah has recently observed the form in which, in the United States, the weakening of the cultural content of identities has generated a growing stridency in their demands. Something similar has taken place in Mexico. See Appiah, "The Multiculturalist Misunderstanding," *New York Review of Books,* 9 October 1997.

run the risk of being disdained for never having climbed aboard a UFO. More dangerous still would have been placing in doubt in thirties Berlin the alleged Indo-European origins of the Nazi myths about Aryan identity. Debating with Iranian or Algerian fundamentalists is even more dangerous, and the exercise of critique can cost you your life. Critics are usually disqualified because of their otherness, their outsider position, or their lack of lived experiences, and they end up bombarded by a hail of stones: the critique of customs—of morals—is a dangerous intellectual exercise. Experience tells me that it is difficult to debate with the dancers of the Holy Child of Atocha who exalt Mexicanness, with the obedient chieftains of the Zapatista periphery, or with the practitioners of officially Indian customs.[34]

But despite everything, we must not give up the moral debate on which Antonio García de León, among others, has insisted.[35] Building on the debate about customs, habits, and conduct—that is, morals—we can now turn to the problem of the consequences of making legal in indigenous regions or communities governmental, electoral, representational, and judicial systems which differ from those governing the political life of the country as a whole. This option has seemed attractive, above all after the failure of assimilationist indigenous policy, but it obviously comes into conflict with the classical Enlightenment definition of the modern nation, according to which the nation is a political expression within a territorial space where all citizens are subject to the same laws, without regard for their color, religion, ethnicity, or sex. In this case, the state is based on a civil society that includes men and women who freely choose to subject themselves to the same laws. This conception contrasts with the political

34. One example of intolerance: one inquisitor covered me with insults for failing to see among indigenous peoples what Marcel Mauss called "facts of civilization." According to this denouncer, my supposed disdain came from a lack of experience living with indigenous peoples—and he has the gall to invoke a French anthropologist who never did any field research, just like his master Émile Durkheim, who never even set foot in the Australia he wrote so much about! See Bartolomé, "El antropólogo y sus indios imaginarios." Bartolomé's attack was published in Ojarasca, which is the indigenist supplement of the newspaper La Jornada. A year later, an editor of this same publication took intolerance to the extreme of completely misstating my ideas in order to "prove" that I had joined a campaign against the Huichol Indians. See Ojarasca, January 1999. When I protested this libel, the editor simply answered back with a slew of insults.
35. Antonio García de León, "Chiapas, estado de ánimo," Fractal 8 (1998). I am not convinced by the pragmatism that Luis Hernández Navarro invokes, inspired by John Dewey, to resolve the conflicts between the concrete ethical values proclaimed by the Zapatistas and the universal or scientific dimension of certain moral postulates. See Hernández Navarro, "Zapatismo: La esperanza de lo incierto," Fractal 8 (1998).

tradition, sometimes termed "romantic," according to which the form of government emerges organically and historically from the national, ethnic, and cultural unity of a people. In that case, the basis of the government is the *Volksgeist*, not civil society. In reality, there have been various combinations of these two principles, at times with catastrophic results in regions of pronounced ethnic differences, since the democratic blindness toward multiculturalism or, above all, the smothering of minorities in the name of an ethnocentric nationalism has been a constant source of violence.

In recent years the idea has been gaining ground that, to avoid these forms of violence, we must accept forms of self-determination and autonomy within already constituted states, in addition to promoting forms of representation and support (called affirmative action in the United States) directed against the multiple expressions of discrimination—economic, racial, religious, sexual, ethnic, and others. Of course, this proposal emerges in very particular situations, since we can suppose that Catalans, the Northern Irish, and the Basques would never think of invoking the protection of International Labor Organization (ILO) Convention 169.[36] Under the protection of multiculturalism, international organizations, and the spirit of affirmative action, a growing tendency postulates indigenous self-determination and autonomy the new solution to ancestral problems. This idea usually assumes that a formula can be found in the traditional customs and mores of indigenous peoples that not only will pacify conflicts but also will lead indigenous societies toward liberation. But we should ask ourselves: Can integralist, sexist, discriminatory, religious, corporatist, and authoritarian forms of government stop violence? Aren't we confusing indigenous character with colonial and postcolonial forms of domination? Clearly the COCOPA, in its 20 November 1996 initiative for constitutional reforms (approved by the EZLN), took a critical approach and recognized that certain customs and mores would threaten the development of a democratic civil society. After establishing that indigenous peoples have the right to apply their own normative systems, for example, it prudently added the phrase "respecting individual civil rights, human rights and, in particular, women's dignity and integrity." Isn't COCOPA recognizing that

36. That is, that they would not consider themselves "indigenous" or "tribal" peoples. The ILO is a United Nations organization whose primary function is to develop international standards, called conventions, for labor and civil rights, which are adopted by national governments. ILO Convention 169, approved in 1989, pertains to the civil, labor, and political rights of tribal and indigenous peoples. Emphasizing self-determination and autonomy for tribal and indigenous peoples within nation-states, it supplants the earlier, "assimilationist" Convention 107, passed in 1957. The text of all ILO conventions is available on-line at www.ilo.org. [Trans.]

these supposedly indigenous normative systems violate those civil and human rights? Clearly, introducing such rights strikes a great blow against the essential elements of the indigenous system of customs and mores. What does this imply? This proposal certainly does try to avoid turning indigenous regions into the Bantustans of a Mexican version of apartheid and instead locates them in the modern space of civil society. It civilizes the savage tendency of Indians, as Clastres and Lipovetsky might say. Even though, we might add, that savagery was in reality brought by the civilized Spanish colonizers.[37]

This and other hybrid proposals might end up translating self-determination and autonomy into a sui generis regulation of separated zones, condemned to marginality and segregation, veritable reservations forced to live off the marginal income generated by exploiting natural resources, tourist concessions, and, at worst, illicit activities such as drug trafficking. I fear we are witnessing the transition from an assimilationist paternalism to a multicultural segregationist mode of patronage, a mode just as corrupt as nationalist indigenism, if not more so. We are watching a complex and thorny transition in the forms of articulating central power with indigenous communities. This transition is driven forward by a paradoxical spectrum of political forces, from the technocrats of the PRI government to the neo-Zapatista guerrillas, with the objective of establishing certain forms of local, municipal, and perhaps regional government that supposedly are originally derived from traditional culture.[38] In Oaxaca, for

---

37. Another problem is that of restricting autonomy to the narrow limits of the community, as is reflected in the San Andrés agreements. Although they define the "indigenous peoples" as the subject of "self-determination" and "autonomy," in practice the application of "traditional political practices" is reduced to each municipality, community, auxiliary agency of the township, and similar legal settings. In a debate about this question, Luis Violloro pointed out to me that this reduction in the autonomy of communities is only made in the official proposal by the president of the republic. This is not the case, as can be seen in the general proposals by both sides, and specifically in the initiatives and observations to change article 115, paragraph 10, of the Constitution. Both the COCOPA and the government agree on this reduction. The debate I am referring to, which also included Federico Reyes Heroles and José del Val, was published as "Ruinas étnicas o nación inexistente," ed. Luis Enrique López, El Ángel 240 (supplement to Reforma, 16 August 1998).

38. Sociologist Yvon Le Bot, who knows Zapatismo and the Chiapas situation well, warns that in Chiapas there is "a tendency to put an end to conflicts resorting to imposition by force. The Zapatistas themselves have perpetrated various forms of authoritarianism, of the authoritarianism of consensus. . . . The danger exists in Chiapas of reproducing the disastrous experience of the Communities of Population in Resistance (CPR) of Guatemala, which lived—in some cases

example, forms of government have already been implemented in many munici-palities that based on customs and mores, exclude, among other things, any par-ticipation by political parties. In other places, following the same logic, non-Catholic religious groups have been excluded. This preoccupation with rescuing political forms of dubiously indigenous origin contrasts with the great neglect of implementing exacting legal standards for promoting multilingualism. In-digenous languages are an extremely valuable heritage of undoubtedly pre-Columbian origins, and their spread across Mexican society could become a powerful amplifier of their speakers' demands.

Little by little, the Mexican government has been refining the idea that, in the case of indigenous peoples, the conditioning of individual rights by collective rights must be accepted and, furthermore, that collective patrimonial expres-sions are precisely the basis of the traditional forms that must be legalized. These collective expressions are collective decisions in assemblies, respect for the councils of elders that represent the spirit of the hive, communal use of natu-ral resources, joint defense of ethnic and religious identity, and so forth. What re-mains in dispute, of course, is how far this standard reaches.

I have a very critical interpretation of this process. It seems to me that this is not the makings of a new national model but rather the rotting of the old authori-tarian one. The implementation of governments based on customs and mores is one of the ills, not the remedies. Far from strengthening civil society, I think that in many cases this is sowing the seeds of violence. These are not democratic seeds; they are sources of conflict. That is why the governing logic comes from confrontation and violence, a logic of contention, of lobbying and negotiation that overshadows the desirable logic of a deep reform of the essentially segregat-ing and discriminatory political system ruling Mexico. I think that the indige-nous problem is so far-ranging that it obliges every serious attempt at a solution to address it on a national level, not on a regional or municipal one. While we usually look for solutions to come from below, this one must be found from above. It is the brain of the system that is sick, and that generates violence. The indigenous problem is located primarily in government structures. The Indians are not silent: it is the government that is deaf, the government and the entire economic and bureaucratic elite. In my judgment, what is necessary is not a con-

---

for fifteen years—turned in on themselves, captives (with or without permission) of the guerril-las and dependent on international aid, practicing a kind of primitive communism, encouraged by a millenarianism fed by certain liberation theologists." Yvon Le Bot, "La autonomía según los Zapatistas," *Masiosare* (supplement to *La Jornada*), 29 March 1998.

servation but a profound reformation of customs and mores—for Indians and for savage politicians alike—to ensure the expansion of a civil society based on individual freedom and political democracy.

Moby-Dick in the Lacandon Jungle

One of the most notable aspects of the uprising led by the EZLN is the flood of metaphors of a moral flavor that has inundated civil society, washing away the stagnant slogans and concepts of traditional leftist rhetoric. A goodly number of these metaphors revolve around the figure of the boat or the ship: there has been talk of the jungle boat of Fitzcarraldo, of Noah's ark, of pirate ships, of the ship of the mad, and so on. An interesting mythology has also developed, speaking of anchors, sails, rudders, winds lashing the stern, furious waves, storms, and ports awaiting the longed-for arrival of the lost boat.

A few years back, while I was enduring the blows of an enraged sea, after hearing the nautical allusions in the speech Subcomandante Marcos made to the National Democratic Convention on 8 August 1994, it occurred to me that what was happening certainly had been written and codified in the mythical images that seemed to blossom out of the Bible, film, and literary novels. But I realized that everything had already been spelled out in a novel that, as far as I know, has not been cited as a metaphorical source for the strange happenings in Chiapas. "It must be because of the pessimism that is flooding over us now that the main sail has collapsed," I thought to myself, recalling Captain Ahab fighting against Moby-Dick. Soaked by the rain and frightened by the spectacle of a Ship of Babel of the Left wrecking against the coffee fields of Aguascalientes, I thought that I should head down to the makeshift EZLN library to see if they had Herman Melville's novel. The wind and mud kept me from it.

The stalling of negotiations between the government and the EZLN, the growing militarization of Chiapas, and the terrible massacre at Acteal have caused a wave of pessimism to wash over our spirits once more, and confirmed to me that the demiurges of the Chiapas tragedy are using Melville's novel as their basic textbook. I recommend that Subcomandante Marcos and the president of the republic reread the final chapter of *Moby-Dick*. And I ask them, for the love of God, not to take that text as their script for acting out the final acts of this drama.

In that book, the subcomandante will find his boat and his pipe, his Indians and his obsessive hopes. In the whale, the president will find the Leviathan he wants to save at all costs. But this is the story of a shipwreck: of the sinking of Ahab's boat, of the death of the White Whale, of the bitter and bloody struggle of whalers whose primitive industry is condemned to extinction.

Many of us ask ourselves, terrified: what the hell is Captain Ahab's ship doing lost in Chiapas? Will the Mexican government never stop releasing white whales into the Lacandon jungle?

I only want to quote the final paragraphs of Melville's novel so that in between the lines, we might imagine what could happen if Captain Ahab doesn't abandon his harpoons and President Moby-Dick doesn't stop swishing about in his death throes:

> But as the last whelmings intermixingly poured themselves over the sunken head of the Indian at the mainmast, leaving a few inches of the erect spar yet visible, together with long streaming yards of the flag, which calmly undulated, with ironical coincidings, over the destroying billows they almost touched—at that instant, a red arm and a hammer hovered backwardly uplifted in the open air, in the act of nailing the flag faster and yet faster to the subsiding spar. A sky-hawk that tauntingly had followed the main-truck downwards from its natural home among the stars, pecking at the flag . . . this bird now chanced to intercept its broad fluttering wing between the hammer and the wood; and simultaneously feeling that ethereal thrill, the submerged savage beneath, in his death-grasp, kept his hammer frozen there; and so the bird of heaven, with archangelic shrieks, and his imperial beak thrust upwards, and his whole captive form folded into the flag of Ahab, went down with his ship, which, like Satan, would not sink to hell till she had dragged a living part of heaven along with her, and helmeted herself with it.
>
> Now small fowls flew screaming over the yet yawning gulf; a sullen white surf beat against its steep sides; then all collapsed, and the great shroud of the sea rolled on as it rolled five thousand years ago.[39]

Lest we be covered by a giant shroud, we must bury our weapons, leave the ship in the jungle, and abandon the white night of forgetfulness to slide over toward the shadows of democratic civility (as I once counseled Subcomandante Marcos, in a letter that may have been swallowed by the whale).

Postscript: A Tale of a Tub

In early 2001 the leadership of the EZLN decided to abandon the white night of forgetfulness to march to Mexico City, setting in motion what seemed to be a

---

39. Herman Melville, *Moby-Dick, or The Whale* (New York: Penguin, 1992), 623–24.

long journey to the heart of the republic. But the journey did not prove as long, politically speaking, as had been expected, because the marchers happened upon an entirely new situation. With the PRI loss in the 2000 elections, Mexican politics had changed significantly. The EZLN march had a tougher time crossing the democratic ocean than confronting old PRI authoritarianism: the rebels received a friendly welcome from the new Vicente Fox administration, the Catholic Church, leftist groups, the press, local governments, the Congress, the police, and even certain business organizations. The new president of the republic had sent the COCOPA proposal supported by the Zapatistas to the Senate, and Mexican society was preparing itself for a complex and democratic debate on the indigenous law. People who seriously thought the 1996 COCOPA initiative on indigenous culture and rights could undermine national sovereignty or encourage fragmentation of the nation were few and far between. The major lobbies and various interest groups—all with right-wing leanings—certainly had nothing to lose from the approval of modifications to the Constitution inspired by the San Andrés Accords. Do bankers care whether the regulation of internal conflicts in indigenous zones is governed by indigenous normative systems? Could collective use of the natural resources surrounding indigenous villages affect industrialists in any way? Is the vast hegemony of the former ruling party (the PRI) over rural areas threatened if some indigenous governments opt for traditional political practices? Does it bother the big companies exploiting natural resources to pay royalties to local indigenous governments rather than to state or communal bodies? Is the church affected by the preservation of indigenous tongues? Do merchants have any interest in opposing changes in electoral district boundaries? Are large unions threatened by the formation of associations of indigenous communities? Do the great radio and television monopolies see any danger of serious competition if indigenous peoples operate their own means of communication? Will trying to bring indigenous prisoners closer to their communities shatter the judicial or military bureaucracy? We can answer all these questions with an emphatic no.

The fact that the COCOPA initiative is inoffensive is so evident that the president of the republic himself—who is no leftist—firmly supported it and sent it to the Senate for approval, while his predecessor, Ernesto Zedillo, had accepted the San Andrés Accords. Reforms in a similar spirit have been introduced into the law in Oaxaca with PRI approval. In addition, the proposals are protected by an international organization—and not exactly a subversive one—dedicated to defending the rights and living standards of the working population. I am referring to ILO Convention 169, which implicitly connects the identities of indigenous and tribal groups to their existence as protected labor.

Nevertheless, the original proposal inspired by the San Andrés Accords would clearly not be approved without important modifications. Sympathy for Zapatista rebels did not mean unified and acritical support for the COCOPA proposal, since that project embodied a strange yet fascinating contradiction. The San Andrés Accords appear in the symbolic imaginary as an expression of the most rebellious and advanced impulses of the people. Yet in terms of legislative mechanisms, these proposals irritate (at most) only the most backward economic interests of a few marginal sectors of parasitical merchants, companies dedicated to the savage exploitation of natural resources, and similar groups. Who else might they affect? In the first place, beyond any doubt, indigenous peoples themselves. In the second place, the democratic system of political parties. There are aspects of the proposed law that could disturb mechanisms for representation and therefore would bother democratic political parties. Here lies the heart of the problem: under new democratic conditions, the parties represented in the Congress could hardly approve the most conservative and even reactionary aspects of the COCOPA proposal—despite the progressive imaginary shining like an aura around the San Andrés Accords. In those accords, the forms of indigenous government are linked to populations who *conserve* their ancient institutions, who define their political practice according to *tradition,* who use (or want to use) their surrounding habitat in a *traditional* collective manner, and who exercise forms of justice based on *custom.* The conservative, traditionalist, and customary spirit of the accords is evident, although it is attenuated by symptomatic conditional additions about the necessary respect for individual rights, human rights, constitutional precepts, and, especially, women's dignity.

We can sense the dangers of this conservatism for the indigenous populations themselves: it may keep out the political parties and new institutions that contain the seeds of change, blur the boundaries between political and Catholic religious roles, marginalize women, dissidents, and the young from the everyday practice of an assembly-based direct democracy, transform the collective use of natural resources into corporatist usufruct of rents and royalties collected from private companies, and produce countless other dangers. These conservative aspects of the COCOPA initiative are not imaginary inferences: anyone could confirm their existence in the Zapatistas' appearance before the Congress on 28 March 2001, which was broadcast live. There they offered a defense for an unsettling "juridical pluralism." In keeping with this pluralism, we should accept, as Adelfo Regino said, the normative systems now existing in communities. We should legitimate the uses and customs considered to be "good," according to the delegate of the National Indigenous Congress, María de Jesús Patricio, such as recognizing that when a husband goes to a community assembly he brings with him "the participation of his wife" (who stays home), accepting that in those assemblies "there is no vote" but unanimous agreements imposed by the "true word" of the elders, or admitting that justice is better served "repairing the harm than punishing the guilty" (a practice that includes a great variety of traditions, from public exhibition of the presumed guilty party in order to shame him, to lynching, to forced labor on behalf of victims). Facing the doubts that were in the air, Commander Ester of the EZLN defended the COCOPA proposal by pointing out that the criticisms made of it are in fact problems for all of society: indigenous people already live on reservations, isolated from all other Mexicans; the country has a backward legal system that encourages racism and confrontation; the government creates exceptions in the political process by turning posts and offices into spaces for impunity and the corrupt accumulation of wealth. All this is true, and must be fought against: these are precisely those "uses and customs" that have to be changed, even when they take on the appearance of supposedly indigenous "normative systems." Their presence throughout Mexican society offers still more proof that these are not values inherited from our elders but a dreadful poison of colonial and authoritarian traditions that have been accumulating for centuries. All this should not obscure the extraordinary and welcome fact that, by their presence in Congress and their speeches before deputies and senators, the EZLN seemed to have formally accepted the initiation of dialogue with the executive and legislative branches. With the collapse of the authoritarian system, the EZLN found itself confronted with the need to make a grand turnabout in order to direct its march toward the democratic heart of republican civil society.

But that was not what happened. In an absurd gesture, the leadership of the EZLN chose to return to the sea of Chiapas and to withdraw from debate. The Congress approved an indigenous law that avoids the most conservative aspects of the San Andrés Accords, yet introduces some uncomfortable federalist principles: each state will define the forms of autonomy of indigenous groups.

So the guerrillas ended up like a tub that can float on the sea because it is empty. To understand the situation, we could resort to whaling metaphors once more—this time to the one Swift used ironically to refer to Hobbes's Leviathan. "Sea-men have a Custom when they meet a Whale, to fling him out an empty Tub, by way of Amusement, to divert him from laying violent Hands upon the Ship." Swift explains that the whale could be seen as Hobbes's Leviathan, an immense animal who tosses and plays dangerously with various alternatives for government and religion. The boat would be the Commonwealth, a republican civil society threatened by the swishing of the State's tail. To avoid damage to the republic, the spectacle of a battle must be staged: the governmental whale has to be busied in fighting off a simulacrum—an empty threat—to achieve the tranquility and legitimacy of the Commonwealth. Thus the tub is like those political proposals that are "hollow, and dry, and empty, and noisy, and wooden, and given to Rotation."

With this I mean to say that the fall of the authoritarian political system has opened the door to reorganizing the processes of legitimation and cohesion: now the Zapatista guerrillas in Chiapas—along with other armed groups—play the role in the political imaginary of dangerous liminal actors whose presence sparks "normal" society to close ranks around the democratic establishment. This is the spectacle I have called the "Jezebel syndrome," a postmodern expression of the imaginary networks of political power. With the new millennium, this syndrome appears like a Mexican version of the game of a tub described by Swift: "in order to prevent these Leviathans from tossing and sporting with the Commonwealth, (which of itself is too apt to fluctuate) they should be diverted from that Game by a Tale of a Tub."

The Bridge, the Border, and the Cage:
Cultural Crisis and Identity in the
Post-Mexican Condition

I n Mexico, just as in the rest of North America, sociology is going through
a period of crisis and turbulence. The interest in building interdisciplin-
ary bridges has become a pressing need. At the same time, powerful political
and economic trends are weaving new forms of interaction that overcome traditional limitations. One result of these trends is NAFTA.[1]

Taking these facts as my starting point, I will try to briefly offer some thoughts
on both the crisis of national identities and the worries and hopes I can see growing in contemporary sociology in North America. The need to synthesize has
forced me to use metaphors—which is actually a pleasure—that freely express
the themes I want to address. When I speak of the bridge, the border, and the cage,
I will be using these images more as the ingredients of a fable than as scientific
concepts. And yet I do intend for this fable to lead us into science.

I picture the sociologist as trapped inside a kind of hermeneutic cage framed
by the bars of a border. That border marks off our space, but it also limits our en-
deavors. In the face of this distressing contradiction between identity and freedom, we long to build a bridge to the outside, but we worry that it might collapse
after we cross it, cutting off our way back. This has been bothering sociologists
for many decades. Half a century ago, at the beginning of the postwar period,
Robert Merton declared his distrust of grand theories and issued a call to concentrate on developing middle-range social theories. With this, sociologists could

Presented at the opening session of the 92d Meeting of the American Sociological Association in
Toronto, Canada, 9 August 1997.

1. The North American Free Trade Agreement, which went into effect on 1 January 1994, and
was the culmination of the strategy of headlong economic opening pursued by the administration of Carlos Salinas de Gortari (1988–1994). [Trans.]

avoid the dangers of flying too high and too far, and also justify their growing specialization. But the trouble with this path toward the *aurea mediocritas,* the golden mean, was its ever-diminishing returns in producing meaningful statements about society. Forty years ago, Paul Lazarsfeld asked himself: "What has social research all added up to in the past fifty years? Is there any sociological finding that has not been anticipated by philosophers or novelists?" He was not only hinting that very little had been achieved but also auguring an equally mediocre future. "It is unlikely," he said, "that any surprising 'discoveries' will be made for quite some time to come."[2]

Sociologists south of the Río Bravo were more ready to accept that their science might long remain an ambiguous, impressionistic discipline, and less bothered that the borders between the social sciences and the literary works of Carlos Fuentes, Octavio Paz, or Juan Rulfo were blurry. By contrast, they were rigid on the matter of national borders, so much so that, for instance, they adopted and refined a theory of dependency—to explain underdevelopment—that only made full sense if one took for granted that the borders inherited from colonialism were physically real. Sociology locked itself up inside a nationalistic cage.

Some social scientists laid bridges to the north, only to discover that sociology in the United States had built itself a different cage out of an almost medieval obsession with classifying, codifying, and quantifying and was living in confinement behind nearly impenetrable post-Weberian jargon. To make the claustrophobia of some sociologists even worse, the use of sophisticated statistical techniques drew sociology closer to the natural sciences, only to make some mathematicians suspect that their hopes for a flowering of the social sciences had been in vain, as most of the phenomena under study were of a highly indeterminate nature. Confirming social structures might demand far more mathematical work than had been required for physicists to confirm indeterminacy in quantum mechanics—and it did not promise terribly significant results.[3]

For their part, the social sciences in Mexico—as in some other Latin American countries—had jumped onto the nation-state bandwagon. Driven by the forces unleashed by an agrarian revolution that crystallized into a state that was particularly complex and sophisticated, although authoritarian and undemocratic, the social sciences had developed and refined certain theories, especially for studying politics and rural phenomena. Yet sociology was trapped in a

2. Paul Lazarsfeld, "Problems in Methodology," in *Sociology Today,* ed. R. K. Broom, L. Cottrell, and R. Merton (New York: Basic Books, 1959), 39.

3. Gunther Stent, *The Coming of the Golden Age: A View of the End of Progress* (New York: American Museum of Natural History, 1969), chap. 6.

strange paradox: although it rested on a nationalist base, for many years it disdained the study of cultural symbols. Thus instead of being interested in how the phenomenon of the nation was expressed culturally, sociology preferred to look closely at how it was formulated economically. Here too some had the uncomfortable suspicion that sociology, interested primarily in studying dependency and the global system of domination, might find itself entangled in the law of diminishing returns. As sociology looked to economics in search of a firmer scientific basis, it fell into a trap without having cleared up the mystery it was obsessed by—the causes of underdevelopment. The sociologists who inherited and carried on this tradition generally came to the conclusion that dependency and globalization (or, as some prefer to call them, underdevelopment and neoliberalism) had prevented a cohesive and strong civil society from developing in Mexico. According to them, this process would lead to disaster: fascism or chaos would threaten the system, and the solution—if any could be glimpsed —would lie either in supporting a soft form of authoritarianism, semidemocratic and populist, or in opting for a more or less revolutionary project for national salvation, which would open the way to a new form of economic development. These sociologists naively hoped that globalization would bring about a crisis that would weaken the imperial power of the United States.

In contrast to these interpretations, another sociological approach emerged that looked closely at culture and symbols and came to the opposite conclusion: the Mexican system was based on a strange but solid civil society whose very complexity could account for the legitimacy of nationalist authoritarianism. In addition to reaching this conclusion, this approach also theorized that certain changes were taking place in how national identity was constituted within this civil society, changes that seemed to suggest a deep systemic crisis was drawing near. Some of us also believed this would be a crisis of legitimacy, with basic mediating devices going haywire. These studies of identity and "Mexicanness" linked up with approaches that analyzed power relationships from what we now call "postmodern" points of view. From our perspective, the alternatives for the future were to be found within changing civil society itself and had to form a part of globalization, instead of opposing it. Paradoxically, globalization seemed to strengthen civic culture, rather than weaken it. By contrast, it was the authoritarian state that could not hold out against the winds of globalization.

I cannot resist the temptation of assuming a connection between the critical situation of sociology and the cultural tensions observable in North American societies. I think this connection is to be found primarily in the ways in which traditional identities are losing legitimacy. As far as Mexico is concerned, I am convinced that we are faced with the problem of constructing postnational forms of identity, to use Habermas's formula.[4] In this sense, I think we can speak of a post-Mexican condition, not only because the NAFTA era has plunged us into so-called globalization, but primarily because the crisis of the political system has put an end to specifically "Mexican" forms of legitimation and identity. We can understand this process better if we compare it with the fall of the Iron Curtain and the collapse of the Soviet socialist bloc. Without a doubt, "Westernization"—and "Americanization," in the Mexican case—are important effects induced from the outside, but derived from the huge internal breakdown of a complex system of legitimation and consensus.[5]

However one chooses to read it, the collapse of political systems born at the beginning of the twentieth century was a great surprise to many. While the social sciences may not have made any surprising discoveries, vast regions of the world have undergone amazing social changes. Latin America has ceased to be a mosaic of dictatorships, the socialist world has evaporated into thin air, and Europe has traveled far down the road to unification. It is no wonder then that, looking out over this rapidly changing world, the social sciences feel as if they are locked up inside an anachronistic cage and are looking for bridges to get out. Perhaps sociology made no great discoveries, but its subject of study underwent spectacular transformations. Remember that during the nineteenth century the most important achievements in the social sciences—symbolized by Marx and Tocqueville—had the spectacle of the new world inaugurated by the modern revolutions as their motor or magnet. After all, Marx and Tocqueville had the privilege of dissecting a world in transition, societies whose convulsions revealed their inner workings and allowed the curious eye to pry into their most intimate secrets. Should we not expect this new century to draw new gazes to discover unknown social dimensions?

The fact that the old Mexican system finally lies dying on the sociologists' dissecting table is a cause for celebration: not only because its body is laying a bridge to democracy but also because examining its body may—as I fervently hope—spur the social sciences forward.

A profound crisis of identity and legitimacy that began to ripen in 1968 has destroyed the old Mexican regime. This kind of crisis offers a privileged opportunity for research and reflection. The breakdowns of a system are for sociologists what eclipses are for astronomers: in these moments, we can get a better look at

---

4. See Jürgen Habermas, *The Postnational Constellation: Political Essays,* trans. and ed. Max Pensky (Cambridge: MIT Press, 2001).

5. "Americanization" refers here to a "United States of Americanization," or "North Americanization," as Latin Americans would have it.

the outline of a society and the great tensions traversing it. All of a sudden, the sociologist realizes that the borders have vanished and the bars have fallen off the cage, and he gazes out at the exterior space lit by the strange light of the eclipse. This pale glow seems to be inviting us to the macabre but fascinating task of examining the social body *in articulo mortis*, listening to its death rattles, and beginning to write out its death certificate.

At this moment we ask ourselves: can we tune our instruments to locate certain organs, mechanisms, systems, devices, and processes, to learn how they function and to predict how they malfunction? Can we determine whether any of these organs or devices is responsible, say, for functions of legitimation? Perhaps the magical effects of the twilight are what make me think that we can do this—or will be able to, in the near future.

For the moment, I think we can understand that the end of the Mexican political system is part of the great worldwide transformations that have shaken regimes built on revolutionary traditions, signaling the end of the twentieth century. Up to a point, the Mexican democratic reform is an aftershock of the great 1989 earthquake. Not even NAFTA could prevent this shock—and it may even have accelerated it. Looking at this from the shaky Mexican point of view, we can now ask ourselves: Will these great worldwide changes affect the U.S. political system as well? To what extent has the fall of the Berlin Wall affected the legitimating devices of the United States? These are questions that some of us bewildered Mexicans ask ourselves as we accept the invitation to cross the border on the bridges laid by U.S. social science. But we cannot arrive as academic wetbacks; instead, we come as intellectual wet blankets to dampen American enthusiasm for the golden end of history that seems to be drawing near.

I am convinced that creating and stimulating public feelings about otherness is one of the most important functions of the legitimizing apparatuses. I find it hard to believe that the end of the Cold War and the extinction of Communism as the great embodiment of menacing alterity will not bring about significant shake-ups or changes in the political system of the United States, at some point in the near future.[6]

But let us leave this wishful thinking aside and return to Mexico, where for many years the embodiment of menacing alterity was the United States. NAFTA marked the end of this myth, which was worn out already, and helped open the doors of what I have called "the cage of melancholy." I coined the term as a contrast to the modern and disenchanted "iron cage" Max Weber spoke of,

6. On this problem, see my book *The Imaginary Networks of Political Power.*

to explain the peculiar political and cultural structure that defined postrevolutionary national identity.[7] But the way in which NAFTA was approved not only laid a bridge and opened the cage. It also opened Pandora's box. The process was swift, and a commercial opening that should have begun years before but had stubbornly been blocked by a nationalist ruling class was negotiated at breakneck speed. The trade liberalization process caught an unwary elite by surprise, without the ability to effectively handle it or the time to learn to navigate the waters of free trade. As an irony of history, inner threats sprang up suddenly along with NAFTA and acquired unexpected force and resonance, pushing the vague menace of the northern giant into the background. An imaginative Indian guerrilla movement challenged the government, provoked a political crisis, and put democratic reform on the agenda. Also, an obscure coalition of hidden interests, including drug dealers, sponsored a few spectacular political murders that shocked Mexican society. The 1994 presidential elections were extremely tense, and they were followed by new economic problems. Overnight, it seemed as though NAFTA had eradicated external menaces but summoned internal dangers that were dispelled not so much by the prowess of governing politicians as by the steadiness of a civil society that drove the transition toward a democratic regime.

The identity crisis that has opened the Mexican cage, built bridges, and knocked down borders has also had some unsettling and perverse effects. Let's look at one example. Up until this point, Mexican national identity was based on an integrationist model that promoted the fusion of Indians and Europeans and exalted the unifying process of mestizaje (there is no exact English translation for this word, meaning racial and cultural mixing, hybridization, and crossbreeding). Racial and ethnic problems were allegedly solved by dissolving into a racial continuum colored by paternalistic forms of building national unity. While this policy took shape in Mexico during the thirties, in the United States the laws governing Indian reservations were changed to preserve ethnic separation by establishing forms of self-government that combined traditional mechanisms and modern legislative methods. Both these so-called solutions failed, each in its own way.

Today Mexico is moving from integrationist paternalism to patrimonialism (to use Weber's term) with multicultural and segregationist overtones. This is a strange cocktail of two failures: Soviet attempts to organize national autonomy and U.S. efforts to keep ethnic and racial groups apart. The result is that in many

7. See my book *The Cage of Melancholy*.

rural areas in southern Mexico, governments are being set up based on so-called customs and mores, which are actually little more than the residue of the political and religious practices of Spanish colonialism—this justified at times with the brand of cultural relativism usually called "political correctness" in the United States.

This is just one example of the ways in which the traditional ruling class seeks to promote postdemocratic means of representation in order to keep the collapse of the old system from reducing its power. Just as it attempts to replace votes with supposedly traditional councils of elders in indigenous areas, so in the rest of society it tries to replace elections with negotiations, congressional debates with lobbying, citizens with corporations, and individuals with nongovernmental organizations, grassroots movements, or virtual guerrillas. This bizarre postdemocratic threat is broadly similar to the abandonment of the color-blind civil rights ideals that were still dominant in the United States during the sixties and have partially been supplanted by the multicultural and multiracial affirmative action programs we know today.

As we stand at this point where the processes taking place in Mexico and the United States meet, halfway across the bridge, we may ask ourselves if this is not in fact a turning point, a sign of significant changes for both nations—changes affecting not only political machinery but also certain aspects of the cultural underpinnings of what we like to call the modern West.

Method in a Cage: How to Escape from the Hermeneutic Circle?

When I was invited to publicly perform a methodological dissection of some project I had done on political culture, two possibilities for the macabre task occurred to me. The first was the design and publication of a journal: more than fifteen years ago, the Mexican Communist Party asked me to direct a new publication and gave me, at first, plenty of leeway in setting its orientation. But I did not get to choose the name, since I lost a vote; I wanted to call it *Hopscotch* (in honor of Julio Cortázar), but the majority decided that it should be called *El Machete*, just like the thirties review founded by Diego Rivera, David Alfaro Siqueiros, and Xavier Guerrero. I should add that I was able to pick a subtitle for *El Machete:* "A Monthly Journal of Political Culture."[1] So I had an intense practical experience in what it means for a myth to endure, and even more, in what it's like to be trapped inside one. In this case, the plot was all too evident: I had to continue editing an old myth from within, making use, if not of the same strategies and hermeneutic codes, then of very similar ones. The journal lasted

This essay was first prepared at the invitation of Larissa Adler for the seminar "Political Culture in Mexico" at the Center of Latin American Studies of the University of Chicago, 26–28 April 1996. Some of the ideas had been developed in a series of talks for the seminar "Mythology of Identity and Savagery" at the National Autonomous University of Mexico (UNAM) in November 1995. Short pieces of this essay were later incorporated into my book *The Artificial Savage*. An earlier translation by R. Lane Kauffman was published in the journal *Transculture* in 1996.
1. Within the committee organizing the journal there was a group, led by Jorge G. Castañeda, who were opposed to widely distributing it commercially and allowing contributors complete editorial freedom. They proposed that it be distributed only to party activists, that its contents be submitted before publication for the approval of the Political Commission of the Mexican Communist Party, and that it be called *El Machete*. All that was approved was the name, symbolic of an old, hard, and conspiratorial idea.

only fifteen months, as the owners of the cage changed course. I won't carry out a dissection of that experience here, since the hermeneutic circle was broken prematurely.[2]

My other idea was a research project, and that experience was—I hope—a more lasting one, although in one sense it was not all that different. While I was writing up the results of my study of Mexican political culture—*The Cage of Melancholy*, which was originally published in Spanish in 1987, I came to understand that I was myself trapped inside the cage I was trying to understand (and critique). Now, ten years later, I would like to offer some methodological reflections on the cage in which those of us who study political culture find ourselves entrapped.

I will address in turn four problems here: research, analysis, interpretation, and presentation.

On Research

I don't want to offer a full definition of political culture now. But I should clarify at the outset that from my point of view, political culture is not made up, on a fundamental level, of what we usually call ideology. What I mean is that its political functions cannot be explained "politically," in terms of interests that are generated in state realms and in social classes. Its functions in legitimating the political order can only be explained "culturally," that is to say, in terms of a set of symbols.[3] There is ideology in political culture, to be sure, but above all there is mythology.

The method I used for my research was not designed to resolve the contradictions that lie nested inside political myths. Because myths are not ideological creatures imposed by the state or the ruling classes, nothing could be further from my thinking than trying to wipe out myths in order to replace them with rational democratic forms. That old Enlightenment commonplace is all worn out. Just because political myths are inserted in complex processes of legitimation does not make them mere cogs of a machine to trick or distract the masses.

All of this raises many problems, but I want to emphasize one in particular:

2. Those interested in this rupture can consult the following: Humberto Musacchio, "¿Por qué hiberna *El Machete*?" *Nexos* 46 (1981); and Daniel Cazés, "El Machete: Recuerdo, un sexenio después," *La Jornada*, 12 July 1987. Arnoldo Martínez criticized Cazés in the same paper later that week, with a response from Daniel Cazés.

3. I have discussed the theoretical bases of the symbolic, cultural, and mythological dimensions of political power in *The Imaginary Networks of Political Power*.

political culture can only be understood over what Fernand Braudel called the *longue durée*. Political culture builds and matures over an extended period, under the decisive intervention of elaborate mythic structures. Political culture, with its trail of myths, usually occupies a long and sometimes thin band of time, extending for many years across the history of a country or region. This peculiarity makes for obvious practical problems in research. To study Mexican political culture, I chose the method that seemed most appropriate: to focus my lens directly on one aspect (which I called the *canon*, or myth of identity) like someone spying through the keyhole, patiently and for a long time, to discover the bedroom secrets of cultural history. It's like seeing a peep show at a fair. I must confess that secrets must be paid for, in this case by giving up the grand panoramic vista, the wide-angle view of the whole spectacle. But this has its advantages: one is not dazzled by the grandiose staging, with all its falsifications, of what Calderón de la Barca called the great theater of the world.

How to investigate the myth of Mexican identity? I set out to take it as a spectacle, as a peep show; I needed to find a "crack" to get inside. I found it following the example of so-called savage thought. I found an animal that was, as Claude Lévi-Strauss would put it, not only good to eat but also good to think: the axolotl. This animal would be entrusted with guiding me through the crack to the keyhole from which I could study the shameless doings of our national culture.

On Analysis

What is it we see through the keyhole? So many things are going on, and in such confusion, that we must choose some way to sort through this avalanche of signs, deeds, and symbols. Let's go back to the example of history. On the one hand, we have what Braudel mockingly called *histoire événementielle.* In the field that interests me, this takes the form of a history of ideas mainly concerned with tracing sequences by narrating successive feats of intellectual prowess, feats that can be documented thanks to the testimony of their protagonists. On the other hand, we find the structuralist focus characteristic of the anthropology of myths, which privileges the study of whole cultural fabrics and the functions of their subcomponents.

The history of ideas tends to limit itself too much by studying key ideas as events, which makes it difficult to understand ideas as expressions of broader cultural networks. For example, the myth of identity has been interpreted as an ideological manifestation of class interests. In contrast, the anthropology of myths tends to see identity as the immanent expression of structural polarities.

Let me offer an example that illustrates the problem: one of the mythemes making up the canon of national identity refers to Mexicans' alleged primitivism. This savage ancestral side is now back in circulation, thanks to the impulse of the indigenous uprising in Chiapas headed by the neo-Zapatistas.

The mytheme of primitivism has a long trajectory in Europe. Studies of primitivism from the perspective of the history of ideas have generally reduced the interpretation of natural man to its noble and benign variants: a paradisiacal life without hardship (soft primitivism), a sober existence without civilized luxuries (hard primitivism), a primordial golden age of human history (chronological primitivism), or the natural condition onto which noxious artificial supplements are imposed (cultural primitivism).[4] This perspective overlooks, among other things, all the myth's malign, aggressive, and dangerous facets, and without these one loses the possibility of understanding both the myth's extraordinary complexity and its enormous plasticity. It is true, on the other hand, that the structuralists' interpretations of the myth of the wild man have produced static visions not helpful in understanding the changes this alloy of figures, ideas, metaphors, fables, and legend has undergone throughout Western history.

It seems to me that we need an evolutionary perspective able to produce a history of myths (or, if we prefer, an anthropology of ideas) so that we can understand long sequences of events without failing to notice the presence of structures: an evolutionary perspective that tries to go behind sequential narration, but doesn't stop at the formal study of mythological structures. I think we also need to focus our attention on certain transitional moments during which symptomatic changes take place both in the myth's composition and in its function within the surrounding cultural fabric. Ten years ago, I was convinced that Mexican political culture was at a moment of transition. I don't think I was wrong.

For this very reason, I find the example of Mexican national identity, and of what I called the axolotl canon, to be revealing. What determines the peculiar composition of mythic elements that makes up the canon? From the point of view of the history of ideas, we could assert this is a stage, developing out of nineteenth-century nationalism, in the invention or construction of a national community. Another interpretation could be the following: a mythic structure deeply embedded in the human spirit emits signals or messages that each cul-

4. As expressed by George Boas and Arthur O. Lovejoy, *A Documentary History of Primitivism and Related Ideas* (Baltimore: Johns Hopkins University Press, 1935). I've studied the problem in my books *Wild Men in the Looking Glass* and *The Artificial Savage.*

ture or individual (in this case, Mexican national consciousness) translates into concrete forms.

The first line of interpretation doesn't allow us to understand the reasons why a given idea is embodied in the work of, say, Samuel Ramos or Octavio Paz. The second line of interpretation assumes the existence of what we could call a message system: the texts of Ramos or Paz (or the murals of Diego Rivera) would be mythic constructions whose peculiarities came from the encoded reception of certain "instructions" produced by a deep structure (a kind of generative grammar) into which the opposition between individual and society, or nature and culture, would have crystallized.[5]

These ways of analyzing myths complicate an evolutionist interpretation. To understand this difficulty, we should take a leap into biology. The genetic code of each organism does not contain the instructions for evolutionary change; changes and variations are not programmed into genetic messages. What is programmed is the stability of the species, not its evolution. It seems to me that evolutionary neurobiology has faced a similar dilemma. As Gerald M. Edelman phrases it, neural maps cannot be explained by the operation of preestablished genetic codes that would supposedly send instructions on how to weave the synapse networks. According to Edelman, we should understand the neural network based on a system of selection, in which the connection happens ex post facto based on a preexisting repertoire. In other words, connections are woven not according to a set of instructions—as with a loom or a computer—but according to a prior repertoire, which in turn is shaped by a process of selecting the most functional connections.[6] The comparison between biological and cultural phenomena is stimulating and illustrative but can only go so far. What I want to point out is the theoretical problem an evolutionary interpretation faces.

In *The Cage of Melancholy* I began the task of drawing the still-blurry map of the evolution of the myth of Mexican identity. The peculiarities of this map do not come from a structural code impressed in the minds of Mexicans; the links, meanders, paths, frontiers, and connections have been formed thanks to a kind of cultural selection, not as a process determined by the preestablished instructions of a symbolic message system. There is no fundamental substance of identity.

5. Authors Octavio Paz and Samuel Ramos and painter Diego Rivera all produced crucial texts in the middle decades of the century on Mexican national identity. [Trans.]
6. Gerald Edelman, *Bright Air, Brilliant Fire: On the Matter of the Mind* (New York: Basic Books, 1992), 81.

On Interpretation

As we interpret the texts describing national identity, we are endlessly tormented by one question: if we listen to their voices, might we not fall under the spell of their myth? If we break into the hermeneutic circle, as Paul Ricoeur recommends, we accept becoming a part of the very semantic field we are trying to understand.[7] Symbolic textures wrap around us and transfer their meanings to us, leaving us entranced. We may be condemned to die if we listen to the siren's song, like the ancient Greek sailors who—to their misfortune—managed to hear the beautiful voices of those dangerous wild women. We could have recourse to the advice Circe gave Odysseus: tie ourselves firmly to the mast of our ship to make sure that after deciphering the siren's song we might continue our travels. In this case, we come back to where we started from, and the long trip could turn into nothing more than the circuitous, accident-prone path back to Ithaca. This option horrified Emmanuel Lévinas, who preferred the example of Abraham accepting Yahweh's peremptory order to leave his homeland forever. In his exodus without return, Abraham even agreed to give his beautiful wife over to the amorous demands of the Egyptian pharaoh—the Other, the stranger —in order to save his life. This option means accepting that the Other escapes our sphere of intelligibility, even if he remains near enough to allow for contact.[8] But Western tradition has done the exact opposite: it has invented and constituted the Other even before hearing his voice.

Thus we face the double difficulty of deciphering texts that in turn interpret identity; my notion of text of course includes the plastic textures of artists. If in our hermeneutic drive we let ourselves be entranced by the texts we analyze, we cannot be certain that our interpretation will not reproduce the mythical invented image of an identity that replaces and displaces our perception of a real identity. But if we don't allow ourselves to be subject to the textual charms of the

---

7. See Paul Ricoeur's polemic with Claude Lévi-Strauss, "Structure et herméneutique," *Esprit* 322 (1963): 596–628.

8. Emmanuel Lévinas, *En découvrant l'existence avec Husserl et Heidegger* (Paris: Vrin, 1984), 191. It is surprising that Lévinas, who has argued for laying oneself bare beyond all nudity before the other whom one must respect as inviolable and irreducible, should accept the existence of that "primitive mentality" invented by French anthropology (see his essay dedicated to Lévy-Bruhl, originally published in 1957, in the book *Entre Nous: On Thinking-of-the-Other*, trans. Michael B. Harshav and Barbara Smith [New York: Columbia University Press, 1998]). Note that in contrast to the "Yahwist" version (Gen. 12:11–20), in the "Elohist" version (Gen. 20:4–6), King Guerar, who takes Sarah as a wife, never touches the wife of Abraham.

images and figures of the identities we are trying to decipher, we run the risk of returning to the Ithaca we already knew, having discovered merely that Mexicans are our very selves.

This research could lead us to conclude that identities live in the fragile mirror of a power that can quickly disappear. This interpretation retransmits the original myth to us: the mask of identity hides, and at the same time reveals, Mexican identity. Now if for some reason this analysis doesn't satisfy us, we can opt to escape from the hermeneutic circle to try to understand identities as part of an unconscious system that acts through Mexican writers without their awareness (as Lévi-Strauss would recommend). And if we search for the roots of Mexican backwardness in national identity, we could say it has to do with the "shadow" Carl Jung spoke of to refer to the dark, repressed, unconscious, and often destructive aspects of personality.

Maybe we should reconsider the advice Circe gives her lover for escaping the sirens' spell. It's an invitation to give up for a moment the deep truths that nest in our inner fortress, in order to lose ourselves in the marvelous labyrinth of meanings and signifiers. But Odysseus avoids losing his way in the hermeneutic maze because he is strongly moored to his inner being: he dares to decode the sirens' song, but he reencodes each fragment he interprets, burying it in his memory. By his bonds he is saved, and with them he binds the madness of signs to the hermeticism of memories. So Odysseus, both hermeneutic and hermetic, both decoder and encoder, returns to Ithaca with his heart broken in pieces and his soul split apart by the experiences of the voyage: a hermeneutic flight and a hermetic return, after which Odysseus is no longer the same.

On Presentation

I have praised the viewpoint of the voyeur who spies on myths through the keyhole; I have proposed an evolutionary interpretation of myths that studies both their duration and mutations; and I have suggested this requires a process of decoding/reencoding in which each deciphered sign of cultural identity is then disguised once more with signs of our own (the process that proceeds from the unmasking of Mexican inferiorities, hypocrisies, and lonelinesses to the reconstruction of the axolotl canon).

But an important problem remains: Doesn't reencoding hide the truth? Why pretend? Why make such an effort to decipher a myth if we are only going to bury it in a crypt? It seems to me that we are facing a problem of presentation, or representation, if you wish. To tackle this problem, I've made use of one of the oldest methods, with origins in Greek theater: irony. In its classical version, irony is a way of saying something different from (and even opposite to) what is meant. It's a rhetorical and allegorical device by which we say one thing to convey another. It's a matter not of deception but of inviting the reader to do the work of interpretation. But to what end? I think the romantics, who were fascinated by irony, gave a good answer to this question: Friedrich Schlegel thought we had to recognize that the world is essentially paradoxical, and can therefore only be understood with an ambivalent attitude. I believe that irony is the expression of a polyvalent method that includes the peep show, the strange mutations, the dangers of otherness, and the mirror play of hermeneutics. The ironic method allows us to be hermeneutic and hermetic at the same time. That way we can escape from the hermeneutic cage, just as long as we have been able first to climb inside and carry off the myths it encloses. Sometimes getting into the cage is harder than getting out. And the most difficult thing of all is ensuring that we do not make a disorderly escape but instead take flight with a grace befitting our adventures in the territories of political culture. Rather than disdainfully burying all that we have brought out of the cage, like the carnivalesque Spanish burial of sardines at the beginning of Lent, we must bring it along with us, in ironic and playful flight.

II

THE

POST-MEXICAN

CONDITION

The Malinche's Revenge: Toward a
Postnational Identity

After a few decades of nationalist delirium, the time has come for the great opening to the outside world. Since the beginning of the eighties there have been signs that Mexico is no longer the paradise of patriotic and chauvinistic politicians. The great crisis of 1982 confirmed the worst prognosis: even when it was awash with oil, the postrevolutionary system could not manage to bring the country out of underdevelopment. We could apply to the eighties what General de Gaulle said about the difficult fifties in France: "It's no longer a matter of seizing power, but of picking up the pieces."

Certainly the Mexican political system, once famous for its stability, has been seriously battered. To this day, the PRI government has not found any other way out than a rushed integration into the North American economy. The Free Trade Agreement with the United States and Canada is something that should have been calmly debated and firmly negotiated at least twenty years ago. But in the early seventies, the Mexican government was as far from opening negotiations on a free trade agreement as it was from promoting a regime with democratic freedoms, multiple parties, and a healthy parliamentary system. Both things were seen as an ominous surrender of our sovereignty: Mexico should follow its own nationalist path, without imitating the classical forms of capitalist accumulation and democratic representation. As long as business prospered in the shade of protectionism and corruption, the Right kept quiet. The marginalized

This essay appeared in the first issue of *Este País* magazine, in April 1991, as a comment on the unsettling results of a poll: 59 percent of Mexicans would agree to integrate with the United States to form a single country if that would improve their quality of life. Other survey results confirmed the weakening of traditional Mexican nationalism.

Left lived in the depths of statolatry and hostility toward the tentacles of imperialism.

Twenty years later, we carry on, still lacking classical capitalist development or a formally democratic system. By force of our originality, we have come to the most crude backwardness: patriotic excesses have led us to where we have to import capital and electoral observers from the United States to watch over our curious postmodern path toward modernity.

These ironies would only make us smile if they weren't hiding sharp discontent at the deepest layers of Mexican culture. What I mean is that, as in many countries with a colonial past, this discontent reveals the presence of deep cultural contradictions and not merely obstacles on the path of social and economic progress. This discontent has grown since the fall of the Berlin Wall, which has further confused the situation.

The results of these surveys on nationalism, sovereignty, free trade, and ties with neighboring countries lead us straight to thinking about the problems of civilization I've been talking about (which I discussed at length in my book *The Cage of Melancholy*). If we begin with the idea that we are passing through a period of sharp cultural tensions, we should not be surprised that the great majority of those surveyed wish to form a single country with the United States, opt for closer economic ties, and want to eliminate border restrictions on the free flow of goods and services. A certain portion of those surveyed even declare themselves in favor of the complete elimination of the border with the United States.

We should not be alarmed by the results of these surveys. But we could wonder whether revolutionary nationalism—hegemonic official ideology—still remains one of the bases of the Mexican system. The political thinking that sustained the authoritarian system is fatally wounded, and this is something we should celebrate, since it helps to accelerate the democratic transition. And yet this has other dramatic consequences: the cultural structures that symbolically bound Mexicanness to authoritarian forms of government are also breaking apart. This has meant that part of the population is experiencing the political crisis as a true existential problem—not so much a political shake-up that makes the government totter as a great earthquake that threatens all of national reality.

Because of the way it was constituted, postrevolutionary political culture in Mexico suffers from an original sin: it creates the illusion that implanting political democracy and economic development would be an assault on Mexican idiosyncrasy. It is thought necessary that the government administer external modernity in careful doses, mixing and diluting it into the pure veins of the national soul. The result is supposedly a mixed socioeconomic structure that is potentially explosive (like the mythical mestizo), whose secret formula is jealously guarded by the custodians of the system. These are the nationalist myths that are collapsing. The great crack in political culture in 1988 allowed many Mexicans to gaze into the fissure and observe the secret inner workings of the system. What Mexicans saw in the deep hiding places of revolutionary nationalism confirmed the urgent need to close up those hiding places and cover them over with earth, in order to begin the journey toward democracy. It seems to me that this is further confirmed by the surveys, which show how in recent years national pride and the resulting willingness to go to war for the fatherland have declined, a trend that unfortunately is not evident in the United States and Canada. We did not need this survey to see that willingness to go to war has risen in the United States; we need only observe the course of the conflict in the Persian Gulf to confirm that nationalism and patriotic militarism are powerful and growing tendencies in our neighbor to the north.

Mexican culture is ailing because a large portion of Mexicans refuse to keep playing the role of artificial savages in the theater of politics. Mexicans are accepting the inevitable arrival of modernity, without any masks to conceal their fears or to try to fool foreigners. In fact, modernity arrived long ago, but it took the form of a revolutionary nationalism that put up symbolic barriers against the spread of Western values. That is why a culture of hypocrisy and dissimulation spread so far.

I hope I am properly understood: when I point out the need to overcome cultural unease, I am not proposing as a cure an integration to the Anglo-American world parallel to the economic agreements on free trade with the United States and Canada. By affirming the need to face up to the Western condition of Mexican culture, we can free ourselves of the now useless weight of duplicity, to open up the way toward a rich and democratic multiplicity. Both in the mixed economy and in mestizo culture, duality has concealed how ironfisted nationalist unification smothered multicolored Mexican society and legitimized underdevelopment and authoritarianism.

Mexican culture is facing a tension similar to that faced by Germans and Spaniards. In regions where ethnic frontiers do not match political ones, regions that have also passed through a nationalist and fascist period, it is necessary to find the bases for what Jürgen Habermas has termed a postnational identity.[1]

For Habermas the alternative can be found in what he calls "constitutional patriotism," that is to say, pride in having managed to overcome fascism demo-

1. See his stimulating little book *The Postnational Constellation.*

cratically and enduringly. Clearly other European countries are facing this option, such as Greece and Portugal, as are the countries of Eastern Europe, whose 1989 revolutions have led to a democratic transition. There are also a few—not many—countries in the so-called Third World that glimpse a similar challenge, although in addition to democratically overcoming authoritarianism, they also must overcome the immense problems of economic backwardness. In such cases—like Mexico—we are faced with the problem of overcoming nationalist pride to build a postnational identity based on the multicultural and democratic forms of a civic life that forms part of the Western world.

The transition toward a postnational political culture is already taking place, and a large part of the Mexican population has initiated this change, as the surveys show. What we need to know now—to follow Habermas's line of thinking —is whether the political and intellectual class will accept these changes pragmatically, as a mere reorganization of their alliances, or whether it will accept them as a new beginning for our political culture. Habermas places all his hopes in the universal spirit of modernity and the Enlightenment as the foundation of the new forms of political culture. I, on the other hand, fear that modernity, together with nationalism, is deathly wounded and that we have no choice but to face the postmodernity of the fragmented Western world of which we form a part.

Missing Democracy

Mexico is heavenly and undoubtedly hellish, Malcolm Lowry once said. Under the volcano that so fascinated that English writer, we should add, there exists a strange territory which separates heaven from hell. In that territory lives and reigns unrivaled a beast that political zoology has not yet managed to classify: the Mexican state. Heaven is just up there; one can see it and dream about it. Up there are the fruits of the Mexican Revolution, the heroes of the fatherland, the nationalized nation, the *ejidos* of the agrarian reform, popular culture, the expropriation of foreign oil companies, social security, rescued indigenous traditions, the murals of Diego Rivera . . . Down here, we daily suffer the inclemencies of a hell of despotism and authoritarianism, of corruption and social misery, of repression and violence, of an old revolution institutionalized by political bureaucracy and hemmed in by monopolies and bankers. In between rises up the all-powerful sixty-year-old state, balancing tensions and pacifying conflicts. Various authors have baptized it with different names: the Creole Leviathan, the Philanthropic Ogre, the Despotic Power, the Populist Government, the Six-Year Monarchy, and other curious terms that point up the difficulty of understanding the complex space of political hegemony in Mexico. Yet one thing is clear: it is evident to all serious analysts that the Mexican state *does not have a democratic character.* Anyone could recognize some democratic aspects here or there, but only the self-satisfaction of the dominant bureaucracy is capable of affirming that a democratic regime exists in Mexico.

This article was originally presented on 7 June 1982 at a conference organized by the city government of Florence, Italy, entitled "Structures of Power in the Third World: Between Authoritarianism and Democracy." My title is a play on a book by Umberto Eco whose title would translate as "The Missing Structure," although it has not been published in English.

For many years, a large part of the Mexican Left passively tolerated the precariousness of political democracy—"formal" democracy, it was called—in the name of a "superior" democracy of a social nature. This was particularly dramatic at moments of crisis, when the state apparatus was shaken by either popular upheaval or the voracity of the ruling classes. A few years ago, the novelist Carlos Fuentes signaled the existence of two dangers for the Mexican political system: in the first place, the repressive leanings of the business class, and in the second, the danger of political democracy. To the degree that one holds—following the famous thesis of Albert Hirschman—that practically every underdeveloped country must sacrifice democracy for stability, the only viable option seems to be strengthening the state's capacity to negotiate and arbitrate.[1] This means opting for the governing autonomy of the public sector, stability lightly seasoned with social justice, but without democracy, to achieve "an honorably optimistic national future" that exploited and exploiters must peacefully share.

Carlos Fuentes's ideas about political democracy illustrate the blindness that the Mexican Left has inherited, as a double burden, from the Mexican version of populism (Cardenismo, a kind of social democratic populism) and from orthodox Stalinist Marxism. For many years, this double inheritance has kept us from presenting alternatives to the Mexican system. In December 1935, during the political crisis that pitted him against former president Calles, Lázaro Cárdenas—the president who carried out the agrarian reform and expropriated the oil wealth from foreign companies[2]—wrote in his notes that "Mexican conservatives, enemies of the social program of the Revolution, wish government policy to be the democracy practiced in capitalist States, that is, freedom for their interests and impositions of their criteria."[3]

On the same page, he also wrote two theses that could have come out of the mouth of any thirties Marxist: "In capitalist States, democracy will only be theoretical, since the strongest will always have the influence," and "political democracy cannot exist unless economic democracy is imposed."[4]

We now know that economic democracy cannot exist without political de-

---

1. See Albert O. Hirschman, *Journeys toward Progress: Studies of Economic Policy-Making in Latin America* (New York: Greenwood Press, 1963).

2. Cárdenas presided over the most "revolutionary" administration in postrevolutionary Mexico (1934–1940), not only in its social programs but also—and more importantly here—in its institutionalization of one-party rule. [Trans.]

3. Lázaro Cárdenas, *Obras, I: Apuntes 1913–1940* (Mexico: UNAM, 1972), 334.

4. Ibid.

mocracy, and that so-called formal—or bourgeois—democracy is not so contemptible as was once thought. From the dramatic experiences of the peoples of the socialist countries, and also from our own tragic 1968, we now know that the two forms of democracy are closely connected. We know that separating them is a sign and an instrument of complex mechanisms of exploitation. The idea that democracy is something connected to conservative and business interests opposed to the nationalist social justice of the ruling party (the PRI) makes no sense today.

The Trilateral Commission, a high-level organization of the capitalist states, has also discovered that "an excess of democracy" makes rich countries "ungovernable."[5] The exercise of political democracy tends to corrode and subvert not just the authoritarian systems of so-called underdeveloped countries but every system of exploitation. Carlos Fuentes aimed to make us believe that the "very wide spectrum of ideological tendencies" sheltered by the PRI is a good substitute (because it is "stabilizing") for the true multiparty system that only exists in a few countries. The self-proclaimed or self-injected multiplicity of the PRI would be better than the disguised monolithic unity of Anglo-American countries. And yet Fuentes warned us right away that "the PRI's range of options is as wide as stability allows." Very true. The bad part is that the defense of "stability" leaves popular options with a narrow field of manuever, since the "stability" of the system is nothing more than the preservation of the order established by the ruling class to save us from the "anarchy" of independent struggles by the exploited classes.

The Political Labyrinth

The debates about the question of democracy revolve around a central problem: what is the relationship between society and the state? The way we resolve this problem determines our interpretation of the whole of the Mexican political system. The problem is that since the 1910 revolution, Mexican society has not fragmented into sociopolitical currents that represent the various interests in play through a system of parties, unions, and other organizations. In Mexico, the great political currents of our times have not really crystallized into parties: there is no conservative right-wing party, in the classical sense of the concept,

5. Samuel P. Huntington, "The United States," in *The Crisis of Democracy: Report on the Governability of Democracies to the Trilateral Commission*, ed. Michel J. Crozier, Samuel P. Huntington, and Joji Watanuki (New York: New York University Press, 1975), 113.

and we do not find an organic expression of Social Democracy, much less Christian Democracy. We could say that the objective social bases are given for the existence of each: we have a large and extremely reactionary sector of the bourgeoisie, along with conservative middle sectors; we have a reformist labor movement; and we have a population that overwhelmingly—95 percent—professes the Catholic faith. On the other hand, the Mexican Communist Party traditionally suffers from a weak working-class base and has been the object of multiple persecutions. In addition, Mexico has also not seen the populist/militarist split that in some Latin American countries has produced a peculiar repeating pattern of coups led by military groups who react to the real or imagined dangers of popular upheaval. This is true even though Mexican populism had its base in an enormous radicalized peasant mass, and the army was a very important factor in postrevolutionary politics until the mid-forties (the executive branch was in the hands of generals until 1946).

It would seem that the ample bosom of the Mexican state can shelter conservative bourgeois groups, social democratic currents, Marxists, Catholics, unions, organizations of peasants and of middling groups, populists, and soldiers. There is room for everything inside the Mexican Leviathan.

But let us explore, if only briefly, the historical process that has shaped the extraordinary expansion of the Mexican state. The institutionalization of the authoritarian political system that has lasted down to the present day began more than a half century ago. At the end of the twenties, in the midst of a deep political crisis sparked by the assassination of General Obregón, General Plutarco Elías Calles managed to domesticate revolutionary forces and place them under the close vigilance and control of a new government bureaucracy. That was the goal of creating the National Revolutionary Party (ancestor of the PRI).[6] As a biting critic of the time, Luis Cabrera, put it, the objective was "taking care of the elections that the secretary of government was in charge of before." Uneasily watching this course of events from afar, Peruvian socialist thinker José Carlos Mariátegui rightly affirmed that "the least astute energies of reaction had spent themselves in attacking the revolution from without, while the wisest operated from within the revolution, waiting for the hour for Thermidorean action."[7]

6. On this period, see Thomas Benjamin, "Rebuilding the Nation," in Meyer and Beezley, *The Oxford History of Mexico*, 467–502, esp. 471–77. [Trans.]

7. José Carlos Mariátegui (1884–1930) was an innovative socialist thinker and the founder of the Peruvian Communist Party. "Thermidor" refers to the month, in the revolutionary calendar, in which conservatives wrested control of the French Revolution from the Jacobins. [Trans.]

Today, with the perspective a half century of history gives us, we can understand that the hour for counterrevolutionary action sounded in 1929, and that action managed to put in place an institutional Thermidor designed to guarantee the hegemony of the ruling classes for several decades. The institutional government inaugurated by Calles was in reality the dictatorship of a bureaucracy that administered the process of capital accumulation. Unlike the Thermidor of Carranza, which had involved open and violent struggle against the rural masses, this second version was a bureaucratic Thermidor that opened the door to the most grotesque forms of class struggle: dubious pacts and alliances, assassinations, and corruption. The class confrontations grew sharper in this era, but they were led into the dark factional pact that gave birth to the PNR, grandfather of the PRI.[8]

Despite everything, the great global crisis that began in 1929—and greatly affected Mexico—brought to the fore much sooner than expected the need to advance social and economic reforms that, even considering their capitalist orientation, shored up the bases of popular legitimation of the new state. The faction led by Calles was incapable of leading those reforms. It was Lázaro Cárdenas who openly confronted Calles and carried them out. Thus the great nationalizations and redistributions of land consolidated the worker and peasant base of the government and laid the basis for the development of a modern capitalist state.[9]

But the Cárdenas reforms did not manage to halt the process of institutionalization of the authoritarian political apparatus. On the contrary, the socioeconomic reforms of Cárdenas complemented the political reforms of Calles. If we observe the later course of Mexican political life, essentially directed by right-wing governments, we can understand that the roots of the authoritarian state

8. As head of the ultimately victorious "Constitutionalist" forces during the Mexican Revolution, Venustiano Carranza defeated the forces of Pancho Villa and Emiliano Zapata—the "Thermidor of Carranza"—and later became president (1917–1920), leading the revolution in a conservative direction that prompted forces under his ally Álvaro Obregón to rebel and depose him in 1920. It was the group around Obregón who, in a violent and unstable political setting, drew up the blueprint for the bureaucratic revolutionary state—the "institutional Thermidor." See Thomas Benjamin, "Rebuilding the Nation." [Trans.]

9. On the importance of Cardenismo in consolidating the Mexican revolutionary state, see the essays in Gilbert Joseph and Daniel Nugent, eds., *Everyday Forms of State Formation: Revolution and the Negotiation of Rule in Modern Mexico* (Durham: Duke University Press, 1994); and Alan Knight, "Cardenismo: Juggernaut or Jalopy?" *Journal of Latin American Studies* 26 (February 1994): 73–107. [Trans.]

are to be found in the peculiar fusion of political uniformity and social reform-ism that took place in the thirties.[10]

The political transition of 1940, when the Cárdenas administration came to an end, is perhaps the most important moment in understanding the form in which the control of the PRI government was established. The forces of the Right, rudely shaken by the Cárdenas reforms, made one last attempt to regroup in opposition to the state: for the 1940 elections, they tried to come together be-hind the candidacy of Juan Andrew Almazán, who enjoyed significant support from urban middle sectors and even from certain popular groups. At the same time, a powerful rural movement, of a Catholic and reactionary bent, came back to life headed by *sinarquistas*. But the true general staff of these forces, the Mon-terrey bourgeoisie and the Catholic Church, came to terms with the govern-ment: they thought that in the long term their interests would be better served and protected by the authoritarianism of the Mexican revolutionary state than by the development of an alternative oppositional political space. Within a few years, the government would tolerate and even encourage the existence of a party that symbolically—and only symbolically—expressed the interests of the Right, the PAN, founded in 1939.[11]

Something similar happened at the other end of the political spectrum. The

10. As Knight closes his article about the machinery of state constructed in these years, "the in-stitutional shell of Cardenismo remained, but its internal dynamic was lost. In other words, the jalopy was hi-jacked by new drivers; they retuned the engine, took on new passengers, and then drove it in a quite different direction." Knight, "Cardenismo," 107. [Trans.]

11. As Carlos Monsiváis has written, "the most notorious Utopia of the Right in twentieth-century Mexico was represented by the Cristero War (1926–1929), an effect of clerical anger at the policies of the post-revolutionary State, whose monopolization of power entailed the secu-larization of education, and thus an anticlerical offensive." As many as 70,000 died, including President Obregón, who was assassinated by a clerical sympathizer, before "the rebellion even-tually died out, while the Church hierarchy comes to an agreement with the State behind the backs of the Cristeros." Monsiváis, *Mexican Postcards*, ed. and trans. Jon Kraniauskas (New York: Verso, 1997), 131–32. The nonaggression pact reached at the end of the struggle led the church to check the growth of the sinarquista movement at the end of the thirties, and set the tone for church-state relations for the next half century. A similar course was taken by the Mon-terrey bourgeoisie, the Catholic-allied elite dominating the interlocking network of industrial firms in the Northeast who played a powerful role in Mexican industrialization. See John Sher-man, *The Mexican Right: The End of Revolutionary Reform* (Westport, Conn.: Praeger, 1997). These points are addressed in more detail in the essay "Journey to the Center of the Right." [Trans.]

Left was represented primarily by a relatively strong Communist Party, influential in the countryside and in broad sectors of intellectuals and the bureaucracy, and by the organized labor movement headed by Vicente Lombardo Toledano. Both currents, for different reasons, agreed to give their support to the new president of the republic, General Manuel Ávila Camacho. The result was that within a few months, both the Lombardistas and the Communists lost their hegemony over the forces they represented and found themselves almost completely marginalized from the labor and peasant movements. Later on, Lombardo founded the Partido Popular, which symbolized the Left—with official permission—in this puppet theater of a political system. For its part, the Communist Party was driven underground into more than three decades of illegality.[12]

The outcome was that different social forces were impelled to negotiate their conflicts inside the state as corporatist groups, not as political currents. The Workers' Confederation of Mexico, the National Peasant Confederation, the Catholic Church, and businessmen came to build direct and stable channels of communication with the government apparatus. This was how the reformist and social democratic impulses of the labor movement represented by Lombardo were incorporated into the state machinery. The same happened to the populist currents that led the peasant movement. The Catholic Church agreed to negotiate the faith at the highest levels of the administration and renounced all organic links to the sinarquista political movement. The various business groups lost any interest in promoting the formation of a genuine conservative party but gradually broadened their interests in finances and mass media.

In general terms, a sharp line was drawn between the machinery of government and the leaders of large social forces. It is true that at times the political bureaucracy swallowed figures coming out of social groups, especially from the labor and peasant movements, but that was not the norm. In the opposite direction, the business class was also fattened by politicians who had been enriched by corruption. Yet despite all this, the enormous and complex political bureaucracy developed its own systems for reproduction. That is why it is interesting to introduce into the analysis of the Mexican state Antonio Gramsci's famous equation by which the state = political society + civil society. Only by examining the state in its broadest sense can we understand the dynamics of the Mexican political system. One example is enough to illustrate this situation: one hardworking U.S. professor, Peter H. Smith, spent many years compiling the bi-

12. See the essays "Lombardo or Revueltas?" and "Marxism on the Gallows." [Trans.]

ographies of every individual who occupied important public posts in Mexico between 1900 and 1976, with the aim of inputting this voluminous data into a computer and finding the patterns of behavior of the political elite.[13] More than six thousand members of the elite were processed, classified, and correlated in search of the hidden logic of the system. The results the computer spit out can be summed up in a single word: *nothing*. Nothing, that is, that is not completely obvious to any reasonably informed observer of the peculiar style of Mexican politics—much less every well-trained politician. With this I do not mean to discount in any way the patient and arduous labor of Peter H. Smith. I mean to underscore the fact that no technical refinements will manage to discover a *hidden structure* in the government machinery that could explain the rules of the Mexican state's game. That is the true finding of Professor Smith's detailed research, although he may not have fully realized it. It turns out that the rules of the political game make sense only if they are studied inside the network that links the machine of government to civil society or, more concretely, to the organizations of the labor movement, the peasant movement, business, and the Catholic Church, to mention only the most obvious links. We should add— among other factors—the ways that culture and education are structured, which are no less important for all their subtlety. This is how we would complement the elements of Gramsci's equation.

But here another difficulty arises. The presence of an overwhelming authoritarianism and the absence of democratic traditions in Mexico have made many think—following Gramsci—that we find ourselves facing a typical "Oriental" situation in which a war of movement is dominant, and civil society is "primitive and gelatinous."[14] In reality there is nothing primitive or gelatinous about Mexican civil society. The seeming paradox lies in that, despite the absence of a democratic structure, the processes of political mediation—which have their distant roots in the Mexican Revolution—are extraordinarily strong and provide the state with a solid and broad basis of consensus. This mediating civil society is authoritarian and antidemocratic, but it is not a fruit of backwardness. On the contrary, it has grown stronger as the most advanced and modern forms of capitalism have expanded. As a result, we can say that the choice between authoritarianism and democracy does not run parallel to the duality of underdevelopment and development. To put it in other words, Mexican authoritarianism is

13. Peter H. Smith, *Labyrinths of Power: Political Recruitment in Twentieth-Century Mexico* (Princeton, N.J.: Princeton University Press, 1979).

14. This was opposed, in Gramsci's thinking, to the patient, parliamentary war of position a more "developed" civil society called for. [Trans.]

not a consequence of backwardness that will gradually be overcome in nearly direct proportion to the advance of modernization. This could be tied to a more general thesis: political democracy is not simply the normal superstructural product of capitalist development. In large measure, it is a political and cultural conquest of popular movements.

On this point it is worth mentioning, if only in passing, the problem of the army and the military. From after the revolution to the end of the thirties, the army's political interventions took the form of the struggles and alliances between military *caudillos* and caciques. Unification into a single official party slowly brought this to an end. At a certain point, the military sector of the official party even disappeared (and it was then composed of only three sectors: workers, peasants, and the "popular" sector). It was only in the sixties that the Mexican army was almost totally marginalized from politics. From then on, the eruption of new social contradictions—typical of rapid capitalist modernization—slowly and almost imperceptibly returned the army to an important position in government policy. It so happened that the government could no longer manage in a "civil" manner the rural and urban upheavals that shook a society rapidly entering a phase of capitalist expansion. It became more and more necessary to resort to the army to control and repress the peasants who invaded lands and gave shelter to guerrillas, to keep the unions shackled to the government, or to persecute students who rebelled. The collateral phenomena of drug trafficking and terrorism contributed to technically modernizing the army and strengthening its position, placing it in an important strategic position inside the dense correlation of forces within the Mexican state. If the specter of a military coup has been frightening us for some time, this is not due to the country's backwardness but, on the contrary, is a product of capitalist modernization. We do not know exactly how far the politicization and lobbying capacity of the Mexican army have increased. What is certain is that it has ceased to be a mere instrument of the civilian bureaucracy.

The Heads of the Minotaur

Instead of losing ourselves in the mechanical labyrinth of the machinery of government, perhaps it would be more useful to try to study the anatomy of Mexican civil society. But here we run into an obstacle: the political party system does not reflect the true makeup of civil society. On the contrary, the political party system almost exclusively reflects the despotic, centralized, and authoritarian character of the Minotaur—the government apparatus. Various sociopolitical forces are barely reflected in political parties, since the system is composed of an enormous and omnipresent official ruling party (the PRI), which operates under a single-party logic, and a dozen little parties, some of which are not even legally recognized.

In Mexico we find four great sociopolitical forces that are hegemonic in the capitalist system, properly speaking. None of them are expressed by means of a political party (not even the PRI). These forces are the technocracy, tied to state capitalism; the bankers, headed by the two large banks, BANAMEX and BAN-COMER; the traditional bourgeoisie, led by the old Monterrey group; and the new businessmen who have developed under state protectionism since the forties. These are four *political forces* (or tendencies), not distinct social strata, and since they are political forces, they promote various options and bring together very different segments of the bourgeoisie and petty bourgeoisie. The technocracy is not organized as such: it holds positions in the government apparatus and in businesses owned wholly or in part by the state.[15] Bankers are organized, of course, and they enjoy enormous negotiating power. Because they control the nervous system of the monopolistic economy, they try to assume a leading role over various groups of businessmen, and they serve as a privileged bridge crossing all the mechanisms of negotiation between the government and the private sector.[16] The Monterrey group, for its part, heads up the oldest sectors of the bourgeoisie, which take a more independent stance toward the government and are more tied to the production of intermediate and capital goods in close association with foreign capital. This group is expressed in a certain way through the Employers' Confederation of the Mexican Republic (COPARMEX). Finally, the new businessmen, who tend to represent the producers of consumer goods, were favored and even fostered by government subsidies and policies favoring import substitution industrialization. They organized themselves in the National Chamber of Manufacturing Industries (CANACINTRA) and have had considerable influence over the governments of the state of Mexico and the Federal District.[17]

Probably the most important political event in the last ten years has been the

15. On the technocracy and its growing power, see Miguel Angel Centeno, *Democracy within Reason: Technocratic Revolution in Mexico* (University Park: Pennsylvania State University Press, 1994); and Roderic Ai Camp, "The Time of the Technocrats and the Deconstruction of the Revolution," in Meyer and Beezley, *The Oxford History of Mexico*, 609–36. [Trans.]

16. This situation ended, obviously, with the nationalization of banks in 1982, which put the task of determining financial policy in the hands of the technocrats.

17. On the differences between these organizations, see Roderic Ai Camp, *Entrepreneurs and Politics in Twentieth-Century Mexico* (New York: Oxford University Press, 1989), 146–66. [Trans.]

process of rapprochement between these four political forces, with the gradual erasure of the social and political boundaries separating them and the progressive coordination and centralization of their interests. Undoubtedly the massive production and export of oil were a crucial factor in accelerating this process. Signs of this phenomenon can be seen principally in three facts: (1) the openly intransigent and aggressive attitude of one portion of businessmen during moments of crisis and transition (1976 and 1982); (2) the frankly monetarist and antipopular economic policies of the technocrats and their every day greater hegemony over the government apparatus; and (3) the creation in the late seventies of the Mexican Businessmen's Council (CMHN), which gathers together the elite of the bourgeoisie—thirty persons—and of the Coordinating Council of Businessmen (CCE), which brings together the chambers and associations of industrialists and merchants.[18]

So technocrats, bankers, the traditional bourgeoisie, and the new businessmen are the four great pillars of bourgeois civil society, properly speaking. To finish off this sketch, we should add the pillars supporting the civil bureaucracy associated with specific sociopolitical interests: the populist bureaucracy tied to peasant organizations, the union bureaucracy that directs the labor movement, and the bureaucracy bureaucracy—that is, the leaders and organizations that direct the masses of government employees and related middle sectors. These three forces are expressed in the PRI and make up the peasant, worker, and "popular" sectors, respectively, of the ruling party. Only three decades ago, the political bureaucracy within the Mexican state—especially the part connected with the control of peasants and middle classes—had considerable strength and enjoyed great autonomy. But things have changed in the course of recent years: the gradual strengthening of the technocratic current—progressively more tied to business interests, but also with a growing power of its own—has placed the various sectors of the political bureaucracy under its hegemony.[19] The might of the state economy grew with the exploitation of the immense recently discovered oil reserves while at the same time a deep agricultural crisis weakened the agrar-

18. Camp notes that "on paper, the CCE appears to be the apex organization of the Mexican private sector." Yet "the power behind the throne is the semisecret CMHN." Camp, *Entrepreneurs and Politics in Twentieth-Century Mexico*, 166–67. Both organizations represent an attempt to centralize and concentrate lobbying power in the hands of larger, more capital-intensive business. [Trans.]

19. This tendency toward technocratization was brutally sped up by the nationalization of banks. The future rearticulation of the hegemonic bloc—hard to foresee, since it is taking place during a crisis—will indicate what situation other political forces will be left in.

ian sector and helped to erode the strength of peasant organizations. The new contradictions in the countryside, which involved a profound proletarianization and impoverishment of the peasantry, could no longer be controlled, and the old force of the official peasant organizations crumbled in many regions and faded away nationally. With this, the populist sector was pushed aside, and the technocracy took the agrarian policies of the government into its own hands. On the other hand, the urban middle sectors, whose core are white-collar workers in the service of the state, have tended to break up politically. One large group accepted the political guidance of the technocracy, but another group swung to the right and became clients of the PAN, which is the second-largest electoral force in the country, and certain segments became radicalized and turned to the Left.

In contrast, the political influence of the union bureaucracy has grown considerably during recent years. This evolution has led to a greater polarization of forces within the state, in the measure that intermediate groups of a populist or petty bourgeois type have lost influence or been dispersed. For this reason, the increased influence of labor has meant a loss of maneuvering room and deal-making capacity for the union bureaucracy, which finds itself besieged in its organized fortress, apparently impregnable but with great difficulties in taking a position on other areas of political life.[20]

At the opening of this piece, I wanted to play with the Manichaean impression that the political inferno is separated from the paradise of civil society, and that the state—an intermediary organ—is a place of equilibrium. This is the image the governing bureaucracy has of itself. But in truth we find that inferno and paradise form a single space, which is the space of the state. In Mexico the state seems omnipresent, but as I've pointed out, its omnipresence is not simply the outgrowth of strong roots of violence and coercion in the "gelatinous" terrain of civil society. It is a vast territory, solid and structured, but inhospitable to democratic options.

To bring these reflections to a close, I would like to point to one problem for democracy's prospects in Mexico. As we have seen, I do not start from the idea that democracy is some natural subproduct of the modernization of the capitalist system. Better stated, I think the opposite is true: the way in which capitalist development takes place in Latin American countries offers significant obstacles to the democratization of the state. In Mexico, economic modernization is eating away at the old forms of mediation and legitimation of the authoritarian

20. See Kevin Middlebrook, *The Paradox of Revolution: Labor, the State, and Authoritarianism in Mexico* (Baltimore: Johns Hopkins University Press, 1995). [Trans.]

state, and this tendency, by itself, seems to be strengthening a brand of authoritarianism without any social base. It is true that the opening of new democratic space must necessarily involve the breaking up of old mediations, but if that break is not accompanied by an irreversible and stable rise in popular movements, the consolidation of a democratic alternative seems difficult.

Given its evolution, the political system could be drawing near a dangerous situation. The electoral reform of the late seventies, which legalized various parties, was the result of the significant accumulation of strength by the Left opposition since 1968. But it was also an effect of the erosion of the state's mediating mechanisms. If in the future that erosion advances more swiftly than the popular space of the Left expands, the political system could harden to a considerable degree.

The Political Crisis of 1982

At long last, the crisis is here. The crisis! So feared, so foretold, so deferred or controlled, but so long invisible, slippery, shapeless, or hidden: now the crisis arrives decked out in the most spectacular garb. The nationalization of the banks and the general freeze on currency exchange were the surprising measures the president announced on 1 September 1982, when he revealed—not without some sobs and anguish—the existence of the deepest political and economic crisis Mexico has lived through in the last fifty years.[1]

Suddenly the themes most argued about on the Left—the state, democracy, socialism—have taken on a real, dramatic, present, and tangible dimension. And against all predictions, the remedies decreed by the government came from the Left's recipe book: from one day to the next, without prior warning, the Mexican Left—which was already readying itself to defend against the technocratic moralism the next government seemed to promise—has been pushed into the forum

This article was originally written as the prologue to my 1982 book *El reto de la izquierda* (The Challenge for the Left), which took its title from the last line of the second paragraph.

1. This essay emphasizes the political underpinnings of the economic crisis of 1982, when the state-centered model of import-substitution industrialization that had produced the "Mexican Miracle" of the forties, fifties, and sixties, and had held together through the seventies thanks to populist measures and the oil boom, finally broke apart. A deepening balance-of-payments crisis led President José López Portillo (1976–1982) to decree the establishment of strict currency controls and the nationalization of nearly all private banks. As ever, the exceptions are revealing: the two banks left in private hands were the U.S.-owned Citibank Mexico and the union-owned Banco Obrero. For a firsthand account of the crisis, see Carlos Tello, *La nacionalización de la banca en México* (Mexico: Siglo Veintiuno Editores, 1984). For a broader sense of what provoked it and what was at stake, see Nora Lustig, *Mexico, the Remaking of an Economy*, 2d ed. (Washington, D.C.: Brookings Institution, 1998), chaps. 1 and 2. [Trans.]

as the spiritual, if not material, protagonist of the crisis. The Mexican Left has never experienced such a singular mix of great strength and extreme weakness: theoretical strength, political weakness; cultural strength, social weakness; or, as a military officer would put it, strategic strength, tactical weakness. This is the challenge for the Left.

He Who Cries Last, Cries Best

But it was not just the Left that was getting ready for conservative times. The Right was already licking its lips and rubbing its hands before a weak government, a devalued president, and a technocratic and complacent future ruler. In fact, the bourgeoisie had already begun serving itself big helpings, without realizing that the business boom hidden behind the "Alliance for Production"—a sinister memory—was in reality one of those typical fictitious bonanzas that come before financial crises. Most dramatic of all is that one could hardly imagine a more ineffective economic policy strategy to lead the country through a critical juncture in the international economy than the one put into practice by the government of José López Portillo during nearly six years (1976–1982). The problem was not only that he set a reactionary, monetarist, and antipopular economic policy but that he carried it out with great ineffectiveness and much wavering. Despite everything, oil managed to cover up the problems, for a time.[2]

The economic policies of the López Portillo administration promoted the expansion and autonomy of a financial sector that attracted enormous volumes of capital fleeing productive areas. It generated intense stock market activity based on stocks and bonds whose price had nothing to do with the process by which industrial capital was valued. This set off a speculative and rent-seeking euphoria that invented all kinds of businesses without any real productive base. The difficulties of the Alfa group were a typical sign of a crisis situation in which monetary flows expanded in inverse relation to the devaluation of capital, creating a spiral of debt and inflation.[3] For various reasons, undoubtedly including

2. The "Alliance for Production" was the set of populist policies López Portillo had enacted in the late seventies, which played an important role in bringing on the crisis. [Trans.]

3. The Alfa group was the most powerful element within the interlocking network of companies known as the Monterrey Group, and the political favor and overexpansion it experienced in the seventies led it into a deep crisis in 1982. As Roderic Camp puts it, "For the average Mexican, Alfa's failure affected confidence in the private sector. It would be comparable to General Motors or Exxon going under in the United States." See Camp, *Entrepreneurs*, 215–19. [Trans.]

the political necessity of delaying all economic measures until after the presidential elections, the government allowed the conditions for a financial panic to emerge: capital began to flee overseas in exorbitant amounts, in search of peace and tranquillity. When the government decided to freeze capital movements, it was already too late: the vaults of the central bank were empty, and the country was in no shape to pay off the external debt.

The results were extremely chaotic: the government dedicated itself to misgoverning, the bankers started definancing, businessmen undertook nothing but business trips, capital was decapitalized, unions were stunned, technocrats were contradicting each other, politicians—just in case—were depoliticized, and the future president was speaking about . . . moral renewal. Even so, bankers and big businessmen did not cease to mourn and weep over the paradise lost. President López Portillo, who finally came to understand that the financial crisis would not be stopped with pacts and begging, cried himself on 1 September 1982, but his tears were spilled over the remains of the private banks, which he had just expropriated by means of a stunning decree.[4]

Paradigms and Surprises

Nearly the entire Left supported the nationalization of the banks. It could hardly do otherwise: only extreme sectarian blindness could reject such a deep and significant step in the life of the country. Early interpretations of the event varied, although they could be reduced to two extremes: orthodox and nationalist. Later on, other nuances were introduced.

The first explanation argues that the state adapted to the functional needs of the capitalist system: that is to say, the financial crisis forced the government to take extreme measures to save the global interests of the capitalist class. In contrast, the second explanation suggests that the measure came from the governmental source of national values and interests, the inexhaustible constitutional fount of the Mexican Revolution that continues to bubble up inside the state. All

4. Among other things, López Portillo claimed that "in a few, recent years, a group of Mexicans . . . led, advised and aided by the private banks, have withdrawn more money from this country than all of the empires that have exploited us from the beginnings of our history. We cannot continue to risk that those resources be channeled through the same conduits that have contributed in such a dynamic fashion to generate the severe situation we are going through. We have to organize ourselves to save our productive structure . . . we have to stop the injustice of this perverse process." In consequence, he argued, he had nationalized the banks and set exchange controls. Quoted in John Adams Jr., *Mexican Banking and Investment in Transition* (Westport, Conn.: Quorom Books, 1997), 4–5. [Trans.]

through this book, the reader will read many critiques of the false choice expressed in the question "Lombardo or Revueltas?"[5]

The first explanation resolves the problem by resorting to the traditional economistic paradigm: political and juridical superstructures respond to the determinations of the capitalist economic base. The former adapt to the latter thanks to that chain of "last instances" with which every concrete instance is supposedly explained. Of course, the economistic interpretation can "explain" that there is a structural agreement or logical continuity between the Mexican state and capitalist development. But it does not allow us to understand *why* the banks were nationalized at precisely this moment and in this particular, concrete, and unique way.

The nationalist explanation fits the problem into another paradigm: the polarized presence within the state of two "models" of development—neoliberal and national-popular—allows us to suppose that each political measure derives tangentially from one of the two poles or, more exactly, from the balance of power between them. Here, by the same token, every government measure can logically be explained quickly and easily as a product or combination of one of the two models. But what we cannot understand well is *why*, at any given moment, the balance of power changes.

There is one element both interpretations coincide on, which might lead us to suspect that these paradigms have grown somewhat outdated: we all agree that the nationalization of private banks was a *surprising and totally unexpected event*. I am not aiming to develop a third explanation here, but I am convinced that we must overcome the two traditional paradigms of the Left. I want to emphasize the importance of one thing: the unexpected (and welcome) expropriation of the private bankers happened because of the concurrence or confluence of the financial crisis with the political crisis. More exactly, the erosion of the financial system coincided with the exhaustion of the political system at a transitional moment. To put it another way: *The convergence of the devaluation of the president with the devaluation of the currency provoked a sudden strengthening of the state apparatus.* This situation could not be foreseen based on either of the two paradigms.

The End of the Alliance and the Scapegoat

Undoubtedly those most surprised by the nationalization of the banks and the freezing of currency exchange were the bankers themselves, big business and the

5. See especially the essay of the same title in this volume.

parties of the Right. The only explanation the PAN could mumble made reference to the "visceral" quality of the decision. The most reactionary employer groups (in Monterrey, Guadalajara, Sinaloa, and so on) immediately tried to launch a strike to aggressively confront the government. Rogelio Sada Zambrano, director of the Vitro Group of Monterrey and an owner of BANPAÍS (a bank), understood right away that the expropriatory measure had nothing to do with the economic policy set by López Portillo during nearly six years. The day after the decrees were made, Zambrano complained: "Yesterday the government unilaterally shattered the Alliance for Production." It was true: the hegemonic political bloc—which included bankers and monopoly capital in a privileged place—broke into pieces before the shocked bourgeoisie. For his part, President López Portillo placed the blame on the bankers, explaining how they had betrayed the nation.

The frightened Right could not help but point out the incongruence of the government action: Abel Vicencio Tovar of the PAN stressed that "many of those now applauding wildly are the same ones who for months, perhaps for years, were filling their pockets with dollars to send abroad." In fact, the expropriation of the private banks and currency exchange controls meant a 180-degree turnaround from the economic policy of López Portillo. Commentator José Antonio Pérez Stuart, in open support of the bankers, pointed out immediately that the private banks had in fact been backed up by the government. And the Coordinating Council of Businessmen (CCE), in a manifesto signed by its president, Manuel J. Clouthier, explained in a bout of hypocrisy that the López Portillo administration had contributed to the crisis by generating an inflationary policy that kept the peso overvalued (and cheapened the dollar), discouraged saving, stimulated overconsumption, resorted to budget deficits covered up by issuing more currency, and arbitrarily delayed changes in the exchange rate. What Clouthier did not say was that all those "errors" formed part of the "Alliance for Production," which sadly ended up promoting speculation and rent seeking among bankers and businessmen who took advantage of the critical juncture to make extraordinary profits.[6]

In this manifesto the CCE pointed out the government's responsibility for the behavior of private banks: "The control the government had over the banks ensured their strict functioning within national objectives and policies." Why did

6. The president of both the CCE and COPARMEX, Manuel J. Clouthier, was a leading figure of Mexican business. Over the course of the following years, he also became increasingly important within the right-wing opposition party, the PAN, and ultimately would be its candidate in the 1988 elections. [Trans.]

the nationalization take place, then? The only possible explanation, the businessmen responded, is that when its economic policies failed "the government looked for someone to blame for a situation for which the banks are not responsible." According to the CCE, the banks were López Portillo's scapegoat.

On the other hand, some leftist commentators have assumed that the nationalization of the banks was a response to popular demands. This illusory and mistaken idea was taken to absurd lengths. Pérez Stuart himself, the spokesman for the Right, immediately contrasted the course of events in Mexico with the electoral path by which the Mitterrand administration, with the support of a broad democratic consensus, had carried out nationalizations in France. The unilateral and authoritarian way in which nationalization was decreed helped the Right once more spread the idea that socialism has a dictatorial, totalitarian, and antidemocratic character. The CCE manifesto declared: "The nationalization of the banks is a definitive blow against private free enterprise and *a clear sign of the country's entrance into socialism.*" The businessmen held that socialism "unites in the government all political power and all economic power," allowing it to be stigmatized as a "totalitarian" process. It is fundamental to point out not only that the nationalization of the banks is not a step toward socialism—as Carlos Tello, appointed head of the Bank of Mexico, immediately declared—but also that *the situation described by the businessmen has nothing to do with the democratic socialism that the most important organizations of the Mexican Left were fighting for.* Even so, we must recognize that the socialism the businessmen are referring to did exist, in the most backward expressions of Lombardism that sought support in the authoritarian and despotic ways of the Mexican government and confused statism for socialism.

The businessmen were clearly not attempting, with their absurd declarations, to offer an explanation for what had happened. What they wanted to do was create panic in the middle sectors, and especially in the electoral mass of four million Mexicans who had voted for the candidate of the Right in the recent elections. The idea that the onset of socialism might be sparked by a presidential fit only soothed by the slaying of a scapegoat is so unhinged that all it reveals is the bewilderment and political aphasia of those who expressed it.

Splitters and Splits

Within the government almost no one wanted it, and very few believed in it, but the nationalization of the banks happened anyway. Part of the union bureaucracy and some Lombardists believed in it the way that many Catholics believe in the gospel, as a merely ritual act that allows the official pastors of proletarian minds to be symbolically and spiritually identified. Neither President López Portillo nor his economic staff believed in the measure, much less incoming president Miguel de la Madrid or his team. Hardly anyone in the government took a clear, public, and honest political stance toward the problems of the country. One of the few who did was Carlos Tello.[7] Nevertheless the banks were nationalized, and the architect of this process was none other than Carlos Tello himself, the politician who seemed condemned to loneliness and marginality because he openly defended his political principles. What had taken place inside the hegemonic bloc to produce this surprising outcome? Over the previous years the conditions for a crisis had emerged, little by little, and not only in financial terms: the cracks splitting the apparatus of political domination also deepened. The sixth (and final) presidential report by López Portillo contained, camouflaged in odd metaphors, hostile gestures toward the groups and currents that were splitting off, breaking up and thereby weakening state power. Frequent changes in the cabinet makeup were symptoms of this erosion of political power, as were the enormous tensions surrounding the presidential succession of 1982. López Portillo asserted that private banks had lost their sense of national solidarity (did they ever really have any?) and promoted speculation and plundering. The president also spoke of the ruling political circles, "the weeping of those who were applauding a short while ago," the "complaints of those who won't take responsibility now but were shooting off firecrackers a little while back," and "those who split on me." In sum: he was speaking of all the politicians who like rats jumped off the ship that threatened to sink and shamelessly grabbed on to the lifeboats of the next six-year term before the captain had even turned over the helm. He also made references to "technocratic orthodoxies," the "transnationalized," and the "critical pontiffs."[8]

The beginning of the crisis was accompanied by political upheavals: a four-dollar reduction of the export price of oil on 3 June 1981 provoked the firing of the head of Pemex, the state-owned oil company, for having taken a "rushed" ac-

---

7. Carlos Tello (b. 1938) is a distinguished structuralist economist and government official, although not—significantly—a member of the PRI. A few years earlier, President López Portillo had centralized control over government spending in a new Secretariat of Planning and Budget (SPP) and appointed Tello to head it. But Tello's ideas quickly ran into resistance from more conservative monetarist economists, and he resigned within a year. Three later monetarist heads of the SPP—Miguel de la Madrid, Carlos Salinas, and Ernesto Zedillo—have gone on to become president. Tello's tenure as governor of the Bank of Mexico was similarly tumultuous and short-lived: he was ousted within ninety days. [Trans.]

8. These phrases came from López Portillo's address on 1 September 1982. [Trans.]

tion, in the words of López Portillo. In July 1981 the president claimed that a "sea of distrust was beginning to be created in the country." A few days later he emphatically declared that this was not exactly a "problem of trust" but, openly, a "conflict of interests." During the following months, and especially after the future president had been selected, centrifugal political tensions grew, and a financial crisis rabidly bit at the national economy. Each event followed another in a dizzying spiral, with a particularly complicated electoral struggle in the background: inflation took off, short-term external loans were required, the flight of dollars overseas sped up, and finally, in February 1982, the peso was devalued 75 percent and the price of oil dropped again. One month later, the secretary of finance, David Ibarra, quit after announcing an austerity program; the director of the Bank of Mexico was also forced to accept retirement. The new secretary of finance, Jesús Silva Herzog, was a politician tied to incoming president Miguel de la Madrid, and the new director of the central bank was considered to be openly conservative and opposed to currency controls. Nevertheless once the elections were over, they established partial currency controls, based on a dual exchange rate. A little while later, they created a third exchange rate, freezing the so-called Mexdollars, and on 20 August 1982 they won a ninety-day extension to meet the external debt that had come due.

By this point, the government and the hegemonic apparatus had fallen into such a state of disorder and confusion that it hardly seems strange that the very head of state had to resort to nearly conspiratorial methods to find solutions to the crisis. What produced this curious event? The certainty that (incoming president) Miguel de la Madrid would be unable—and perhaps unwilling—to take drastic measures to reorder and redirect the chaotic situation? The nerve and prepotency of the bankers and some officials who responded to every presidential request by spiriting fabulous sums of dollars out of the country? Whatever it was, clearly almost uncontrollable divisions and antagonisms had been generated inside the state: the financial sector rejected the orders of the politicians, the technocrats turned their backs on the populist leaders, the union bureaucracy seemed opposed to the future president's team, part of the political class deeply disliked the new technocratic morality, the president couldn't manage to control his own cabinet, and each little group's bickering for its own piece of power helped to atomize the mechanisms for making political decisions. In short, a marked state of misrule governed the ruling class.

For the first time in many years the symptoms of a hegemonic crisis had appeared, but they remained hidden behind a dense web of rumors. With great difficulty, we began to discover, in the astute words of Carlos Monsiváis, that this time, reality was much more alarming than the rumors.

But perhaps the most important part of the political crisis was the cold and cautious attitude Miguel de la Madrid took toward the nationalization of the banks. He did not declare his support for López Portillo's move until three weeks after it was announced. The brief communiqué he put out the day that nationalization was announced simply stated what had happened: "These measures respond to critical circumstances," he said, and immediately broke off and took his distance: "The report demonstrates the president's great efforts to carry out with authority, responsibility and patriotism his elevated function of *firmly leading the country up until the last day of his term*."

We should add that from the very first day, two different and opposing control centers in financial policy could be glimpsed: the Bank of Mexico with Carlos Tello in charge, and the Secretariat of Finance with Jesús Silva Herzog at its head. The latter was opposed to what he called a "policy of ineffective subsidies" and underscored the essentially profitable character that the financial system had to have. This position was reinforced by Mario Ramón Beteta, who argued that the banking system should remain within its traditional operative limits "*no matter who owns it.*" They argued forcefully that the state-owned banks should do the same thing they did when they were privately owned, but better: this was the guiding principle in the government technocracy.

The nationalization of the banks happened within a state context in which a significant polarizing process had taken place. The technocracy had been enormously strengthened, and with the expansion of state capitalism (thanks to oil), it had drawn closer to industrialists and financiers and imposed its designs on a progressively more cornered segment of more or less populist politicians. On the other extreme, the union bureaucracy had also been notably strengthened. We should add that the nationalization of the banks was like an unexpected and undesired gift from the heavens for the technocrats, increasing their already important influence. But it was also a hot potato in their hands, since it had its origins in the hardest blow to the Mexican bourgeoisie since the days of Lázaro Cárdenas. Their relationships with the business sector had to be reorganized in a tense and difficult atmosphere.

Don't You Wrinkle, Old Skin

Suddenly awakening from long rhetorical dreams, nationalism reemerged. This was a nationalism that doubted the existence of Mexico except when revealed by the state: the state lives, therefore Mexico exists . . . The expropriation of the banks caused a wave of jingoism that obscured the basis of the problem: as Monsiváis has pointed out, official revolutionary nationalism reaches its limits in its lack of a democratic impulse. Nationalism conceals the authoritarian and despotic state in the background. This is true even at the moments when the government puts into practice important economic reforms that have an undeniably progressive character, because, I must say once more, democracy cannot be reduced to its economic aspects. The enormous difficulty the Left faced was that this critical juncture split its program in two: the government took up the reformist side of its demands and the parties of the Right seized the democratic side. When government despotism turned against its interests, the bourgeoisie angrily called for its "democratic rights." The Left saw some of its demands partially satisfied and suddenly found itself shackled to the logic of the state apparatus. The situation was difficult, but the only thing that could guarantee the Left a distinct profile and a revolutionary character was precisely a program joining deep social reforms with broadened political democracy.

For one passing moment, we had the happy illusion of a magical swap: the Left would take the seat the financial bourgeoisie had been occupying. The naming of rather conservative directors at the heads of the nationalized banks did not banish this concern: as the *Wall Street Journal* rushed to publish, at that point even John Gavin, the ambassador of the United States, was concerned at the "leftist tendencies" of the new director of the central bank and warned of a "disaster." The new head of the Bank of Mexico seems to have caused not only concern but also terrified paralysis among businessmen.

And their terror only grew because the government opened the doors to the mass movement. Here, by the way, there was also a curious switch: popular struggle, conveniently measured and channeled, came after the act of expropriation. The class struggle was so domesticated in our surreal country that it seemed to take place post facto, only when the government called for it. Business groups had threatened an employers' strike—a true lockout—in protest, but now they pulled back. On 8 September, the day the strike was to take place, the CONCANACO explained its reasons for taking it back: "Our action could be used as a pretext for bringing down public order." As proof, the organization pointed to the attacks businessmen had suffered on state television, the police harassment business leaders had been subjected to "as if they were criminals," the threats to dissolve business organizations, and the announcements of violence by the union bureaucracy, which was stirring up workers against employers. Poor little bourgeoisie, treated as if they were subversive leftists!

But no, things took a different path. The businessmen decided to begin negotiations: two days after the planned strike, the head of the CCE, Manuel J. Clouthier, met with the president of the republic. Leaving the Los Pinos palace, Clouthier declared that he had spoken with López Portillo "about the appropriateness of halting everything having to do with the class struggle." The response from the maximum leader of the official labor movement was not long in coming: the new position adopted by Clouthier was "nationalist and patriotic," Fidel Velázquez declared. And so all of a sudden, the class struggle went back to its bureaucratic and governmental underground retreat, swallowed once again by the state, which had seemed to have lost much of its mediating capacity. With the little class struggle party over, civil society would have to watch from a distance as the ogre digested the conflict. Once again, we were all patriots and nationalists . . . almost by decree. The state assigned everyone the task of stretching out the old skin of nationalism. The great question of that moment was whether the march of the new forms of class struggle could resist the call of the drum.

The nationalization of the banks suddenly resuscitated the problem of "popular," "revolutionary," or "leftist" nationalism. We should specify the terms of the debate more precisely. First of all, we must clarify that from a socialist perspective, at that point more than ever we needed to develop a coherent set of demands and reforms that might strengthen economic independence and national sovereignty and promote the integration and consolidation of the Mexican social and economic space in the face of the disaggregating tendencies to which our immersion in global capitalism made us subject. The discrepancies came from trying to define the character of the *basic articulating axis* of what had been called, a little confusingly, "a project for national development." The most widespread idea—in official unions, some sectors of government bureaucracy, and certain nationalist groups—located the possibility of an independent project in the *strengthening and expansion of the existing Mexican state.* This began from the idea that the state "represents" the nation, that the state is the principal organized social force capable of mobilizing human and economic potential to develop the country, and that, as a result, "alliances" between the state and the labor and peasant movements must be strengthened. This thesis had made some sense during the processes of decolonization that had produced powerful movements of national liberation, but it corresponded to political processes taking place in very *backward* countries. Without any doubt, these political formulations had their place in Mexico a half century ago, but by the beginning of the eighties, revising these ideas was essential. Mexico seemed on the cusp of a new era in which the combination of expanding state power and increasing state incorporation of popular movements could no longer be the motor of a "national project" leading toward a democratic and socialist transition. We also had to meditate not only on whether a statist path to national development was *possible,* but also on whether it was *desirable.* We knew the difficulties and deformations this path had produced in countries where a socialist transition had occurred based on a statist model: the results greatly undermined the possibilities for broadening democracy. From that viewpoint, I want to question—let me be clear—not the broadening of state economic authority but the bureaucratic and authoritarian incorporation of the popular movement into the machinery of government (which is usually called the "alliance" between the state and the popular movement). The bureaucratized presence of the masses in the state is no guarantee that the "national project" will take a course independent of the interests of the bourgeoisie and the logic of the capitalist system. That presence of the masses inside the state has ceased to be a steady forward impulse. It has placed critical limits on state administration, and when the government overstepped those limits, as in recent years, political crisis occurred. This would seem to be something new in Mexican politics: the integration of the mass movement into the state apparatus was becoming unstable, opening up a new period of rearticulation and renegotiation that might turn quite ugly. It was becoming increasingly clear that the only guarantee that a reform project might take on a truly national direction was not an "alliance" of the state with social movements but rather a separation of the two. This was nothing like the liberal proposals that wished to limit the functions of the state to such a degree as to make it nothing more than a distant regulator of economic activities. But making the state a *political force* guiding economic development was not the same as allowing the state to reproduce itself as a corporatist force of social bonding. The necessary socialization of the state—extending its role as a social planner—must never be shackled to a statization of society.

Journey to the Center of the Right

Power and domination seem to have a will to symmetry: being at the center, even if only hypothetically, produces a sense of stability, order, and tranquillity.[1] When St. Matthew speaks of the Final Judgment, he describes how the Son of Man takes his seat on the throne and divides men into two, some to the left, and some to the right:

> Then the King will say to those on his right: "Come, you who are blessed by my father, take your inheritance, the kingdom prepared for you since the creation of the world." . . . And he will say to those on his left: "Depart from me, you who are cursed, into the eternal fire prepared for the devil and his angels."[2]

And so in the French Assembly, when the conservatives placed themselves to the right of the presidency, and the revolutionaries to the left, they were in some way reproducing the ancient symbolic symmetry of power. In Mexico things apparently take place differently: the symbology of the 1910 revolution has spurred

In 1982 I edited a special issue of *Nexos* on the Left (no. 54) and included an essay—"Lombardo or Revueltas?"—found in part 3 of this book. In 1983 I edited a special issue of *Nexos* on the Right (no. 64) and wrote this essay for it. I was to edit a special issue of *Nexos* on the Center—that is, on the PRI—but my proposal was rejected as excessively critical of the government.

1. "Symmetry signifies rest and binding, asymmetry motion and loosening; the one order and law, the second arbitrariness and accident; the one formal rigidity and constraint, the other life, play and freedom." Dagobert Frey, "On the Problem of Symmetry in Art," quoted in Hermann Weyl, "Symmetry," in *The World of Mathematics*, vol. 1, ed. James Roy Newman (New York: Simon and Schuster, 1956), 678.

2. Matt. 25:33, 41.

a great repugnance among all politicians to seeing themselves classified as "right-wing." And even though the existence of a central balancing and mediating point is an essential ingredient in the Mexican political system, nearly everyone flees in terror from the space reserved for the Right and tries to place himself in the Center or even on the Left. Exemplary and memorable was that statement made in 1975 by Jorge Sánchez Mejorada, at the time president of CONCAMIN: "Mexican businessmen are leftists, although I admit that some are from the conformist bourgeoisie, which includes people from all sectors, including the political area."[3] Equally memorable were the declarations made in 1960 by Alfonso Corona del Rosal, president of the PRI, and by Adolfo López Mateos, president of the republic. The former had the charming idea of defining the government as "well-tempered leftism," and the latter classified it as "extremely left-wing, within the Constitution." That sparked the "nonexistent" right wing to get a little frightened and hurriedly rush some capital out of the country, despite the security given by a repressive government that persecuted railroad workers, kept Campa, Siquieros, and Vallejo in jail, and two years later would commit one of the most atrocious political assassinations of recent history: the liquidation of Rubén Jaramillo and all his family outside Xochicalco on 23 May 1962.[4]

If the bourgeoisie isn't right-wing, and neither are repressive politicians, does the Right even exist in Mexico? Let's leave the realm of appearances behind: the Right exists and is well established in our terribly unjust political system. The illusion that it does not exist is due to the fact that the Mexican Right is not found exclusively, or even primarily, to the right of the central power of the "government of the Mexican Revolution." *The Right is simultaneously in power and in the opposition,* in the government and in society.

I want to warn that I am using what might be a lax and general definition of

3. He also affirmed: "I believe that in Mexico now very few people are on the Right, in its older sense of total liberalism. If we understand 'the Left' as the people who are concerned about the well-being of the majority, then most Mexicans are leftists." *Excelsior,* 10 June 1975. CONCAMIN is another national business organization.

4. A wave of dissident labor agitation and two strikes by railworkers in 1958 and 1959 had called the regime's control of the labor movement into question, sparking brutal repression. Painter David Siqueiros was jailed for his involvement in the movement, although—famously—he was released during the day to paint nationalist murals at Chapultepec Castle. As a counterpoint to this repressive tolerance, Valentín Campa and Demetrio Vallejo would serve more than ten years in prison for advocating democracy in union affairs, and a few years later, Rubén Jaramillo's dissidence would cost him and his family their lives. [Trans.]

the Right: those conservative forces who strive to maintain order and the currently governing system or who struggle to restore a past order, motivated by the defense of the privileged positions they occupy (or occupied).[5] This allows us to locate the Right with a certain realism and escape the mythological image that the discourses of official demagoguery give us: the horrendously antinational, aggressively antidemocratic, and frighteningly antirevolutionary Right is nearly nonexistent. The *nation, democracy,* and *revolution* can be symbols of conservatism; in fact, as we will see, these three concepts have become integral elements of various currents of the Right: the traditionalist Catholicism that defends the Guadalupan nation, the liberal Anglophilia that proclaims democracy, or the authoritarianism that practices repression in the name of the revolution.

Merely spelling out these problems already indicates that to reach a better definition of what the Mexican Right is, it would be worthwhile to sketch out a brief description of its anatomy and the key elements in the historical process that constituted it. With these preliminary anatomical and taxonomical ends, we can define four great currents or sectors of the Right:

1. the conservative Catholic Right
2. the liberal bourgeois Right
3. the protofascist petty bourgeois Right
4. the "revolutionary" *carrancista* Right

One of the peculiarities of the Mexican Right—and this is in keeping with, and well adapted to, our hardly democratic political system—is that its various currents have not crystallized into political parties, much less unified into a great conservative and bourgeois party. The various currents of the Right are expressed in each one of the conservative parties, within the state, and in groups of various kinds that operate in society with relative autonomy.

The clearest example is the PAN, the largest party of the Right. Since its origins it has been divided into two currents. On the one side are those who, like Manuel Gómez Morin or Efraín González Morfín, take up the old Mexican Catholic conservative traditions in order to adapt them to the social teaching of the post-Vatican church. On the other, there is the liberal reactionary current led by José Ángel Conchello and Pablio Emilio Madero.[6] This division is expressed concretely as a showdown between those who want to abstain from elections and

---

5. See Norberto Bobbio, Nicola Matteucci, and Gianfranco Pasquino, eds., *Diccionario de política* (Mexico: Siglo Veintiuno, 1991).

6. On the formative currents of the PAN, see Donald Mabry, *Mexico's Accion Nacional: A Catholic Alternative to Revolution* (Syracuse, N.Y.: Syracuse University Press, 1973). [Trans.]

those who want to participate—this has been so strong at times as to paralyze the party, as in 1975 and 1976. The conservatives conceive of the party as an instrument for the common good of society and "not a passing or permanent agent of partial interests, classes or groups as a function of varying opportunities."[7] These ideas, deeply marked by Christian social thought, produce an emphasis on solidarity that accepts certain forms of state control and intervention in the economy within an overall private enterprise framework while promoting worker participation in managing individual companies and recommending worker ownership of company stock. From this perspective, PAN participation in elections would only strengthen the dominant political system. In contrast, solidarity looks to promote a "civic consciousness" that might eat away at the legitimacy of the governing group and enable "the strengthening of the social, as the indispensable foundation of the political."[8]

God's Own Little Shop

By contrast, the pro-electoral current accepts the rules of the Mexican political game. Conchello's pragmatism led him to try to form a strong pressure group on the basis of the inorganic strength of votes won. This group constantly criticizes the PRI government, without offering an overall programmatic challenge, in order to defend the spaces and interests of bourgeois liberalism through permanent opposition. It should be underscored that the PAN also shelters, although only in embryonic form, potentially fascist petty bourgeois tendencies of a Poujadist bent. Conchello himself tried to represent the interests of an offended and aggrieved urban middle class when he came out in defense of small businesspeople and those he called "shopkeepers." But behind the ideology of the little shop lurked the aggressive appetites of a part of the haute bourgeoisie of Monterrey that was deeply unhappy with official "populism." This line has not been abandoned by the PAN: today there clearly are tendencies within the party that try to project it as representing the interests of the bourgeoisie as a whole, shored up by the support of the urban middle class, which has been affected deeply by the economic crisis. If those who claim to represent Christian solidarity bless the political project of the New Right, the PAN might become a powerful party and cease to be God's own sad little shop on Mexican soil.

Nonetheless in recent years the PAN has seen the growth, on its right, of an

7. Efraín González Morfín, quoted in *Excelsior*, 8 March 1975.
8. Ibid.

aggressive party that has reclaimed the old fighting traditions of Catholic si-narquistas. The Mexican Democratic Party has shown a certain dynamism in combining the nationalist Guadalupanism inherited from sinarquista ideology with the provincial petty bourgeoisie's longing for social and economic secur-ity. This combination has given it a relatively modern look, and even a few re-formist and populist touches, concealing its conservative roots and its origins in the thirties and forties struggles of the radical and clerical Right. At the same time, this has also obscured sinarquismo's flirtations with fascism. Nonethe-less the mix of sinarquista nationalism and social Christian reformism has gen-erated powerful disputes and contradictions within the PDM.[9] Some of these dis-putes have resembled those within the PAN: they have pitted the "abstainers" against the (electoral) "participators," although the latter have clearly predom-inated.[10]

Seen as a whole, the organized political parties of the Right are wrestling with an internal conflict between two opposing tendencies that is very difficult to re-solve. The Mexican Right finds itself facing the great problem of reconciling conservative Hispanist Catholicism with bourgeois liberal pragmatism; this is a question of reconciling not only two different kinds of socioeconomic interests but two different and even opposing cultural worlds. How to blend the corporat-ist interests of the traditional castes of the Hispanophile and Catholic neo-Porfirian bourgeoisie with the modern individualist appetites of the pro-U.S. new bourgeoisie? It is true that from a strictly socioeconomic point of view, the aged and backward rentier bourgeoisie barely exists and seems to have no future at all, but its sociocultural aura—conservative Catholicism—continues to be a powerful force with a base in broad sectors of the rural and urban petty bourgeoi-sie, the peasantry, and even the working class.

Conservative Catholicism and bourgeois liberalism are backed up by the church and the business class, respectively; evidently the interests of one do not always coincide with the interests of the other. In addition, the Mexican gov-ernment has traditionally striven to place itself between the church and the bourgeoisie, negotiating separately with each and repressing with greater or

9. Carlos Monsiváis has stressed the millenarian aspects of sinarquismo: "During the 1930s, and influenced both by the Cristero War and Spanish Falangism, the second great utopian moment of the twentieth-century Mexican Right emerges: Sinarquism (meaning the opposite of anarchism: with order). It celebrates sacrifice, opposes the atheistic State, and sympathizes with Fascism (al-though it does later distance itself from Nazism)." Monsiváis, *Mexican Postcards*, 132. [Trans.]
10. Since this essay was written, the PDM has faded in power and eventually—in 1998—ceased to exist, with its more modern stances and supporters being taken up by the PAN. [Trans.]

lesser severity any attempt to reconcile clerical with business interests in an organized way. The result is that the church has always preferred to block the impulses of the Catholic masses in order to negotiate with the government. Similarly, the employers and business associations have chosen to contain the political aggressiveness and particular interests of the bourgeoisie in order to discuss problems at the highest level. So the antistatism of Catholic and liberal traditions (each with very different characteristics) has collided with the statist behavior of their leaders, the shameful and unadmitted statolatry of the institutional powers of the church and business, who have always sacrificed the autonomy of their class and institutional interests for a negotiated and relatively passive insertion in the political system. In sum, business and the church have preferred to act as *corporations* and have disdained promoting the representation of their interests through political parties within a parliamentary democratic system. To explain here the reasons why the social Right has given up the subtlety of political mediations in order to insert itself into the state apparatus through a corporatist relationship would go beyond the objectives of this essay. Suffice it to say that certain right-wing extremists have claimed that Archbishop Ernesto Corripio Ahumada and COPARMEX leader José Luis Coindreau, among others, were nothing more than a unique variety of *charro* leaders.

This situation has become not only a great dam blocking the fusion of the two currents of the Right but also a serious obstacle to the broader development of bourgeois democratic thinking and practice in the parties of reactionary roots. The credibility of the Right's "democratic" criticisms of government authoritarianism is seriously damaged by the traditional negotiating attitude of church and business leadership.

Historically, the contradictory relationship between conservative Catholicism and bourgeois liberalism has been the great challenge the Mexican Right has proven unable to resolve. The Right has sought two kinds of solutions to its great historical split. The first kind have attempted to build a ferociously nationalist, corporatist, and Catholic autonomous movement, with fascist leanings, on the basis of the petty bourgeois masses. The second have produced the union of conservative and liberal traditions within the Thermidorean space of the state, with the blessing and legitimacy of the reactionary strand of the Institutional Revolutionary Family (which I prefer to call the "Carranza" strand).

The Banging of the Pots

Let's take a look at the first option. This appears at critical junctures, when the radical extremes of Catholic conservatism and bourgeois liberalism come into contact, and they come into contact precisely along the social fringe that is especially sensitive to the cries of those who call for the combined values of *individualism* and *order*. The work and life of José Vasconcelos are, in a certain sense, a veritable x ray of this phenomenon of the unification of political extremes. Vasconcelos lived his life torn apart by the contradiction between conservative Catholicism and modern culture. One confirmation of this can be found in the interesting declarations of his son Héctor, who said his father always lived in a polarity opposing the nineteenth-century Catholic provinces to the cosmopolitan world of the Ateneo. It is interesting to confirm how a parallel to the historical process can be found on a biographical level: this contradiction drew Vasconcelos close to positions of a fascist tinge.[11] It's also worth pointing out that the political and philosophical evolution of Vasconcelos is a wonderful example of how right-wing ideas on democracy lead to irrationalism.

The different landmarks in the protofascist tradition in Mexico are illustrative: one line goes from the "golden shirts" to Saturnino Cedillo, passes through Almazán and the sinarquistas, and extends to various associations of the Far Right (from the pious ACJM to the fearsome MURO, from the Christian Family Movement, the Missionary League, the Perpetual Veil, or the League of Mary to the Mexican Youth Movement, Yunque, or Guía). On this terrain, favorable conditions are created for an alliance of the most conservative proposals of a Catholic social order with ultraliberal interests and, above all, with a middle class frightened of the end of its not very secure privileges. To put it differently: the crisis of bipolarity produced a breeding ground that encouraged the mix of the Catholic ultrarightist tradition of Salvador Abascal with the ultraliberal, Poujadist and pot-banging mumblings of a Luis Pazos. A strange combination of this nature can be observed in the PDM and in certain segments of the PAN. Yet it is highly unlikely that this forced marriage between the cape of the Indian Juan Diego and the manuals of the economist Milton Friedman will manage to come together as a solid and coherent alternative.[12]

Up until now, across a broad range of reactionary political alternatives, every attempt at fusing Catholic and liberal values has failed. The many attempts have left a great amount of wreckage behind them and on more than one occasion have deposited the little eggs of the fascist serpent in some corner of society. But

11. Héctor Vasconcelos, interview by Roberto Vallarino, *Unomásuno*, 18 February 1983.

12. The cape of the Indian Juan Diego was where the Virgin of Guadalupe made her first appearance; Milton Friedman is of course the founder of monetarist economics and a saint in the neoliberal firmament. [Trans.]

they have not prospered. Those on the Far Right still stubbornly think that there is no such thing as outdated and new ideas: there are only true ideas and false ones. Salvador Abascal claims:

> Liberal democracy is false and it engenders the worst of all evils: Marxism, which is no less evil for presenting itself under the name of socialism. There is only one remedy: Catholic social order, which adores and adheres to the supreme wisdom of God, which recognizes no rights but those of Truth, which prevents the concentration of economic power and political power in the same hands, which multiplies private property—both individual and cooperative—to the maximum even in production goods, which is hierarchical and healthily nationalist.[13]

This sort of extremist political formulation openly clashes with the practice and interests of the modern bourgeoisie, but at certain critical junctures, certain segments of the business class and the petty bourgeoisie develop ultraliberal ideas that reject all state initiatives based on democratic consensus, reject the very mechanisms of consensus, and draw close to the views of the traditional clerical Right.

The *Carranclanes*

Without any doubt, the meeting of Hispanizing and criollo conservatism with modern business pragmatism at the heart of the Mexican state has been, until now, the most successful means of resolving (or concealing) this ancestral polarity.[14] The most repugnant political symbol of this singular alliance is President Gustavo Díaz Ordaz: the massacre of Tlatelolco on 2 October 1968 consecrated him as the most recent hero of the history of the "institutional and revolutionary" Right. This history is a long one and has its starting point in the Thermidorean reaction that emerged at the heart of the governments descended from the Mexican Revolution. What would become the Right's principal means of participation in the institutional government took form during the rule of Carranza and Calles. With the additional benefits of the restoration of Ávila Camacho (1940–1946), the developmentalist pragmatism of Miguel Alemán (1946–1952),

13. Salvador Abascal, "Presentación," in Jacques Ploncard d'Assac, *Rousseau, Marx y Lenin* (Paris: Editorial Tradicion, 1978). Abascal was the founder of sinarquismo.
14. The term *carranclanes* (in the section title) is a mocking way of referring to the carrancista Right, the statist internal reaction. [Trans.]

and the tolerance of Ruiz Cortinez (1952–1958), a wide space for the Right opened up within the state. The party of government, at exactly the point when it changed its name for the paradoxical designation it uses today ("The Institutional Revolutionary Party"), entered a long reactionary phase. The second president of the PRI (after the fleeting and undistinguished presidency of Rafael Pascasio Gamboa) was none other than General Sánchez Taboada, who had been one of the assassins of Emiliano Zapata. He stated:

> I did in fact form part of the forces which liquidated Zapata, and I was one of the first to see his cadaver. I want to express to you that at the time he had taken up arms against the government of the Republic and it was the Republic's soldiers who killed him.[15]

The rest of his declaration reveals the peculiar conservative mentality developing within the "revolutionary" party:[16]

> If the dearest and most respected of my friends were to take up arms against the Republic and its institutions and I as a soldier were entrusted with the task of pursuing and exterminating him, I would do it, following my duty. Yes, I saw Zapata fall. By the way, he had very big and beautiful eyes.[17]

Precisely the brand of politicians who helped to extinguish those big and beautiful eyes spread like a plague inside the government and the official party. There is a line that ties Sánchez Taboada to Corona del Rosal or Alfonso Martínez Domínguez.[18] The local power bases of the great politicians of the institutionalized revolution have been protective umbrellas for the provincial Right: Gonzalo N. Santos in San Luis Potosí, Leobardo Reynoso in Zacatecas, Javier Rojo Gómez in Nayarit, the Ruiz Cortines in Veracruz, and the list could grow con-

---

15. Rodolfo Sánchez Taboada, in conversation with Gonzalo N. Santos and Leobardo Reynoso, who had claimed that he was not present at the Chinameca hacienda where Zapata was killed. Miguel Osorio Marbán writes, "there is a telegram addressed to the Secretary of War and the Navy on 1 July 1919, ordering the promotion of Colonel Jesús Galardo and Infantry Lieutenant Rodolfo Sánchez Taboada for their participation in the armed action at the ex-hacienda of San Juan de Chinameca which cost the life of the 'criminal' Emiliano Zapata." See Miguel Osorio Marbán, *El partido de la revolución mexicana* (Mexico: Impresora del Centro, 1970), 979–80. Sánchez Taboada was president of the PRI from 5 December 1946 to 4 December 1952.
16. See the essay "The Domesticated Revolution" in my book *Agrarian Structure and Political Power in Mexico*.
17. See Osorio Marbán, *El partido de la revolución mexicana*.
18. Both latter-day conservative functionaries of the PRI. [Trans.]

siderably longer with the rich descendants of caudillos of the Northwest or the peculiar offspring or residues of the system such as Almazán (1940), Ezequiel Padilla (1946), and Casas Alemán (1952).[19]

Many volumes could be written about the documented course of the "revolutionary" *carrancista* Right, from its origins down to the present day.[20] One of the guiding threads of this history of the internal Right is the stigma of betrayal: to be able to exist and expand, the institutional Right has betrayed its own popular and revolutionary origins. It has also betrayed, in a certain sense, the business class and, obviously, conservative Catholic tradition. In this sense, the consolidation of the institutional carrancista Right is a false solution to the Right's historical problem: the fusion between traditional conservatism and bourgeois liberalism has taken the form of a pragmatism that could develop only thanks to corruption, cynicism, and repressive practices. It is not a true fusion, and that is why today a large part of the Right, longing for independence, is subjecting its own statist alter ego to bitter and constant criticism. For its part, the institutional Right tries to draw the veil of technocratic efficiency and administrative morality over several decades of infamy. The worst that could happen to it—and it just might happen—would be for its project to crash because of the inefficiency and corruption of the system itself.

A Semibourgeois Subculture

As we have seen, the preference of the church and Right for top-down solutions has narrowed the living space of the parties of the Right. Social forces of a rightist bent have tended to form corporations of various sizes and to take their place inside the state: from that corporation, they do politics, or something like politics. Now, the multiplicity of corporations and the absence of representative political channels have produced high-level forms of organization, like the CCE or the CMHN. These high-level organizations want to become, and in part already are, the rectors of an extensive and mixed variety of right-wing groups: from the large corporations such as CONCAMIN and CONCANACO, down to the Lions and Rotary Clubs, the Masons, parareligious organizations like Opus Dei, ONIR, or the

19. The first group—Santos, Reynoso, Rojo Gómez, and Ruiz Cortines—are conservative regional bosses who stayed inside the PRI; the second group are conservative regional bosses who chose to (unsuccessfully) run for the presidency against the PRI in the 1940, 1946, and 1952 elections. [Trans.]

20. This is called the carrancista Right because of its lineage from Venustiano Carranza, the author of the first Thermidor within the Mexican Revolution. [Trans.]

Knights of Columbus, the great diversity of protective groups (of animals, the elderly, victims . . .), and sports, philanthropic, family, and charity societies. This multitude of groups and associations form a dense fabric reaching far across society: although they have no unifying political or ideological ingredients, all threads are woven together in a semibourgeois subculture. This can be identified by its pragmatic adoration of mediocrity, its worship of the family held together by a Victorian morality that serves as a sure guard against the aggressive individualism of voracious and self-seeking bosses, its unceasing development of a parallel network of jokes and gossip to conceal its enormous ignorance, and its daily commentary on the last tears wept on popular *telenovelas* or alarmist speculations on television news. What is saddest about this bourgeois subculture is the complete lack of aristocratizing or cosmopolitan ingredients that might give it a "respectable" patina. It is crudely middle-brow, narrow-mindedly provincial, given to kitsch and less aware of the outside world than your average traveling salesman. That is why I mockingly dub it "semi-bourgeois."

All these bourgeois and semibourgeois groups aspire to make a connection with the state apparatus, from those who dedicate themselves to protecting whales or the handicapped, down to those who represent the plastics industry or the merchants of La Merced. It is enough just to think of the uncountable sum of meetings and juntas that politicians carry out with the representatives of different pressure groups to realize that the corporatist system can become very inefficient. And that is only taking into account the declining marginal utility of each additional meeting added to the endless agenda of government secretaries and directors, not to mention the president. At such an extreme, political activity becomes mere protocol and theater, and the spectacle tends to become an absurd vicious circle. It is not surprising that the crisis has given many politicians a passion for effectiveness and efficiency. The problem is that each improvement in technical efficiency brings less political effectiveness: that is the rule in a nondemocratic system.

What makes the great social fabric of the Right dangerous and threatening is that despite the ideological dispersion at its core, it has a nervous system of stimulus and control that, under certain conditions, can operate as a political unifying force. This system is basically made up of television and, on a lesser scale, radio and the press. The national mass media system is one of the key axes of the Mexican Right. Without the reactionary press and without Televisa, the Mexican Right would be like a body without nerves or skeleton, a formless and headless civic mass. This situation is terribly harmful, and while it lasts, imagining the extension of a true political democracy in Mexico is absurd. The political parties of the Right themselves have to live like parasites in this corporatized bourgeois civil society, this enormous Noah's ark manned by the mass media who are waiting for the flood to subside so that they can come ashore.

The expansion of the mass media, and especially television, has completely changed the rules of the political game. It is symptomatic that an old traveling representative and shoe salesman like Emilio Azcárraga should be the architect of the monstrous Televisa monopoly, beginning with the modest founding in 1930 of the radio station XEW. In some sense his dull spirit seems to have contaminated the whole system of television broadcasting. The result is that Mexican television—and more exactly, Televisa—has become the main leadership of an inorganic mixture of right-wing social forces that it directs more through bewilderment than signaling, before an audience composed of millions of Mexicans. A situation like this completely negates the symbolic geometry of Left and Right, since one of the poles here is "depoliticized" and, behind the neutral colorlessness of its anchorpeople, seizes the entire space. The key to this seizure lies in the apolitical appearance of radio and television broadcast programming; it is exactly this gray, schlocky, apolitical mediocrity that stimulates and directs the semibourgeois subculture, which is, at the end of the day, the great party of the Right in Mexico.[21]

For all these reasons, the Left's activities in the field of culture and the mass media are especially important. Although they are in general amplifiers of a reactionary subculture, the press, radio, and television are also a space for struggle, where complicated correlations of forces come together. That is why it was a lamentable mistake for the representatives of the Left to vote in Congress (during the 42d Legislature) for the ridiculous "moral law" that the executive branch proposed. The Right used the opportunity to clothe itself in the tunic of democracy by opposing, along with the immense majority of journalists and intellectuals of all tendencies, the so-called gag law. As a gag, the law was clearly not very effective. The reactionary puritanism with which it aimed to very subjectively set standards for "the right to privacy" (and throw freedom of expression into question) should have been enough for the representatives of the Left to oppose it. The incident reached well beyond the technical and legal framework of reforms to the Civil Code and burst with great political spectacle. Since the demand for a "moral renewal" had been one of the principal axes of the election campaign of Miguel de la Madrid, a proposed law that aimed to regulate morality and narrow freedom of opinion would predictably provoke many disputes. The

21. See Rubinstein, "Mass Media."

Right realized this immediately and effectively agitated the enormous subcultural field I have been referring to. It was a good example of the importance of this subculture, and a harsh lesson for the Left.

One of the first things the Mexican Left should do is take the Right seriously. We need to stop denouncing imperialism and reaction in general, in order to carefully analyze the multifarious political universe of the Right. The incomparably greater and more developed cultural and scientific potential of the Left should not make us think that everything on the Right is more or less pedestrian simplification. Behind simple things hide complex worlds. And if the Right has managed—in politics—to reduce its complexity to simple gestures, that should be cause for alarm, since its possible influence and reach have grown.

The Right has grown stronger over the last twenty years, and not simply because it has seen itself obliged to fight off a Left that has expanded notably since 1968. It has also grown stronger since the government is no longer satisfying many of the needs of a bourgeoisie that renews and multiplies its economic power with progressively greater autonomy from the traditional political bureaucracy. The political crisis breaking out in the Mexican state is strengthening the Right. At this moment, the forces of the Left should not allow the Right to advance bearing the banner the Left already captured during the sixties: that banner is called *democracy*. In a capitalist society, democracy is a slippery and marshy terrain, and if we wish, we could even say it is full of traps. But it is the best terrain for struggle that the Left can capture to build socialism as a real possibility. The Left should take the lead in the struggle to form new democratic spaces, and then to push the Right aside.

Today some right-wing forces are advancing for a critical alternative to PRI government authoritarianism, but we must make clear that the democratic element of their struggle has been completely marginal and secondary until now. There is nothing in the interests of the Mexican Right—or in its historical trajectory—that might suggest that democracy would be a fundamental part of the change it is proposing. On the contrary, the Right is the main cause of the despotic climate ruling Mexico during the last decades. When it cries out for democracy, in reality it is demanding a return to the situation before the crisis, when the state had not yet entered into a phase that required certain adjustments in its relationship with the dominant classes. The problem is that those adjustments were produced in the context of a certain weakening of PRI legitimacy, which occasioned the cracking in 1976 and 1982 of the hegemonic bloc. At root, freedom and democracy—for the Right—are synonyms of a return to the "quiet" period before 1968, the date when despotic governmental power began slowly to wear away, and the foundations for broadening freedom and democracy were laid. This unleashed leftist forces that, even though they were small and incipient, frightened the ruling class and made it taste—only taste—the rigors that every modern bourgeoisie faces in countries ruled by democratic political systems. By themselves, these rigors do not mean the weakening of capitalism, but they open the way to setting new rules of the political game, which the Mexican Right does not seem willing to accept.

That is why we are living through a critical juncture that might not repeat itself: under present conditions, the Mexican Left could become the great vehicle of democracy and simultaneously spread its alternatives across society. It is still possible. But we must not forget that the Right is beginning a time of effervescence and intense mutations: the present panorama could change quickly and produce surprising turnabouts.

The Crisis of Nationalism

The idea that nationalism is best understood as an instrument for resolving social conflicts and a means of domination is widely accepted in the social sciences. The evident fact that on countless occasions nationalism carries out the *function* of legitimating modern political systems gives this idea an aura of certainty. Yet if we want to understand the essential nature of the mechanisms of domination and legitimacy that hold up the modern state, we should ask whether the existence of a functional connection demands an *instrumental* explanation. The Mexican nationalism that gave life to the power structures slowly consolidated after the 1910 revolution seems like a good example to illustrate the myth: many "specialists" have concluded that Mexican nationalism is "a means for resolving conflicts between groups," an "extremely useful mechanism for social control,"[1] a project of the revolutionary state to integrate the interests of all classes into capitalist development.[2] It would seem that we

This essay was written in La Jolla, California, between September 1987 and February 1988 while I was a visiting scholar at the Center for U.S.-Mexican Studies of the University of California–San Diego. I am very grateful to Wayne Cornelius and Peter H. Smith for their support while I was there. An earlier version of this essay, translated by William B. Heller, was published in *Mexico's Alternative Political Futures*.

1. Frederick C. Turner, *The Dynamic of Mexican Nationalism* (Chapel Hill: University of North Carolina Press, 1968). A different perspective can be found in Robert Freeman Smith, *The United States and Revolutionary Nationalism in Mexico, 1916–1932* (Chicago: University of Chicago Press, 1972).

2. Carlos Monsiváis, "1968–1978: Notas sobre cultura y sociedad en México," *Cuadernos Políticos* 17 (1978).

are facing a problem of political technique, where the issue is finding the formula for creating what has been called "civic culture," that is to say, a means of participation that brings political culture in line with state structure.[3]

The Function of the Myth and the Myth of the Function

The nationalism that emerged from the Mexican Revolution undoubtedly did perform this vital function of regulating the consensus on which the state is based. It is impossible to understand the stable succession of postrevolutionary governments without recourse to the study of revolutionary nationalism. In this sense, nationalism performs an important ideological function by consolidating as a political tendency that establishes a structural relationship between the nature of Mexican culture and the peculiarities of the Mexican political system. Nonetheless the mere analysis of this ideological function can easily lead us to see the relationship between culture and politics in a way that is unilateral and, in the final instance, instrumental. Like other assemblages of ideas, nationalism would be simply a mediating bridge between society and politics, between culture and coercive institutions. This is a problem of great complexity, since the nationalist myth is inserted in Mexican society in a paradoxical way. On the one hand, nationalism gave the political system stability, but on the other, it fueled a political culture that exalted inefficiency and negated modernization. There are those who have seen this contradiction as an expression of backward and savage capitalism. What is clear is that nationalist mythology is becoming a stumbling block, but its dysfunctionality comes from the populist and, up to a certain point, anticapitalist character of the national myth itself, which has been fed by the protests and bitterness of the exploited. The situation is confusing and marked by the coexistence of functional relationships, expressions of class interests, and disconnects that reveal the dysfunction of the moment.

I find it important to offer an alternative approach that evades the pitfalls of an instrumental and narrowly functionalist interpretation of nationalism. We can fully understand nationalism only if we look at its cultural dimension. What I mean is that the processes by which consensus and legitimacy are achieved are not fundamentally ideological in nature. Even when what we observe is a coming and going of ideas, the form in which they are woven together in a mediating network is governed by cultural canons. The study of political culture offers us a

3. Gabriel A. Almond and Sidney Verba, *The Civic Culture* (Boston: Little, Brown, 1965).

clearer vision of how connections are made between the interests of the dominant classes and nationalism.

Although nationalism offers concrete political solutions at specific historical moments, it must be observed as a trend over the longue durée, as Braudel might say, knitting together myths, legends, customs, ideas, images, and symbols at a pace not completely determined by political and social struggles. Even so, long-term tendencies, with deep and solid cultural roots, also undergo periods of critical transformations. Here I set out to explore this possibility: How close has Mexican nationalism come to reaching a certain edge, beyond which there is nothing? Has it gone so far as to cause deep unease across society?

To even begin to formulate these questions, we must give up the idea that the nation cannot exist without nationalism. Although closely connected, these realities operate on different planes: the territorialization of political power concretized in the nation-state is one thing, and the particular way—among many other possible ways—in which the makeup of national space is legitimated is quite another. It is true that nationalism usually accompanies the creation of a modern state; the modernization that follows is a process that includes the spread of nationalist trends (in the context of the expansion of highly technological urban industrial capitalism). This close relationship between modernization and nationalism will be one of the guiding threads of this essay, since I am pursuing the idea that Mexican national culture is drawing close to what has been called a postmodern (or postcultural) condition.[4]

By announcing my intentions at the outset, I hope to avoid another pitfall that often snags observers of contemporary politics: the temptation to associate nationalism with backwardness and underdevelopment. Those U.S. scholars who, for obvious geopolitical reasons, have taken an enormous interest in Mexican nationalism frequently give the impression that Mexico is a country dominated by powerful national passions, in contrast with a United States conditioned by a cold materialist culture revolving around the world of interests. These judgments have reinforced the false idea that nationalism is an inherent passion of the Mexican people. They have also helped to hide a fact that should not escape our analysis: the United States is today, and has been for decades, one of nationalism's most fertile breeding grounds. In reality, nationalism runs far deeper and more aggressive in the United States than in Mexico. Therefore Mex-

4. Jean-François Lyotard, *The Postmodern Condition* (Minneapolis: University of Minnesota Press, 1984); and George Steiner, *In Bluebeard's Castle* (New Haven: Yale University Press, 1971).

ican nationalism cannot be explained without understanding its counterpart in the United States, where the exaltation of national values is clearly and intimately associated with so-called modernization.[5]

Crisis, Modernization, Technocracy

Faced with the terrible blows of the open economic crisis of 1982 and the symptoms of a latent political crisis, the leaders of the system—especially the technocrats—have proposed a "new policy" that can be summed up in one word: modernization.[6] They tell us some changes must be made in the political system to bring it in line with the new winds blowing across the world. This is an implicit recognition that the structures of power are lagging behind the demands of modern society. As a consequence, they say, they must be modernized so that the state apparatus can return to its traditional efficiency and functionality. The technocratic origins of the modernization policy are evident, if only in the implicit message that the system is no longer as efficient as it once was, because of its relatively dysfunctional relationship with civil society. In reality, modernization is a proposal for making the system functional once again.

On the other hand, the new airs blowing through Mexican society can also be summed up in a single word: democratization. The social forces yearning to exercise democratic forms of political power are growing every day. What is important is that this democratization of civil culture is happening in very different—and even opposing—social sectors. Today we can see that the democratic ideal has taken root across the entire political spectrum, from the far right to the far left. Even the ruling party has been subject to strong internal tensions and an important split: its "democratic" current broke off to support the independent presidential candidacy of Cuauhtémoc Cárdenas in the 1988 elections.

Political conflicts are emerging because of the confluence of two problems. The first is the political elite's increasing difficulties in holding the government machinery together at moments of electoral transition. The second problem is the governing group's increasing difficulties in efficiently managing, much less resolving, the economic crisis. The political crisis of 1982—which sparked the

5. See Hans Kohn, *American Nationalism* (New York: Macmillan, 1957); R. W. Van Alstyne, *Genesis of American Nationalism* (Waltham, Mass.: Blaisdell, 1970); and J. J. Pullen, *Patriotism in America* (New York: American Heritage Press, 1973).
6. See my essay "The Political Crisis of 1982" in this volume, and also Centeno, *Democracy within Reason.*

spectacular nationalization of the banks—plainly revealed the advanced state of dissolution of the ties of cohesion (or the "pacts," to use the term technocrats prefer) that unite the governing group. The most visible aspect of the crisis is the generalized demand for a representative democracy: the tragic fact that the extension of "social democracy" (the elimination of private banks) took place in such a despotic manner is one more symptom of the government's inability to harmonize social democracy with political democracy. The crisis of 1982 has opened an era characterized by the rapid spread of a new phenomenon: the need for a democratic opening has appeared at every level of political society and across progressively wider sectors of civil society. The precariousness of existing democratic mechanisms has become an obstacle for various currents and tendencies at work inside the government. The PRI style of authoritarian government is no longer effective or operative in reproducing the mediating and legitimating functions of the state.

But these conflicts have also been observed and experienced by the technocrats, who are trying to halt the sclerosis of the mediating channels between the state and society. If traditional PRI forms are no longer effective, they must be "modernized," that is to say, a new governing technique must be found that might unblock control processes and clear the political stage of the remains of a useless past. Modern techniques place more emphasis on management, efficiency, and economic measures than on the old approach of making political pacts, manipulating leaders, and dividing up areas of influence.[7]

The critical tensions that characterize the Mexican state today are expressed on the level of political culture in the apparent contradiction between "modernization" and "democratization." This situation has developed because of the important changes in the political elite over the last ten years, which I will only quickly sketch here. The governing group, as it developed in the years after Cárdenas, was essentially made up of the peculiar confluence of the interests of the economically dominant classes and the bureaucracy that holds power in the name of the masses of peasants and blue-collar and white-collar workers.[8] To be more precise, the political elite was composed of three groups: technocrats, "new" businessmen, and bankers. These were three political groups who exercised, in a way, the representation of the motley and complex conglomerate of

7. See my analysis in *Agrarian Structure and Political Power*, as well as "Missing Democracy," in this volume.

8. Lázaro Cárdenas, president between 1934 and 1940, laid the basis for the consolidation of the modern Mexican political system. [Trans.]

interconnected interests arrayed around the "government of the revolution." The technocrats formed the group that led and represented the other portions of the bureaucracy (labor unions, peasant unions, "popular" organizations, and so forth). The new "nationalist" businessmen—especially the bourgeoisie of central Mexico who owed their existence to protectionism—were assigned the role of leading the entire business class, thanks to their solid channels of pressure and influence in the governments of the Federal District of Mexico City and the state of Mexico, in the Secretariat of Industry and Commerce, and so forth. And finally, the bankers had positioned themselves in a powerful and dangerous balancing position between the right-wing businessmen of the north (the "Monterrey Group" et al.) and the political bureaucracy.[9]

But in 1982 it became clear that new factors had appeared, along with the economic crisis:

1. The deepening division between the technocrats and the rest of the political bureaucracy, which has a great deal to do with how income from the oil boom was managed and also with the government's poor response to the economic crisis.

2. The narrowing political divide between the "nationalist" and "rightist" sectors of the business class, principally thanks to the abandonment of populist positions by the progressively less "new" businessmen of the former sector.

3. The elimination of private bankers as a group, with the nationalization of banks in 1982, and as a result, the business class's generalized distrust of the political bureaucracy.

4. The weakening of the agrarian sector of the PRI and of the network of traditional caudillos in the provinces, accompanied by the strengthening of regional bourgeoisies and middle classes.

5. The relative strengthening of the labor bureaucracy, accompanied by increased divisiveness between the various groups and currents fighting for power.

All these factors—and many others left out for lack of space—led to an extraordinary strengthening of the political position of the technocrats after 1982. At the same time, they generated a kind of vacuum around the new power core, since the old pacts knitting together various political factions had either worn thin or been discarded. Therefore the hegemonic technocratic core has had to propose a restoration of the network of pacts, but pressure groups are less interested in restoring the network of alliances than in reformulating it. Many busi-

9. For a more detailed exploration of these points, see "Journey to the Center of the Right," in this volume.

nessmen are suspicious of a restoration of the old alliance with the government; they want substantive changes, and some have even bet on an alternative outside the system. Paradoxically, the labor bureaucracy is perhaps the group that harbors the most conservative elements, as manifested by its desire for renegotiation on a traditional basis and its distrust of all democratizing structural changes in the system. But it has a hard time swallowing the technocratic austerity policies that have so undermined workers' standard of living.

To round out this panorama of crisis, we should stress that two great powers—one material, the other spiritual—have also taken a decisive turn in their relationships with the Mexican state: the United States government and the Catholic Church. The Reagan administration has shown a certain distrust in the stability of the Mexican system—which contributed to its instability—and the high ecclesiastical authorities are beginning to grow tired of the rules of play in force since 1940 that have kept them out of politics. In sum, we have a less statist bourgeoisie, a more resentful middle class, a more fragile labor movement, a less complacent United States government, and a less standoffish church. All this is reflected in recent electoral trends, which show a strengthening of the opposition, especially on the Right.

Grosso modo, this is the context in which the Mexican technocracy has proposed a modernizing project to the country. It has proposed, that is, a project of pacts and alliances that might manage to repair the breaks in the political apparatus, in order to avoid the all too predictable shipwreck and face the stormy winds that will not die down. This is a modernizing project aiming to avoid, or at least manipulate, the looming democratization threatening the immense accumulated privileges of the hegemonic political bureaucracy.[10]

The complexity of these tensions spurs various sides to invoke nationalism, the symbol of the motley conglomerate of pacts that has kept the government of the Mexican Revolution afloat for nearly a half century. On this point, it is worth pausing to ask: Is nationalist political culture capable today of performing the legitimating function that the crisis of the system seems to demand? One part of the political bureaucracy realizes the complexity and enormous difficulties of trying to refunctionalize Mexican nationalism in the critical conditions the country is facing. These bureaucrats realize that Mexican nationalism contains a set of ingredients that are no longer acceptable to large and important sectors of the population, and they see nationalism as the measure of an era that must be overcome. Revolutionary nationalism clashes both with so-called moderniza-

10. For a good synthetic overview of the Mexican transition, see Peter H. Smith, *Mexico: Neighbor in Transition*, Headline Series no. 267 (New York: Foreign Policy Association, 1984).

tion and with representative democracy. Its fundamental assumptions do not adapt well to the unavoidable competitiveness that would be introduced by a free and impartial electoral system. Neither do they adapt to criteria of efficiency in political decision making and in managing public finances. Nationalism is so intimately associated with the corrupt authoritarian system of the dominant official party that it is difficult to hide the contradictions between the paths out of the crisis and the old hegemonic political culture. Overcoming those contradictions and inconsistencies, modernizing nationalism, is the challenge facing the dominant bureaucracy. I will try to look at this problem first, without forgetting that there are strong indications that reestablishing the functional relationship between nationalism and the political system will no longer manage to restore PRI authoritarianism. My suspicion is that not only is nationalism no longer part of the solution, but now it is part of the problem.

The Ironies of Efficiency

In Mexico, the eighties have been the age of the rise of the political technocracy. Many observers of Mexican politics have pointed this out, but few have examined its consequences in the field of political culture, even though the antagonism between traditional nationalist discourse and the technocratic style of government would seem rather evident. Let's examine the problem a little more closely.

Revolutionary nationalism has been defined by at least four broad sets of attitudes and positions:

1. A distrust of great powers—especially the United States—accompanied by variable doses of xenophobia and anti-imperialism.

2. A defense of nationalization as a means for limiting the ownership of land, the control of natural resources, and the concentration of capital. Concrete expressions of this are, for example, the system of ejidos, state control of oil, and legal limits on foreign investment.

3. A wide-ranging strong interventionist state, whose exceptional force is justified by its revolutionary origins and its broad mass base—the "institutionalized revolution."

4. An overvaluation of Mexican identity as an inexhaustible source of political energy.

To be sure, the political technocrats have not renounced the ideals of revolutionary nationalism in their speeches. But if we pull back the curtains of demagoguery and take a peek at *what the technocracy is doing*, it is easy to see that revolutionary nationalism is no longer its source of inspiration. Not only does the technocracy *not* distrust the government of the United States; it has become an active collaborator in so-called Reaganomics. Both in its direction and in its technocratic bent, official Mexican economic policy cannot effectively be understood without an awareness of recent trends at the University of Chicago or Harvard. Among Mexican technocrats, only the wreckage of the old xenophobia remains. Nothing horrifies the new breed of Mexican public servant more than anti-imperialism, which is viewed as an old weapon best locked up behind glass in the Museum of the Revolution. As is becoming more and more obvious, whatever disagreements periodically arise between the governments of the United States and Mexico are handled according to the logic of the set of interests that revolve around the U.S. economy. This set of interests is manifest in a pragmatic movement toward a kind of North American common market, with connections to Asia.[11]

Obviously the technocracy, hoping to pull out of the crisis, is dedicated to "rationalizing" the limits the system places on the ownership of land, the control of natural resources, and the concentration and circulation of capital. Because of this, the technocracy has attempted, with varying success, to dislodge traditional nationalist policies from three key sectors of the economy: agriculture, oil production, and foreign investment. This has meant an assault on three great strongholds of revolutionary nationalism—agrarianism, labor populism, and protectionism—in order to give economic policy a "modern" outlook.

This confrontation has seriously eroded the PRI regime's popular base, producing serious splits and shifts within the unity of the "revolutionary family." Yet "modern policies" have not managed to bring Mexico out of deep economic crisis. The attacks on agrarianism, labor populism, and protectionism reflect more than ideological aggressiveness: they are part of a general trend eroding the state's mass support and undermining the peculiarly Mexican mechanisms of ruling through agrarian caciques, union strongmen, and protectionist corruption. Although clearly agrarianism cannot be reduced to the cacique, unions cannot be reduced to the strongman, and protectionism cannot be reduced to bribes and favoritism, there can be little doubt that without these odious "national" peculiarities, the Mexican political system is unable to function adequately. The tragic paradox of the system is that the mechanisms that reproduce it have an ambiguous character: they guarantee popular support at the same time

11. This essay was originally written before the (fraudulent and highly contested) election of Carlos Salinas de Gortari in 1988; one of Salinas's priorities in office was to negotiate a free trade agreement with the United States, resulting in the North American Free Trade Agreement that has been in force since 1994. [Trans.]

that they generate repression, violence, corruption, and fraud. Correcting these "flaws" without affecting the ties between the government and the mass organizations that support it would seem very difficult, if not impossible.

How can this system be defended as superior, just because it is Mexican, at a time when every official attempt to escape the crisis has failed? Closely tying the government's fate to "Mexican being" was a stabilizing move while the system was going through a long period of growth; now, in times of crisis, it has become a stone tied around the neck of official ideology and a cause of political confusion and fragmentation.

Proposals to modernize the Mexican political system have placed the idea of *efficiency* at the center of the debate. The inevitable question arises: Is efficiency compatible with the political system? Efficiency is usually measured—and for this only English terms will do—in terms of the relationship of "input" to "output," a formula that can be subjected to complex technocratic transfigurations and take the form of sophisticated mathematical models. All this cannot completely hide the fact that setting criteria for efficiency implies making qualitative political decisions about the nature and character of both "inputs" and "outputs," as well as about how to translate them into appropriate mathematical expressions and plug them into the equations that a given model requires. Nonetheless the essence of technocratic thinking lies in the particular way in which efficiency reasoning hides political reality. Let us examine a curious but revealing example.

A few years back, the current PRI candidate for the presidency of the republic, Carlos Salinas de Gortari, carried out a research project in Puebla with the objective of evaluating the relationship between public investment in rural development programs (input) and popular support for the government (output).[12] A survey led him to reach some revealing conclusions: "These results seem to indicate that public investment does not produce intense feelings of support for the system among those benefiting the most from it: ironically, the system seems most efficient in gaining the support of the communities which benefit the least."[13] The tragic irony is that one of the traditional formulas for organizing

12. It is worth noting that Carlos Salinas de Gortari's study was written at, and published by, the same center where this essay was prepared. His brother Raúl, a kingpin in the corruption schemes that later flourished during the Salinas administration, had also been a fellow at this center. [Trans.]

13. Carlos Salinas de Gortari, *Political Participation, Public Investment, and Support for the System*, Research Report Series no. 35 (La Jolla, Calif.: Center for U.S.-Mexican Studies, University of California–San Diego, 1982), 37.

the alchemy of the political system does not seem to be effective. As the author of this study—and future president of Mexico—says, "Public investment does not buy the political support the government was hoping for."[14] Anyone who knows how the Mexican system works might suspect what is concealed behind this kind of irony: public investment does not usually benefit the public in general, but only a small sector of the public, and it particularly benefits the political brokers whose support is indispensable for the system's survival. The Mexican government does not receive support directly from the masses; it is the "natural representatives" of the people—the brokers—who shape and organize the "popular base" of the system.

Now imagine that the government uses the most efficient formula—according to the correlations discovered by Salinas de Gortari—and reduces public spending with the objective of increasing popular support for the system (and, along the way, satisfying the International Monetary Fund). A considerable portion of the population would be pleased with the system for ceasing to feed the caciques, charros, and corrupt officials. But those brokers would begin to get annoyed and would eventually stop offering support for the system (some might even disappear). In this case, the system would suffer a loss of legitimacy with the dissolution of the brokers' ties to the hypothetical population pleased by decreased public spending. With the crumbling of traditional loyalty, the system would have to look to build a consensus among the aforementioned pleased and supportive population by means of the formal processes of electoral democracy. We may very well ask whether, in such an event, the technocrats would dare to risk their power in open elections, trusting in the existence of a PRI majority in society.

In this imaginary model, we can recognize, even so, the principal elements of the difficulties faced by the political elite. The technocratic style tends to exclude traditional mechanisms of corruption, manipulation, and fraud, since the leadership group supposedly has the "know-how" necessary to modify the system's variables according to a political model that should operate efficiently on the basis of the equations generated by the specialists. There is no room here for the intuition or gut feelings of political leaders, whose skill is supposed to come from their Mexicanness, from their deep understanding of the national soul. In this sense, technocratic efficiency clashes openly with revolutionary nationalism: these are two completely different political cultures.[15]

14. Ibid., 4.
15. Part of the reason for the massive repudiation Salinas faced after the 1994 crisis was the proven inefficiency and ineffectiveness of the technocrats in setting a stable course for the fu-

The Matriotic Belt

Revolutionary nationalism is facing other threats as well.[16] One of them is the growing force of regional systems of power. In this we can observe another of the effects of so-called modernization, which has not only increased the longing for efficiency at the heart of the bureaucracy but also spurred the economic and political development of various regional centers of power.

Since nationalism goes hand in hand with centralism, every change in the correlation of forces that increases power in the provinces evidently affects the basic principles on which nationalism is built. The new situation also directly threatens the enormous electoral fraud belt, a region whose existence guarantees the very high voting percentages assigned to the official party. This fraud belt is composed of extensive rural areas controlled by small and medium-sized centers of regional power. These are places where the opposition is completely excluded, and no one exercises the least electoral oversight.

Changes in the relationship between the center and the provinces therefore not only affect the traditional forms of political culture but also contribute to the periodic crises that PRI forms of government experience in various places. The conflicts in Chihuahua, Baja California, and Michoacán are not the only conflicts, but they are perhaps the most spectacular ones, and they also show best how a new era is coming in which the operation of the authoritarian system runs into obstacles.[17]

I want to point out three factors contributing to this new situation. First, the last twenty years have seen a slow but inexorable decline of the traditional forms of rural power consolidated during the Calles and—above all—Cárdenas eras. These mediating structures, with *caciquismo* as a key piece, came together as a strong political fabric that sewed together into a single network agrarian reform institutions, agrarian leaders turned caciques, peasant organizations, and agrarian communities. I have written extensively on this topic in order to show how the processes of political mediation in the countryside have been changing to

---

ture. Even more important was the popular discovery of the massive extent of corruption and fraud of the Salinas regime, which was all the more shocking given Salinas's clean and modern rhetoric. [Trans.]

16. The term "matriotic" (in the section title) reflects a love of the motherland, the native soil, a smaller-scale loyalty that contrasts with the larger-scale love of the fatherland, of the "patria," which is called patriotic. "Belt" is used here in the sense of a cultural or geographic region, like the Sun Belt, Rust Belt, or Bible Belt in the United States. [Trans.]

17. In all three states, the crisis of the PRI allowed opposition groups to win the governorship. [Trans.]

such a degree that the structure of official power finds itself enormously weakened in certain rural areas.[18] In many others, the system of power is in the hands of a new political class of government officials and technical experts that has replaced the old caciques.

This last phenomenon leads me to the second factor that is changing the political panorama in the provinces: the creation of new regional powers, or the expansion of some of the existing powers as economic-technical-administrative conglomerates tied to oil drilling, prosperous irrigation districts, the *maquiladora* industry, the large electrical power plants, big business (steel, chemicals, etc.), centers of tourism, and so on.

These processes have generated the expansion of a dense regional bureaucracy and technocracy, which invades the pores of quiet rural life. Perhaps the most dramatic case is oil production, whose spread has forever changed living conditions in several zones on the Gulf Coast: along with oil came highways, pipelines, engineers, union corruption, pollution, and hordes of merchants. In less spectacular ways, similar processes have happened elsewhere in the provinces.

All this is taking place within the larger setting of the third factor I want to point out: the extraordinary strengthening—above all at the end of the sixties and the beginning of the seventies—of the provincial bourgeoisie, not merely or even mainly in Monterrey, but in a multitude of small and medium-sized cities tied to the economic-technical-administrative conglomerates I mentioned earlier. The economic bonanza that led up to the crisis that erupted in 1982 helped the business class to reproduce itself rapidly all across the country, along with the middle classes that usually revolve around it.[19]

These three factors, along with others not discussed here, have helped to strengthen regional systems of power, producing some paradoxical effects. One of them is what Luis González calls "matriotism," a concept whose resonances I want to comment on here.[20] It is understandable that the strengthening of regional systems of power spurs the emerging social groups in the provinces to turn their gaze to their surrounding context, in search of an inspiration for confronting the authoritarianism emanating from the central authorities. And what do they see when they take a look around? They see hundreds of *matrias;* as

18. See my book *Agrarian Structure and Political Power.*
19. On the Monterrey Group, see footnote 3 in "The Political Crisis of 1982." [Trans.]
20. Luis González y González, "Suave matria." González y González is best known for his micro-historical study of just one such community, *San José de Gracia: Mexican Village in Transition,* trans. John Upton (Austin: University of Texas Press, 1974).

Luis González says, "Half of Mexicans involve themselves in small-town mini-societies, their hometowns, their birthplaces, their parishes, their *patrias chicas* or *matrias*." These are two thousand municipalities of rustic or semirustic scale, where people's lives revolve around agriculture, livestock, and artisanry, where there usually is—or was—a cacique and where a certain Catholic conservatism dominates and, without actually opposing the desire for change, works to keep local customs alive. Luis González offers moving praise for the values of matriotism as opposed to the nationalism or patriotism of the leaders of the Mexican state, which "frequently takes aggressive actions against matriotism, the hometown loyalty, the love for the native soil, and the hopes and dreams of the two thousand municipal minorities."[21]

The opposition between urban authoritarian patriotism and rural conservative matriotism remains more of an ingredient of the cultural imaginary than a contradiction of the political system. Of course the opposition between rural life and the big cities is expressed in a thousand ways and exercises a powerful influence over how politics is done. But this does not conceal the fundamental fact: *one of the major supports of the Mexican political system is to be found precisely in the existence of those two thousand small towns of the matriotic belt.* Luis González himself describes this, in his own fashion:

> The *cacique* is the autocratic strongman of a *matria* or a native soil . . . he counts on the support of the national authorities, who are fearful of democracy. Besides the *cacique*, each town in the Republic has a municipal government. Most *matrias* have a group of councilmen. According to the law, they are freely elected by the majority of the town's citizens; in reality they are designated by the supreme government in connivance with the *cacique* of each *matria*. Around him revolve the local forces: the shopkeepers and other small-time moneybags, the mayor, the jack-of-all-trades, the doctor, the honey-tongued bootlicker, the jokester, the know-it-all and the shyster.[22]

This moving caricature reminds us of the rural world of Balzac, and it corresponds to reality: despite all their confrontations on various levels, there is a close political relationship between municipal matriotism and central patriotism. In no sense is this simply a violent and prideful aggressive imposition of authoritarian patriotism on the clumsy, naive, rustic, and folksy "matriots" who

21. Ibid., 52, 56.
22. Ibid., 53.

live cowering in their rural nooks and crannies. Mexican authoritarianism, wrapped up in nationalism and patriotism, has deep historical roots in the Mexican countryside. In large measure, authoritarian centralism can exist thanks to the presence of the matriotic belt. Beyond this, those two thousand municipalities are, by and large, the same ones that make up what I have called the fraud belt, the immense zone official statistical alchemy leans on to invent overwhelming electoral majorities. So-called patriotic fraud has its natural base in the matriotic belt.

We should clarify that this situation has begun to change, which helps to explain why in recent years various conservative currents have looked for antidotes to the central government's patriotism in the matriotic belt. What Luis González is expressing with his praise for matriotism are the profound political changes that have taken place in Mexican provinces, whose most obvious sign is the expansion and multiplication of new centers of power. Those centers are starting to dispute the central government's hegemony over the rural belt, an area where the traditional ties between the cacique, the community, and state powers have begun to weaken or have disappeared. These tendencies reveal something more than authoritarian centralism's difficulties in reproducing itself. We also find a serious threat to hegemonic nationalist culture, a threat that takes the form of a renovation of a never completely extinguished regionalism, now tenderly baptized as matriotism by Luis González. This renovation is not the reemergence of old centrifugal and localist tendencies but rather a fruit of the modernization of broad rural zones—with the corresponding weight of frustrations—produced in part by the hundreds of thousands of Mexicans who have traveled and worked in the United States. The new matriotism is a new conservatism that looks for its raison d'être more in the moral and religious values of small-town life than in the universe of "major national problems." It is a postmodern conservatism that has lost its faith in progress but still longs for peace. It is a conservatism that is beginning to look more like the conservatism emanating from many small cities and suburbs in the Midwest or Southwest of the United States than like the old-time conservative pull of soldiers such as Almazán or movements like sinarquismo. The quiet evolution of the party that took up the sinarquista tradition (the Mexican Democratic Party) is a symptom of these new conservative spaces: once a quasi-fascist militant group, it has gone on to form what is perhaps the clearest organic political expression of the new forms of matriotism in many regions (the Bajío, Michoacán, etc.). The PAN, especially in the North of Mexico, captures a good part of this regionalist conservative spirit. Nonetheless the matriotic belt still remains, to a considerable degree, a silent fortress of the official party and one of the major bases of support for groups within the government who oppose the technocrats in the name of traditional revolutionary politics.

Fraud and Postmodernity

It is usually thought that the great mass of Mexicans who abstain from voting form a kind of silent support for the PRI government. From this it follows that electoral fraud does nothing more than fill the boxes with ballots that, if they were actually filled out by the abstainers, would support the PRI in any case. This reasoning aims to give a seal of legitimacy to electoral fraud, under the assumption that abstention is hiding forces that really support the PRI.

One survey carried out in 1959 by Almond and Verba, whose interpretation has been influential in academic circles, showed that despite great political indifference in Mexico the system had broad legitimacy ("system affect," in the authors' terms).[23] Political indifference reached a high level: 44 percent of the sample declared they had no interest in politics. In reality, the percentage of indifferents should have been much higher, since the sample excluded all communities with fewer than 10,000 inhabitants. More than twenty years later, another survey done in 1982 showed that in rural areas, 55 percent of those surveyed had no interest in politics.[24] This 1982 study revealed that 70 percent of those surveyed in the entire country had little or no interest in politics.

According to the survey, the situation in 1982 revealed limited sympathy for the PRI. In fact, only 19 percent expressed their support for the ruling party (6 percent for the PAN, and 1.6 percent for the PSUM, the largest party of the Left).[25] The immense majority did not express support for any political party—71.5 percent. Although the survey did not capture voting intentions, there is little doubt that it reflects them indirectly. If we compare these results with electoral results, we can begin to suspect the gigantic extent of fraud: even if we assume that those who don't support any party abstain from voting, the PRI obtained 66 percent in the survey, the PAN 21 percent, and the whole of the Left 10 percent (the PSUM alone, 5.6 percent). But let's look more closely at what is happening in this potentially abstaining and apolitical zone whose silence seems to legitimate the system.

The 1982 survey allows us to get an idea of the political leanings of the silent

23. Almond and Verba, *The Civic Culture*, 372.
24. Alberto Hernández Medina, ed., *¿Cómo somos los Mexicanos?* (Mexico: CREA, 1987).
25. The PSUM was the unified party of the Left that would later merge into the PRD. [Trans.]

Table. Political Leanings versus Party Preferences versus Election Results

	A Political Leaning		B Party Preference		C Election Result	D Support Index $[D = B / A \times 100]$
	No.	Pct.	No.	Pct.	Pct.	Pct.
Left	206	11%	53	10%	10%	26%
Center	604	33%	352	67%	70%	58%
Right	1,027	56%	117	23%	20%	11%
Total	1,837	100%	522	100%	100%	

fraud belt: paradoxically, even though they form a solid foundation for PRI power, most of the population under study has right-wing leanings. According to this survey, 56 percent of those surveyed placed themselves on the Right, 33 percent in the Center, and 11 percent on the Left. It is easily confirmed that this political spectrum is not reflected in their preferences for political parties (nor is it reflected in election results). We can suppose that two phenomena are at work, not necessarily exclusive of each other: (1) the majority of those who expressed support for the Right and the Left abstain from voting, and (2) a significant percentage of those who define themselves as right-wing or left-wing vote for the PRI. There are reasons for supposing that the first case is more significant. The 1982 survey indirectly provides us with the possibility of clearing up this problem. To do so, I have built a table, in which party preferences are compared with political leanings and election results (I have placed the PAN and PDM on the Right, the PRI and the PARM in the Center, and the PSUM and smaller parties on the Left).

This table gives us some indication of the relationship between political parties and their potential electoral strength. The PRI and PARM are the preference of a group of citizens equivalent to 58 percent of those who consider themselves centrists. Of course, this does not mean that all those who prefer the PRI define themselves as centrists, although we could suspect a strong association between the two. This kind of association should be even stronger on the Left, yet there we see that parties so defined gain the preferences of the equivalent of little more than a quarter of those who consider themselves leftists. On the Right, the PAN and PDM capture even less of the potential preferences than the Left: only the equivalent of 11 percent of rightists prefer the parties that usually define themselves as such (even if those parties would reject such a definition).

The data in this table point to the existence of strange paradoxes, that is, of a peculiar political fragmentation on several levels. What is perhaps strangest is the great difference between the spread of political leanings and the distribution of party preferences, so that the official party, in a markedly rightist context, manages to gain more support than the potential strength of the centrist space it supposedly occupies. This can happen because more than 70 percent have no preference for any party. The second strange fact we can point out is the great similarity between the party preferences of those surveyed and the electoral results from that same year. If the sample is representative—and everything indicates that it is—it would seem that those who did not express a party preference voted in very similar proportions to those who did express some party preference, which is not very likely, if we take into account how political leanings are distributed. The explanations for these paradoxes can be found in four facts that are worth stressing:

1. The PRI is the party that shows the greatest effectiveness in capturing the support of its potential voters (58 percent), which makes clear the ruling party's enormous organizational power.

2. The mass of abstainers are mostly right-wing. The idea that the vast mass of Mexicans who do not vote silently support the PRI government has no basis.

3. The PRI attracts a high percentage of the right-wing electorate, of the Mexicans who believe (and arguments are not lacking) that the official party is the best conservative option.

4. The high electoral percentage assigned to the PRI is not completely explained by the preceding factors. There is clearly a significant element of fraud involved in counting the vote.

These paradoxes take on a tragic tonality if we observe the political campaign of the official candidate: he appeared fiercely committed to a nationalist and revolutionary struggle against the Right, although he was surrounded by a "made in the U.S.A." technocratic aura that could please many conservatives. This paradox alone could be the stoic symptom of a hegemonic group that has no intention of respecting the vote: the members of the group would rather keep their revolutionary myths than risk a campaign to build an electoral territory of their own, cleanly marked off by an open rightist turn in their discourse.[26]

The Mexican political elite has adopted postmodern behavior: it has opted for pastiche and simulacra and given itself over to surfaces and appearances. It refuses to accept democratic alternatives; it refuses to admit the existence of a deeper electoral problem. What matters is for Mexican society to think the elections are clean, not for the elections really to be clean. To achieve this, the elite

---

26. Stoic in the sense of resigning themselves to the lonely task of following the course they believe correct, rather than consulting the people. [Trans.]

no longer turns to the restoration of broken chains of signifiers and signifieds, nor to the existential model of authenticity or lack of authenticity. Depth is replaced by surface, as Jameson says, or by multiple surfaces.[27] And there, in the multiple dimensions of appearances, the criterion of efficiency rules as a form of legitimacy.

Since all this implies abandoning classic ideas about political representation, it is understandable to worry for the future of democracy in Mexico. In the United States, postmodern political trends have meant a retreat from the typical forms of the modern state, based on the representative mechanisms that connect the mass of citizens with the machinery of government. Every day in the United States, we see more multilateral negotiations between monopolies, myriad interest groups, and ethnic groups aiming to establish means of representation that are no longer based on the mass of free and equal individuals who make up what the classics termed civil society. Political parties are weakened, and the personalized struggle between personalities moves to the fore in a context in which the mass media and each politician's financial resources are taking the place of society in choosing alternatives. Umberto Eco has called these new tendencies neomedieval—and it is not by chance that his novel *The Name of the Rose* was a best-seller in the United States. But this would be a new Middle Ages, efficient and technocratic—as described by Bell, Galbraith, or Habermas—immersed in a small-minded and parochial society that looks on politics with indifference or scorn.

Could this political tendency, which replaces classic democratic forms with a plurality of techno-structures reaching beyond the limits of citizen (and national) political control, possibly succeed in Mexico? Must we suffer from a postdemocratic regime before we have even managed to reach democracy?

These seem to be the intentions of the political faction led by Salinas de Gortari. There is good reason to suspect that the combination of the much proclaimed "modern politics" with the much feared fraudulent electoral imposition might produce a postmodern (or dismothern) effect.[28] It might put an end to the obsession with innovation and revolution, to open the door to those things usually rejected by modernity—the parochial, the traditional, and the ornamental—as characteristics of a nondemocratic political culture that tolerates soft authoritarianism so long as the channels of negotiation and agreement are not

27. Fredric Jameson, *Postmodernism, or, The Cultural Logic of Late Capitalism* (Durham: Duke University Press, 1991).
28. See footnote 11 in "The Mexican Office" about dismothernity.

closed and Mexico enters much further into the area of consumption and invest-ment dominated by the U.S. economy.

My question is the following: Are the PRI and the system in conditions to col-lect the silent support of the enormous conservative sector that has grown in Mexico, to head up an alternative that is transnational and parochial at the same time? I have strong suspicions that this would be very difficult and, if it were to take place, would be a short-lived and unstable alternative. It is true that the conservative sector coincides on many points with what I would call the fraud belt, those rural and semiurban zones where the opposition cannot even get its foot in the door, except through the church, the Lions Club, or the semiclandes-tine groups of the radical Left. But it seems to me that this belt, which also coin-cides, up to a point, with the two thousand rural municipalities of Luis Gonzá-lez's matriotism, is beginning to mobilize in a direction not exactly matching that of official policy. One part of that rural belt is living postmodernity even more intensely than the majority of PRI technocrats.

The urban portion of the conservative sector is adopting more and more right-ist positions every day, and its tolerance for government corruption is shrinking rapidly. Add to this the Left's reception, not without protest, of an injection of forces coming from the PRI led by Cuauhtémoc Cárdenas. It is impossible to know how much this split will affect the PRI, but there is no doubt it will be sig-nificant.

If present trends continue, the leadership of the PRI might see itself reduced to an alliance between the governmental technocracy and the labor bureaucracy, with decreasing support from peasants, middle sectors, and businessmen. It would still be a significant political force, but it would be tiny in proportion to the enormous power conglomerate the PRI has been for decades.

For these reasons and many others, the possibility of passing into modernity while bypassing democracy would be a losing wager for the Mexican system. The winds of postmodernism have come, creating an atmosphere of crisis and frustration.

The New Right

Mexican political culture finds itself at a crossroads, split by a deep schism sepa-rating revolutionary nationalism from a cluster of conservative leanings. In a sense, this split has existed for many years: it has separated Catholic Guada-lupean traditions from revolutionary institutionalism. But since the end of the Cárdenas era, an agreement had been reached to heal the wounds that the *cris-*

tero wars and sinarquista struggles had caused in the embryonic systems of post-revolutionary power.

But today, after nearly a half century of stability, we can see that the wound is still open, no scar has formed, and new tensions have emerged. They are expressed in many ways, including the growth of a new form of right-wing opposition often called *neopanismo*.[29] It is worth taking a look at the problem. If we compare the doctrinal principles of the PAN with its current electoral platform, we can get a concrete idea of the new trends I'm talking about.

There is a contradiction, or at the very least a large difference, between the doctrinal principles of the PAN and its electoral platform. Its doctrine originates in Christian humanism and essentially proposes reordering or redistributing political power according to a few basic assumptions about the dignity of the human being, the common good, and the family. From there it follows that private initiative is the most lively source of social improvement, that political functions should be ordered in keeping with the common good, and that the family should have a natural predominance over all other social forms.

The doctrinal principles of the PAN do not forget about democracy, but they put several adjectives in front of it: federal democracy, authentic democracy, and so forth. They place great emphasis on the mechanisms for distributing and ordering power, to the detriment of the importance of the principles of representation. Order is what is essential, and if there is misery, ignorance, and injustice, that is due to the reigning disorder. All we need to do to begin a new era of happiness is to enthrone a "just order." Curiously enough, there are two great lacunae in the doctrinal principles of the PAN, approved in 1939: nationalism and the Catholic Church. These lacunae are undoubtedly not due to an absence of opinions among the members of the PAN on these two fundamental themes. They have often stated their position on this matter: the PAN is not a Catholic party, and it is a patriotic party. But the doubts on the matter have never been dispersed. These doctrinal principles are the expression of a conservative Right that agreed to limit itself to being a relatively marginal watchdog pressure group.

By contrast, the electoral platform of the PAN—of neopanismo, we might say—has a completely different character. The axis of the platform's discourse is democracy and structural change. The liberalization of the PAN platform since 1969 is evident. A goodly portion of the proposals come directly from needs for change in the dominant system itself. There is also a notable influence of tradi-

29. The new (neo) version of the PAN party. [Trans.]

tional demands of the Left, whose influence spread across Mexican society after the 1968 movement. The old ideals of Christian solidarity survive with difficulty; now there is more talk of the national common good.

This new attitude of the PAN expresses a change in the political culture of the Right. There is now an aggressive tendency to renounce the old doctrinaire Christian solidarity, which condemned the Right to form anticommunist cells to keep watch over civil society and to pressure the government to keep it from straying to the Left. The new trends are evident in a church less fearful of state authority that has tired of the rules of play set up by Cárdenas and Ávila Camacho. To this less Caesarian church there corresponds a less Bonapartist Right which—especially after the nationalization of private banks—has begun to distrust PRI authoritarianism. Add to this the ill tempers of an extensive middle class that already tasted the honey of modernity, thanks to the "populisms" of the seventies and to the oil boom, but is now subjected to an unbearable austerity regimen.

These changes have been evident in a growing rightward shift of the governing bureaucracy. But the PAN has sparked a curious expansion effect, which is summarized in the fact that it is ceasing to be a party of the Right—to use traditional terms—to convert itself gradually into a party of the Center Right. It is converting itself, in other words, into a bearer of liberal-democratic values.[30]

The New Right has also benefited from significant changes in political culture in the provinces and in rural areas. At first, these changes sparked the reemergence of a Far Right that attempted, without success, to build a mass party, the PDM. The "reemergence" of sinarquismo never managed to come together as a modern party and ended up diluted in the new presence established by the PAN. Similar phenomena to the growth of urban middle classes so important to the emergence of the New Right have taken place in rural or semirural areas and in the provinces—and not just in the Bajío. From a socioeconomic standpoint, these processes are similar: the development of new privileged sectors, the enrichment of sectors of the peasantry, and the expansion of the commercial, artisanal, or small-industrial petty bourgeoisie. But politically this is a different process. Traditional PRI clientelist structures, based on the manipulation of

---

30. In July 2000, the PAN candidate for president, Vicente Fox, won the first fully democratic elections in Mexico. A typical representative of the New Right sketched out here, Fox is a former Coca-Cola executive and the former governor of Guanajato, a state in the heartland of the Bajío, which has long been a stronghold of Catholic activism and, more recently, of the PAN. See the postscript to this volume, "The Dictatorship Was Not Perfect." [Trans.]

ejido authorities and so on, tend to break up, and metropolitan lifestyles expand. The great quantity of Mexicans who have lived in the United States exercise a powerful influence on this process of expansion of the middle and prosperous sectors. This is not only the economic influence of the accumulation of small amounts of capital: contact with life in the United States has a great political influence. The result is that old political structures are dissolving, just as the economic crisis is causing intense suffering. This generates a large amount of resentment, which explains the growth of opposition alternatives. This phenomenon is closely related to the peculiarities of the conservative belt of matriotism discussed earlier.

The End of Nationalist Gesticulations

I do not want to leave the impression that the crisis in Mexican political culture is simply the expression of increasing confrontation between institutional patriotism and conservative matriotism. Hegemonic nationalist culture is facing more than the challenge of "modernizing" or "refunctionalizing" itself to effectively counteract the pressures of a civil society drifting to the Right. We should ask if significant changes have not taken place on the cultural terrain of revolutionary nationalism itself. I am speaking of changes that might complicate its reproduction as the ideological and, above all, cultural glue of the system. If this is so, we are not facing a situation of "backwardness" in nationalism, which could be overcome through a possible modernization and adaptation to new circumstances. Instead nationalism is in increasing contradiction with national culture.

First off, I want to stress a point that I find important: the New Mexican Right is the offspring of revolutionary nationalism. The fact that the conservative mood takes a more clearly antigovernment bent every day should not keep us from sensing that it is precisely the modernization brought by hegemonic nationalism that has promoted the new conservatism. I believe this is a typical postmodern effect: modern society has lost its meaning because of an excess of meaning. This is a true implosion of meanings, opening the way to cultural fragmentation and broadening the spaces of frustration and nostalgia. At this critical juncture, nationalist political culture is facing down a right-wing culture expanding as a result of internal dynamics: this is the product of the evolution of a political culture dominated by nationalist ideas and feelings. The expansion of conservative and right-wing attitudes is a transitional phenomenon closely related to the crisis of nationalism. If there is a break in the authoritarian monopoly exercised by the nationalist PRI, the space for the Left will undoubtedly open up enormously. One sign of this is the recent decision of the PRI that caused the party's left wing to break away from officialdom.

Nationalism was the justification for promoting capitalist industrialization; the postrevolutionary government sponsored urbanization; national unity became the vehicle for transnationalization; the national state established the channels of political secularization and expansion of radio and television broadcasting. In the name of nationalism, independent workers' organizations and peasant movements were smothered, in order to open up space for free enterprise and authoritarian statism. Nationalism brought modernity, and with it the new winds that have reshaped the frontiers of national culture. This change in the limits of national culture—along with the widening splits—is what has brought revolutionary nationalism into crisis. Nationalism not only is ceasing to be an effective means of domination but has reached such a high level of internal inconsistency as to hamper its reproduction as the culture of the hegemonic class. Nationalism is losing its effectiveness at legitimating PRI hegemony and unifying the ruling class. In other words, official nationalism is losing its credibility with the masses and losing its coherence as the ideology and culture of the governing group.

Hand in hand with modernity inevitably came a transnational mass culture marked by particularly strong Anglo-American ingredients. Hollywood films, rock and roll, television series, and thousands of consumer goods designed for "international" tastes have invaded Mexican territory and filled our minds with new kinds of fantasies and frustrations. As a consequence, specifically national spaces were pushed out of their original places; the traditional popular subject of nationalist politics changed position. From the standpoint of mass society, official discourse seems more and more like mute nationalist gesticulations whose signs are understood less and mocked more every day. In particular, Mexican political culture is less and less willing to put up with the expressions of statolatry that mark Mexican nationalism.

So nationalist gesticulations come to an end. The dramatic gestures that evoked revolutionary heroics are turning into tragicomic tics that barely conceal the background of an authoritarian state. Official nationalism built a bridge between the new state and the nation with the bricks of populist and workerist despotism. Underneath the bridge were hidden the frustrated democratic wishes of a popular mass converted into the audience of the great theater of national political unity. Yet in recent years, those spectator-participants have begun to shake the pillars of the nationalist bridge. In 1968 we can see the first signs of a break with the statolatry instituted by the governments that emerged from, and were inspired by, the Mexican Revolution. I am using Gramsci's idea of statolatry, which applies to a situation where "the State can be identified with individuals . . . as elements of active culture . . . to create a new civilization, a new type of man, and of citizen."[31] Gramsci thought that a period of statolatry would be necessary in societies that had not passed through a long stage of independent and self-led cultural development before developing an autonomous state life. As Gramsci wrote, in such situations, "statolatry is nothing other than the normal form of 'State life,' or at least of initiation to autonomous State life and to the creation of a 'civil society' which it was not historically possible to create before the ascent to independent State life."[32] In Mexico the problem is that the period of statolatry has been institutionalized and has taken on nationalist form. The worship of the state has developed an extremely complex network of mediations, to such an omnivorous degree that it has taken the place of the functions of a democratic civil society with a high degree of perfection. Mexico does not have an unformed and gelatinous civil society. The solid institutional basis of its civil society has deep historical and popular roots but utterly lacks that "spontaneity" that its democratic character ought to provide. In Mexico the danger Gramsci warned of has materialized: statolatry has become theoretical fanaticism and has been conceived of as perpetual.[33]

It is worth recalling that I understand nationalism to be a body of political theory that expresses the hegemonic vocation of the ruling class in the form of a multiclass alliance based on the supposed originality of national peculiarities —subjectively reconstructed—and their identification with the nature of the state. It is important to stress the difference between nationalism, and national culture. To simply mark off that distance, without getting trapped in the territory of definitions, I would say that it is one thing to be nationalist, and quite another to be Mexican. In the first case, we run into the cultural and ideological manifestation of a political orientation; in the second case, we are facing a fact of citizenship, which should be inscribed into a democratic process.[34]

Clearly nationalism is not a constant phenomenon in society; it appears only under certain historical conditions, and it takes very different forms. In Mexico the specificity of nationalist politics, with their messy sociocultural base, has

31. Antonio Gramsci, *Selections from the Prison Notebooks*, ed. and trans. Quentin Hoare and G. Nowell Smith (London: Lawrence and Wishart, 1971), 268.

32. Ibid.

33. Ibid.

34. On these points, see Carlos Monsiváis, "Muerte y resurrección del nacionalismo mexicano," *Nexos* 109 (1987): 13–22.

given us a democracy stingily dispensed drop by drop, so as not to give our highly original underdevelopment any indigestion. It has given us the "pro-worker" policies of charros protected by the shadow of the state; it has given us the destruction of indigenous cultures justified as a sacrifice to fuel the life of the tricolor official statist tri-culture; and it has given us an intellectual life that finds itself obliged to beg from the powerful in order to be called "cultured."

In Mexico, differentiating between national culture and nationalism turns out to be especially difficult and complex. And yet these are—I insist—two processes that should be distinguished as clearly as possible, since few countries have experienced the peculiar sequence of historical situations that has led to enormous confusion between the governance of our national space and the domination powerfully legitimated by a nationalist political tendency crystallized in the interests of the modern capitalist state.

It is important to specify the difference between nationalism and national culture, above all if we want to understand the critical situation the Mexican political system is going through. We are not only witnessing the misadaptation of nationalism to modern society that the national state itself has helped to engender. We are also seeing a contradiction between nationalism and the national culture it forms part of, a national culture whose recent evolution consistently rejects more and more the traditional statolatrous and authoritarian ingredients of nationalism.

Democracy, Deterritorialization, and the Bronco State

The postrevolutionary state achieved national unity in the sphere of political structure.[35] But unity was not completely imposed on the space of political culture, despite efforts to confuse national culture with nationalism. We can identify two trends that slowed cultural unification. First, we have the spread of mass culture and transnationalization, as already mentioned. Second, but equally important, we find in Mexico a multiple and heterogeneous political culture whose roots lie not only in long processes of syncretism and mestizaje but also in the long-standing coexistence of political traditions with very different orientations. Cultural transnationalization has not changed this. On the contrary, it has broadened the already rich spectrum of cultural alternatives, adding elements coming from the Anglo-American "global village." The result

35. As any rodeo fan knows, a bronco is a pony that is rough, untamed, and rebellious. [Trans.]

is that in Mexico we find a typically postmodern fragmented culture, housed in a socioeconomic setting that is relatively backward and containing elements sometimes seen as premodern.

Nationalism faces a critical predicament, not only because it has not managed to unify political culture, but also because by becoming the symbol of authoritarianism, it has placed itself at odds with the growing democratization of civil society. Democratizing ideas have been channeled through the two pathways just mentioned, transnational mass culture and the evolution of Mexican cultural multiplicity.

Let us take a brief look at some problems related to mass culture, which nationalists have traditionally accused of being not only a threat to national unity but also a vehicle for antidemocratic imperialist tendencies. It has also irritated cultural elites, who consider it a degenerate, low, and vulgar expression of higher spiritual values. In the face of transnationalization, national unity was supposedly based on "authentic" cultural traditions. The tragedy of Mexican nationalism, as I have indicated, is that the national state, as the most apt means for capitalist modernization, has become the main vehicle of mass culture. In any case, the "authenticity" of the culture explicitly defended by nationalism is as dubious or as valid as the expressions of the new society of urban, migrant, and intensely proletarianized masses.

Jean Franco has rightly pointed out that mass culture—both in the "center" and on the "periphery"—cannot be seen as a unilateral process uniformly adapting individual consciousness to the needs of industrial capitalist society. She states that in Latin America,

> the "transnationalization" of culture can be seen from various standpoints, and not just as a total disaster. This is true above all from those areas and groups who were in a disadvantageous position when culture was articulated around nationality and national identity. Women and indigenous ethnic groups, marginalized and suppressed by nationalism, can now establish networks of alliances across national borders.[36]

We should add that in Mexico it was not only women and Indians who were treated paternalistically by the authoritarian national state. In fact, large sectors of the population find themselves trapped in the system's peculiar corporatist paternalism. The messages of transnational culture can be read in many ways: although in large measure the reading suggested by its producers looks to further

36. Jean Franco, "Recibir a los bárbaros," Nexos 115 (1987): 53–59.

typically ethnocentric, colonialist, and imperialist influences, cultural interaction has actually produced a great variety of effects, including new forms of radicalism and democratic struggle against oppression and the established powers.[37] The fact that many of these new cultural forms have leaned toward the right of the political spectrum is largely because the Left has voiced a cheap anti-imperialism that distanced it from important turning points in contemporary culture. What is interesting about this is that those influences of transnational culture have begun a democratization and liberation from conservative ideas within the space of the Right. The archaic Catholic Hispanicizing prudishness that marked a large segment of the Right has been forced to give way to the influence of deeply sexualized lifestyles replete with ultramodern imaginings and tolerant pragmatism. A curious phenomenon is taking place: what the Left sees as a hateful denationalizing process produces, within the culture of conservatism, a liberalizing effect. To put it another way: the syncretism of Guadalupean traditions with the "American way of life" is producing an implosion of meanings, undermining the traditionalist Right. The result is not only a New Right but also the expansion of a more critical and less easily manipulated civil society.

This paradoxical situation has fed the crisis of nationalism and the expansion of democratic hopes across Mexican society. Yet some unsettling cracks have appeared, which I would like to mention briefly before closing. Mechanisms of democratic representation require, among many other things, the precise delimitation of a territory whose inhabitants are given the right to vote. The definition of these boundaries is fundamental on all levels: local, regional, and national. It is so important that its manipulation (in order to divide groups of voters of the same political allegiance) has been one of the most widely used instruments, in many countries, for blocking opposition parties' access to power.

Clearly, then, all processes of deterritorialization can threaten the functioning of representative democracy. The most obvious example is migrant workers: millions of people across the world cannot fully exercise their democratic rights either in their country of origin or in their country of residence. Another obvious case involves the kind of situation created by major multinational corporations: there are difficulties in gaining an electoral base for making political decisions about them, since the very object of such decisions lacks any precise territorial base.

Thus territories that delimit and direct processes of representation are an

37. For a good example of this, see Guillermo Gómez-Peña, *Warrior for Gringostroika.*

essential aspect of democracy. One could think that the crisis of nationalism weakens self-determination and sovereignty, since the national frontiers that separate Mexico from the United States could blur. But this argument is based on the false assumption that it is nationalism that draws Mexico's borders. It is precisely this identification of nationalism with the nation that, along with other factors, has blocked the spread of a democratic system in Mexico. And we might well ask: How long can we keep up a national distinctiveness based on the absence of democracy? Nationalism has become the symbol of an authoritarian political regime that has not managed to establish a solid economy or to avoid its transnationalization. In spite of revolutionary nationalism, today millions of Mexicans are living in the United States, not only peripheral to democracy but actually outside the law. Millions more inside Mexico find themselves in a similar situation: their vote is manipulated by the authoritarian system. Even worse, they live in an economy deep in a crisis that ballots can do little against: the answers to inflation or to external debt are to be found less and less on the terrain of national political decisions.

Traditional revolutionary nationalism cannot offer a solution to the crisis. Revolutionary discourse is all worn out, and today we can see that the ideological-cultural mechanism identifying the PRI with the nation does not emphasize its "revolutionary" character. On the contrary, it presents the PRI as the only party that can hold back revolution, disorder, and chaos. Revolution is its property, locked up in its Pandora's box. And the PRI seems to be telling the population (and the United States government): "If you support me, I'll keep the box closed." What legitimates the PRI is the fear of revolution. That is why a "revolutionary" opposition is doomed to electoral marginality. The PRI offers tranquillity, not revolution. The PRI is the revolution domesticated, that is, institutionalized. The party's name tells the secret of its legitimacy.

That is why one of the few things it can still point to with dubious pride is the unsettling fact that social peace has been maintained throughout the period of terrible economic crisis that began in 1982. But every day there are more Mexicans who suspect that this peace is due more to the widespread presence of democratic and tolerant trends in civil society than to revolutionary nationalism. Suspicion is spreading that the final redoubt of bronco Mexico can be found not out there in society but inside the state.

From the Charismatic Phallus to the Phallocratic Office

The images that describe the state as an essentially masculine being may be ancient, but they are not out of date. As Henri Lefebre recently reminded us, we are witnessing a true erection of the state that penetrates into civil society—sometimes fleshy, sometimes mushy—until it reaches everyday life, which is the place where women are still being dominated. This is how, rejoicing in its pleasure, bourgeois civil society is continually fertilized by the semen of the state, and manages to reproduce.

From this we get two popular images of doing politics. On the one hand, we have aggressive and violent machismo, which disdains the feminine in the name of power. We have the "revolutionary" and triumphalist politician with his train of mariachis and camp followers who is so good at using his phallus as a political weapon that he ends up castrated, commanded to impotency by the state apparatus. A necessary counterpart emerges from this style: the hypocrisy of the artfully weepy type who vegetates in the quiet structures of comfortable Puritanism. This is the politician who is forever defeated but never kicked out, who lives off inspiring pity for himself or reselling, at a bargain, the pities and miseries of everyone else.

The vox populi often distinguishes the "politician" from the "licenciado." At one end, we have the image of the manliness of the cacique, that fiery winner of speech contests, tamer of the most beautiful flower of the rough countryside, charro on Sundays or in a union. At the other extreme we have the adviser, technician, or lawyer for any six-year (presidential) cause, the endless master of oth-

This essay was written for the Mexican feminist journal *Fem*, as part of a special issue (no. 18, April–May 1981) of articles written by men.

ers' ceremonies, or the personal secretary with a conciliatory style, an exquisite suit, and infinite adoration for his boss of the moment. In sum, on the one hand the political figure who knows how to handle the people with macho passion and masculine vigor and, on the other hand, the frustrated figure who serves as an efficient Celestina in the politician's troubled relationship with the masses.

What do these popular interpretations of politics mean? At first glance we could say they resemble Weber's sophisticated analysis of power. The macho exercise of power would be a derivation of the traditional forms of domination (according to Weber): gerontocracy, patriarchalism, and patrimonialism. In these forms, the patriarchal family tradition embodied by the elders and the control of inherited patrimony sketch a circle of domination centered on the power of the father. He is a kind shepherd to his children, but rigid and despotic with those who stray from the flock. We would need to add a curious syncretism of this form of domination with the charismatic form. So it is said that a politician has "big balls": he enjoys an extraordinary power that is not limited to the mere pair of testicles of ordinary mortal men. This politician would be a representative of the Cosmic Race, facing down the mass of traumatized *malinchistas*, complex-ridden Indians and effeminate pachucos.[1] That mass would be represented by a group of licenciados and "engineers" who would constitute the legal and bureaucratic form of domination, whose origin is to be found in a covenant, in an abstract set of rules based on law, in a modern impersonal order expressed in a hierarchical group of administrative functions. Here one rules not with balls but with logic: the logic of money, interest, science, production, and capital.

There is a problem with these interpretations: they leave us the impression that, with modernization and capitalist development, we are witnessing a desexualizing of politics and the state. That is to say, we are witnessing a gradual retreat of sexism that could bring with it either a loss of legitimacy for established political power or, instead, a new form of legitimacy. But things are not so simple. Just as modernizing the state does not eliminate its class origins, we could say, so a man does not stop being sexist no matter how clever he is.

Nevertheless, something has to change. Whether in administration or in birth control, modern techniques introduce innovations into political and sexual relationships. Politicians like Rubén Figueroa and husbands with the drive of Jorge

1. The Cosmic Race was the invention of conservative intellectual and politician José Vasconcelos, a way of thinking about national identity that exalted both mestizaje and white male authority in guiding it. Malinchistas are those who have opted to follow the "betrayal" of La Malinche, Cortés's indigenous lover and translator, and are therefore lovers of all things foreign and not true Mexicans. The reference to "traumatized malinchistas" is a play on recent empha-

Negrete are starting to become unfashionable.[2] But there are no signs of a retreat of sexism in the crude reality of politics. On the contrary, new forms of government make even clearer the sexual hierarchies that were supposedly a matter of tradition and the past. In a way, the avalanche of women and licenciados into the labor market and into the bureaucratic state apparatus has reinforced the patriarchal character of political structures. As conflicts move inside the state, a readaptation and refunctionalization of traditional forms takes place. The extension of modern bureaucratic mechanisms means a "feminization" of politics in the intermediary portions of state power—fewer strongmen and more secretaries, fewer caciques and more bureaucrats, fewer populists and more technicians—but it has spurred the concentration of political decision making at the highest level. The result is a process of domination spreading outward from those invisible and unreachable centers of high power, transmitted in a "natural" way by the army of women who are abandoning their functions in the reserve army of labor to take up active posts.

What is happening is that politicians no longer need underlings made in their image and likeness. Politicians need fewer assistants who are fawning in their presence but terribly authoritarian when the leader is away. They prefer charming and efficient executive secretaries. Instead of a lieutenant who follows orders with indiscriminate ferocity, they prefer experts trained in the specialized tasks of their job. In this way state policy penetrates much more deeply into civil society: politics gets civilized, the phallus gets feminized, and the dominator gets confused with the dominated. Power gets diffused, and semen gets dispersed.

The problem lies more and more in uncovering the new expressions of sexism and the new forms taken on by class conflicts. These forms and expressions lie hidden: behind the squeaky-clean gentleness of the specialist who never steps outside his turf, behind the reasonable masculine power that wraps itself in the fragrance of modern colognes and conceals its sex in the drawers of a boldly designed desk, barely hinting at its secret existence, and behind the easy pride of a growing multitude of women who take their step on the pyramid of power and surround with smiles the softness of negotiations that nonetheless end with forceful decisions.

---

sis on the "trauma of conquest." Pachucos are Americanized Mexicans from across or along the border. Along with Indians, all these groups are considered inferior and only partly Mexican, to be incorporated and subdued by an elite-led process of mixture. [Trans.]

2. Rubén Figueroa was the long-standing caudillo—and governor—of the state of Guerrero, and Jorge Negrete was a mythical singing charro in the glory days of Mexican cinema. [Trans.]

But this apparent dispersion of domination does not of course eliminate it: on the contrary, the new spread of functions is a faithful, enlarged photograph of the polarity underlying domination. The stage has changed, and the actors have multiplied, but the tragedy reveals the same wounds, and they are still bleeding.

III

MISERIES
AND
SPLENDORS
OF THE
LEFT

Our Own Nineteen Eighty-Four

The socialism we have known does not tolerate disappointment, nor does it allow for desperation. And so it rejects critical thinking. Pain and sacrifice are conceived of as the path toward the creation of the "new man." Even at the worst of times, people are forced to be happy, to keep hope alive, or at least to declare they believe in doing so. There is an attempt to prove the scientific character of socialism by imposing the official utopia. But imposing hope is the same as annihilating it. Enter the ghost of disappointment. Enter anti-utopia.

Forced Happiness

Nineteen eighty-four is the symbol of socialist anti-utopia, thanks to Orwell's well-known novel. But the trend was already there. In 1920 the brand-new press of the Soviet Socialist State published a curious book: *The Journey of My Brother Alexei to the Land of the Peasant Utopia* was its title, and it was authored by Ivan Kremniov. The little book told the story of Alexis's awakening in the Moscow of 1984: a true environmental paradise opened up before his eyes, in which peasants had defeated the Bolsheviks in 1930, seized power, and built a new society. Twenty thousand copies of this book were printed. It included an introduction written by the editor in chief of the state press (N. Orlovskii, a pseudonym for Vatslav Vatslavovich Vorovskii), which clarified for the dear reader that the book reflected the "utopian and reactionary" ideals of the peasants, but that

In March 1984 *Nexos* dedicated a special issue to Orwell's novel. I sent in my article, which was published along with an insulting piece by sociologist Pablo González Casanova. I sent a very brief answer in to the next issue—the final section, entitled "Verdict: Guilty"—and I never wrote for the magazine again, although I didn't take myself off the editorial board.

it should be distributed because "that utopia is a natural, inevitable and interesting phenomenon" in what was still a basically peasant country. The book was being published, the introduction said, so that workers and especially peasants might seriously think utopian arguments through and come to a conscious and critical position toward them. The author of this peasant utopia, who hid behind a pseudonym, was the famous populist economist Aleksandr Chaianov, known for his penetrating analyses of the agrarian question.[1]

Around the time Chaianov published his peasant utopia set in 1984, a well-known Russian writer was writing a corrosive anti-utopia that already revealed a bitter critical reaction against the corporatist tendencies of the new socialist state. This was the novel *We,* by Evgenii Zamiatin, which Orwell took as a model for his celebrated *1984.* In Zamiatin's novel, unlike Chaianov's, the future city has defeated the countryside: people there are identified by coded numbers, not names. The novel tells how engineer D-503, a builder of the Integral spaceship, falls in love with I-330, who is a leader of the underground opposition movements. They live in a giant city surrounded by a green wall, governed by a Benefactor: the state watches over everything and even decides when its citizens should fall in love—and with whom. Written in Russian in 1921, *We* first appeared in English three years later. The first edition in Russian came out in New York in 1952; it was not published in the Soviet Union until 1988.[2]

Both Chaianov and Zamiatin were able to influence the Soviet culture media in their fields during the twenties, above all during the period of the New Economic Plan (NEP). Along with Babel, Esenin, Pilniak, and Alexei Tolstoy, Zamiatin was part of the so-called *popuchiki,* "fellow travelers" of the revolution. For his part, Chaianov was still taking part in the debates at the end of the twenties about the creation of mechanized state farms, and he proposed that these be units of 20,000 to 30,000 acres in size, organized by their management into collectives of 150,000 to 200,000 acres.[3] As this shows, and despite what many

---

1. The works of Aleksandr Chaianov (1888–1939) only became widely known in the West in the 1960s, with the publication of the English translation of his *Theory of Peasant Economy.* The full text of his peasant utopia was published in a special issue of *The Journal of Peasant Studies* in 1976.

2. There was also a crude and abridged back translation into Russian, supposedly based on the English and Czech editions, published in a Russian émigré journal in 1926. Clarence Brown, "Zamyatin and the Rooster," in *We,* by Evgenii Zamiatin (New York: Penguin Books, 1993), xi–xiv.

3. Aleksandr Chaianov, "The Technical Organization of Grain Factories" (1929) and "Large-Scale Farming Today and Tomorrow" (1929), cited in the bibliography of Chaianov, *A. V. Chaya-*

think, Chaianov not only defended the peasant smallholder but also believed it necessary to organize great agricultural enterprises.

Later on, during the thirties, both were persecuted by the Stalinist state. Accused of forming a peasant party with the objective of restoring the capitalist regime, Chaianov was tried and put in prison, where he died, probably of poisoning. His name disappeared from the second edition of the *Great Soviet Encyclopedia*.[4] For his part, Zamiatin had his political rights taken away in 1929, but he managed to go into exile thanks to a letter he wrote to Stalin (and probably to Gorki's support). He died in 1937. In the same way, his name disappeared from all Soviet publications. Curiously enough, Zamiatin was born in 1884.

It seemed necessary and just to me to cite these two—little-known—precedents for the mythology that, thanks to Orwell's famous novel, bears the name "1984." As can be seen, utopia and anti-utopia go hand in hand here, and develop in parallel: they are both the result of something that has withered away *within* socialism. The utopia portrays with deliberate ingenuousness a lovely and calm rural socialism; the anti-utopia describes the horrors of a society in which even feelings are planned by the state.[5] But when Orwell takes up the symbolism of "1984" again, at the end of the forties, he fills his work with a bitterness and desperation that we can understand only if we add to the experiences of Chaianov or Zamiatin in the twenties gigantic Stalinist repression, the Spanish Civil War, and the Second World War. The thirties and forties could not breathe any kind of optimism into a writer of Orwell's sensibility. The novel *1984* was published in 1949; a year later, its author died of tuberculosis.

1984 in 1984

What could *1984* mean in 1984? When I read Orwell's novel, at some point in the sixties, it seemed to me to belong to the past, to the cold gray postwar years. The danger of "1984" did not seem real to my generation, made up as we were of a

---

nov on the Theory of Peasant Economy, ed. and trans. Basile Kerblay, Daniel Thorner, and Robert E. F. Smith (Madison: University of Wisconsin Press, 1986), 291. In 1930 he was imprisoned by the secret police.

4. He reappeared in the 1974 *Literary Encyclopedia*, vol. 8. The article dedicated to him says that he was "illegally condemned" and "posthumously rehabilitated." He is claimed there to have died in Alma-Ata in 1939.

5. Remember that in the 1920s there was an intense debate about eugenics and population control in the U.S.S.R.

critical blend of uneven elements: the Cuban Revolution, Beat poetry, guerrillas, student struggles, the cooling of the Twentieth Congress of the Communist Party of the U.S.S.R., the civil rights struggle, the expansion of leftist fronts, Rubén Jaramillo, the younger Marx, Vietnam, the Beatles . . . The danger of a "1984" did not seem real to us. To continue with this calendar year symbolism, we set "1968" against "1984": better yet, we were too absorbed in our own "1968" to bother with our parents' "1984." Nevertheless, echoes of what some from the older generation insistently repeated reminded us of the existence of "1984": Marxism, they told us, has disdained political democracy by simplistically placing the need for changes in the economic structure first.[6] Unfortunately, nearly all our guides had been swallowed up by "1984": some, the majority, by the state apparatus, and others, a minority, became officious representatives and defenders of "actually existing socialism." Very few had kept critical thinking alive.

That is why it made me very happy to read in an article by Julio Cortázar a defense of a critical thinking capable of recognizing that *1984* is an allegory of the "reaction within the revolution." Cortázar rightly points out that the infinite horror of *1984* is not only because socialism could become like *1984* but also because in a "1984" hope is impossible. Worse yet, hope is only present in order to tear us apart by testifying to its own impossibility.[7] Cortázar does not remind us in vain of that old Dominican prior who, with his eyes full of compassionate tears, applied the "torture of hope" in the cruel story of the same title by Villiers de L'Isle-Adam.[8] Inquisitors like Pedro Arbuez d'Espila exist in the socialist world. But the feelings permanently feeding the desires, ideals, utopias, and dreams of a better world continue to be one of the fundamental ingredients of the critical thinking that rejects all there is of *1984* in actually existing socialism. In a recent attempt to reveal the supposedly metaphysical content of the critical and antidogmatic Marxist currents that fight against "1984," Pablo González Casanova has written a chilling statement that belongs completely to the Orwellian universe: "Critical thinking has no dogmas. Even worse, it has feelings. And it often hides interests."[9]

This statement has the look of a set trap: whoever criticizes actually existing

6. See, for example, Pablo González Casanova, *Estudio de la técnica social* (Mexico: UNAM, 1958), 133.

7. Julio Cortázar, "El destino del nombre era . . . *1984*," *Sábado (Unomásuno* supplement) 314 (3 November 1983).

8. See Auguste Villiers de L'Isle-Adam, *Cruel Tales.*

9. Pablo González Casanova, *La nueva metafísica y el socialismo* (Mexico: Siglo XXI, 1982), 169.

socialism must have dangerous feelings, and we must tighten the noose of scientific logic to discover their hidden interests. On this point, I would like to respond openly to this insinuation about the presence of a chain of critiques, feelings, and interests, since I think that its author—a distinguished man of the Left whom I care for very much—should clarify the exact objective of his insinuations.[10] The reader of Pablo González Casanova's book is warned, at the outset, against the dangerous existence of "counterrevolutionary ideologues [who] *blend in and get mixed up with socialists* in order to attack actually existing socialism in the name of the ideal." Immediately he asserts that "there are *many many Marxists* in Latin America who eliminate the struggle against the system of exploitation [from their thinking]."[11]

These assertions lead us to ask dangerous questions: who are these wolves in sheep's clothing? Are they the same ones as the multitude of Marxists who eliminate exploitation? How many are they, and where are they? If they have gotten mixed up with *true* socialists, how are we going to tell them apart? Here we are, in the middle of "1984"! The weight of these questions imposes the need for a vigilant Big Brother, imposes the logic of suspicion and, even more, like Julia and Winston in Orwell's novel, the horror of those who—as Cortázar put it—"know they have betrayed each other and only look to leave each other, to forget each other, to keep betraying each other down there in the deepest part of them where once there was hope."

Fratricidal Struggle

The horror of fratricidal struggles at the heart of socialism is nothing new. The idea that the "enemy" has infiltrated the ranks of Marxism and the revolution is what has allowed the most atrocious repression to be intellectually justified. Orwell himself took active part in one of the most tragic episodes of the Spanish Revolution: in May 1937 a true civil war within the Civil War broke out in Barcelona, violently pitting Anarchists and Trotskyites against Communists and Socialists. Between 1936 and 1937, Orwell belonged to the militias of the POUM,

10. Pablo González Casanova (b. 1922) is a leading Mexican Marxist sociologist who trained under Fernand Braudel in Paris and has written prolifically on dependency, internal colonialism, and class struggle in Latin America. Between 1970 and 1972, he was the rector of the National Autonomous University of Mexico, the largest university in Latin America, the center of student politics and the place where Bartra teaches. [Trans.]

11. Pablo González Casanova, *La nueva metafísica y el socialismo*, 7–8. On the presence of "reaction" inside of socialism see especially pages 70, 167, and 211.

the Trotskyite party led by Andrés Nin that put itself at the center of the conflicts. Orwell expressed his opinion about the May events in his book *Homage to Catalonia*. This moment is interesting, among other reasons, because it revealed for a fleeting historical moment the drama of the anarchist utopia placed on earth: it unleashed an infernal whirlwind of authoritarianism, censorship, persecutions, and violence.

That whirlwind led, in the middle of the war against Franco, to an uprising against the Popular Front led by the hard-line of the Anarchist FAI (those sinister "friends of Durruti") and the Trotskyite POUM, who proclaimed the need to "destroy the internal enemy," since the time had come "to choose between revolution and counter-revolution."[12] On the other hand, the Socialists and Communists held that the POUM was a "nest of spies in the service of fascism," an obviously preposterous assertion. By the end, after a week of bloody combat—a thousand dead, and three thousand wounded—the militias and hateful anarcho-syndicalist "control patrols" that had rebelled were defeated. A little while later, the government of Largo Caballero fell as a consequence of the May events, and the Anarchists pulled out of the national government. Evidently everyone lost in this struggle . . . except for the Soviet NKVD (forerunner of the KGB), which took advantage of the confusion to extend its reach. Without any doubt, the Soviet secret police was not innocent of the kidnapping of Andrés Nin, the POUM leader accused of being an "agent of Franco and the Gestapo." Obviously the assassination of Nin was the extension to Spain of the sadly famous "Moscow show trials."[13]

The unfortunate paradox here is that in Catalonia both Anarchists and Trotskyites—some utopians, others persecuted—were the most closed-minded agents of authoritarianism and maximalism. Obviously, as they showed in Catalonia, they too were carrying the "1984" virus. Having been defeated does not cleanse or exonerate them.

Orwell transmitted the problem of the deep splits within socialism to his novel. Big Brother's mysterious rival Emmanuel Goldstein was evidently based

---

12. Julián Gorkin, *Caníbales políticos* (Mexico, 1941). Gorkin was a noted leader of the POUM.

13. Although it is obvious that Spanish Communists contributed to Stalinist repressive activities, that should not erase the role played by Krivitsky and, above all, Orlov at the head of the NKVD. Historian Georges Soria holds that Orlov was directly involved in the assassination of Nin. A few years later, Orlov fled to Canada. Later he installed himself in the United States, where he collaborated with the House Un-American Activities Committee, which, guided by McCarthy, carried out an intense anti-Communist witch-hunt. Georges Soria, *Guerra y revolución en España* (Barcelona: Grijalbo, 1978), 79.

on Trotsky, and according to Trotsky's biographer Isaac Deutscher, the fragments of *The Book* that appear in *1984* are a paraphrase of Trotsky's *The Revolution Betrayed* (published in 1937).

But perhaps Mao Tse-tung is the classic on this matter. The Chinese leader dedicated a well-known 1957 article to this: "On the Correct Handling of Contradictions among the People." There he warned against what he would later promote: he criticized the "ultra-leftist" mentality that sees enemies everywhere among the people and "regards as counter-revolutionaries persons who are not really counter-revolutionaries." The contradictions "among the people" exist because of the persistence of classes and social strata with different interests: the proletariat, the peasantry, the national bourgeoisie, and the intellectuals. He also pointed out the contradictions between state, collective, and individual interests. Above all, Mao's text is interesting because it shows the *impossibility of resolving this problem from the standpoint of official Marxism,* and by official Marxism I mean that which establishes as an untouchable basic axiom that exploitation is nonexistent when state power is in the hands of the Communist Party (or its equivalent). This impossibility of explaining the contradictions of "actually existing socialism" is exemplified well in an earlier quote from Mao:

> To criticize the people's shortcomings is necessary, as we have already said, but in doing so we must truly take the side of the people and speak out of whole-hearted eagerness to protect and educate them. To treat comrades like enemies is to go over to the side of the enemy.[14]

If one comrade treats another as an enemy, then the first comrade has passed over to the enemy's side. But if the second comrade, when he realizes this, denounces the first as an enemy of the people, then he in turn passes over to the enemy's side because he treated the first comrade as an enemy. And so we now have two enemies, who are the beginning of a maddening dialectical spiral at the end of which *everyone among the people is an enemy.*

One way to keep from unleashing this dialectical explosion of suspicions and countersuspicions is by establishing, arbitrarily and from above, the parameters of "truth." That is what Mao does in the quoted article, in six points, prominent among which are support for the Communist Party leadership and for building socialism (which implies accepting that relations of exploitation are non-

14. Mao Tse-tung, "Talks at the Yenan Forum on Literature and Art (1942)," in *Selected Writings of Mao Tse-tung* (Peking: Foreign Languages Press, 1966), 92.

existent "among the people"). But at moments of crisis, the logic of the "internal enemy" comes to the surface again, inexorably. So the only way of preventing the spiral from dizzily spinning into an infinite search for the enemy is by achieving the equilibrium of the vicious circle.

Suspicion

Suspicion is floating in the air. Cortázar finds himself obliged to clarify that he is making his critique of Cuba and Nicaragua on behalf of those processes, not against them. The terrible question has been posed: "What difference is there between the critiques of actually existing socialism by conservative liberals, and those by democratic-and-revolutionary socialists?" The question is posed by Pablo González Casanova, who suggests that European Marxist thought could be mistaken for neoconservatism and is apparently tarnished by metaphysics: "The mere fact that it is necessary to clarify the difference indicates the ideological priority of putting an end to ambiguities and confusions."[15] The man who poses such a barbaric question—and suggests such a schematic answer—unavoidably sees before him a broad and dubious array of Eurocommunists, anarchists, Trotskyites, radicals, critics, rebels, social democrats, and reformists confusedly inspired by Della Volpe, Marcuse, Lefebvre, Cerroni, Mandel, Colletti, and Althusser (to cite only the names and currents he mentions).[16] At the end of his book against the "new metaphysics," he points out one of those "priorities" for putting an end to ideological messiness. He writes that "we need to *impose* . . . what we could call a logic of '*socialism in this world*,'" a logic where everything would be in its place: foreign interventions are always imperialist (the other kind are "solidarity"), class struggle is crystal clear, and there is never any doubt about who are the good guys and who are the bad guys.[17]

To the contrary, I think it is time to cultivate the subtleties of "ambiguity" and "confusion," of freedom and critique, of democracy and the struggle for an "ideal" socialism. It is time to escape the logic of "socialism in this world" be-

15. Pablo González Casanova, "La penetración metafísica en el marxismo europeo," *Sábado* (*Unomásuno* supplement) 270 (8 January 1983): 5. It is curious to note how sexual metaphors referring to *penetrated* virgin beings, beings violated by the enemy, have survived in politics since the Middle Ages. See Kraemer and Sprenguer's *Malleus Maleficarum* on this, especially the part referring to the dialectic of the incubi and succubi, in the face of which I frankly prefer the Aristotelian metaphysics to which it is opposed.

16. This list includes many prominent—although often opposing—Marxist dissidents. [Trans.]

17. Pablo González Casanova, *La nueva metafísica y el socialismo*, 214.

cause in reality it is the logic of reasons of state that attack the *hope* for a democratic socialism. It is time to open our eyes and realize that actually existing socialism does not have one logic, but many: socialism in this world is not a single whole all wrapped up and ready to be accepted in its flat and uniform appearance. There is no unity in socialism: there are antagonistic contradictions, there is exploitation, there is despotism. But there is also freedom, democracy, and equality. That is why today we can—and we must—choose between the different options that actually exist, if only in embryonic form, inside the socialist world. These options are produced in a context in which exploitation has not ceased but taken on new forms.[18] The wide "ambiguous" and "confused" field of new Marxisms, in their plurality, reflects the range of options that have emerged inside of socialism. Julio Cortázar is right: "1984" represents *reaction within the revolution,* which reminds us immediately that once there was also *revolution within the revolution,* when we dreamed we were reading Debray, who dreamed he was translating the dreams of Fidel, who dreamed about the dreams of Che, who lived a dream in Cuba and a nightmare in Bolivia . . . Too many intermediary dreams wore away our utopia, which frequently ended up with a *Conversation in the Cathedral.*[19]

There is another question I would like to pose: Is there a "1984" in Latin American socialism? Don't let it be said that in facing the imperialist aggression of a Ronald Reagan, we should not take up this problem *now.* It is precisely because *the main thing* is fighting against the imperialism that is *exploiting* us—the word pales in comparison to the misfortune that threatens us—that today it is essential to strengthen a democratic alternative within socialism and denounce the dangers of a "1984."

Our "1984" is in Cuba and in Nicaragua, too; it is in El Salvador and in Guatemala, in Grenada and in Peru, in so many places of ours where the revolution has

18. Pablo González Casanova's theory according to which "the class struggle survives in socialist countries" (15), in a situation where the system of stratification "is in no case according to class" (17), does not seem convincing. Class struggle without social classes? This does sound a little metaphysical.

19. This is a play on the well-known sixties writings of French Marxist Régis Debray, who penned a book on the Cuban Revolution—*Revolution in the Revolution? Armed Struggle and Political Struggle in Latin America,* trans. Bobbye Oritz (New York: Monthly Review Press, 1967)—and then went off to join Che Guevara in the Bolivian jungle, where Debray was quickly captured and Guevara was soon defeated and executed. The closing reference is to Mario Vargas Llosa's disenchanted novel of politics, *Conversation in the Cathedral,* trans. Gregory Rabassa (New York: Harper and Row, 1975). [Trans.]

been wounded, and where its strange wounds are called purges in communist parties, settling of accounts between revolutionary groups, terrorism against dissidents, Roque Dalton, Maurice Bishop . . . [20]

Everyone knows that at the end of the sixties, changes in Cuba introduced a significant dose of intolerance and hardness into the political system. The so-called Padilla case was a sign of rigid forms of coercion that, as Cortázar rightly states, achieved nothing other than

> a permanent state of terror, a foretaste of everything that in the last instance ends up in the terror of 1984. Cubans know this all too well, and those who deny it today were certainly among those most afraid and most silent back then. . . . My criticisms, however much they were made in solidarity, cost me seven years of silence and absence.[21]

The extraordinary socialist achievements of Cuba can never be obscured by reactionary criticisms: one need only know what has been achieved in extending education and health, to mention just the most spectacular gains, to have an idea of the depth of transformation. But the longest and most flattering list of the achievements of the Cuban Revolution cannot erase its problems: the economic distortions produced by monoculture, the dangerous levels of absenteeism, a high degree of negligence at work among certain sectors, defects in rationing mechanisms, and, what is perhaps the worst, the precariousness of democratic processes in the political system and the lack of tolerance and pluralism in cultural institutions. Can we publicly manifest our total rejection of the existence of isolated camps for the "rehabilitation" of political prisoners without unleashing the ire of the Cuban government? Do we have the right to doubt the need to keep thousands of political prisoners in jail in Cuba?[22] Can we do it without being decried as bourgeois intellectuals, as CIA agents or metaphysical reactionaries?[23]

---

20. Roque Dalton was a Salvadorean poet and revolutionary, killed by a competing faction of the Left; Maurice Bishop was the Marxist leader of the New Jewel Party in Grenada, killed in a 1983 palace coup by a competing faction of the Left. The coup provided the Reagan administration with a justification for its invasion shortly afterward. [Trans.]

21. Cortázar, "El destino del nombre."

22. In 1965 Fidel Castro publicly admitted the existence of 20,000 political prisoners.

23. In an excellent open letter to Cortázar about 1984, Héctor Schmucler reminds us what Fidel Castro told the intellectuals who made criticisms about the "Padilla case." On 30 April 1971, at the closing of the First National Congress of Education and Culture in Havana, Castro said: "But those who are with Cuba can't even defend it. When they do get around to defending it, we'll tell

We know all too well that we have no such right. Anyone who offers criticisms runs the risk of suffering—at the very least—the seven years of banishment, the seven years of thin, absent, and silent socialist cows that were imposed on Cortázar. Whoever criticizes the state is seen as an enemy (or "objectively serves" the enemy, as political jargon puts it). In the eyes of the majority of current governments of actually existing socialism, it is practically impossible to criticize and at the same time defend socialism. From outside the socialist countries, we can hardly understand the reason for this unreason, since over here, in one way or another, we know that the various currents of the Left (from Trotskyites and Maoists to Communists and Socialists) at least tend to be on the same side against imperialism and the Right. Whenever an "internal enemy" is being chased down among us, we can be certain to discover behind it the influence of some reason of state originating in the socialist countries: *because there are antagonistic contradictions "among the people" in those countries*, because there are deep divisions and fractures. A new system of exploitation rules there, generating sharp contradictions. If this were not so, how could we explain the great mass repressions from the time of Stalin, the smothering Soviet interventions in Czechoslovakia and Afghanistan, the persecution of union workers in Poland, the threats of war between socialist countries? We already know the Manichaean explanation: there are no internal contradictions, just the presence of the long arm of imperialism. But who could believe that imperialism convinced the millions of Soviets who were assassinated in the thirties, inspired the Prague Spring, organized Polish workers, or guides Chinese leaders today?

Clouds

Octavio Paz recently published a book on this topic, trying once again to face down Marxist thought, his eternal interlocutor.[24] Unlike many other texts by Paz, this one let me down: clouded minds, clouded view. The present world seems to him submerged in a delirium of pleasure or frivolity, and he finds that everything taking place is a repetition of the past: "We live a true Return of other

---

them: don't defend us, comrade, don't defend us because it's no good for us for you to defend us . . . There will be space in our company only for revolutionaries, now you know, bourgeois intellectual gentlemen and bourgeois liberals and agents of the CIA and imperialist intelligence." See Schmucler, "Carta a Julio Cortázar," *Sábado (Unomásuno Supplement)* (3 December 1983).

24. Octavio Paz, *One Earth, Four or Five Worlds*, trans. Helen Lane (San Diego: Harcourt Brace Jovanovich, 1985). The title of this section comes from the original Spanish title of Paz's book: *Tiempo nublado*, or *Cloudy Times*.

times," he writes. This is an old idea of his, which is now gaining more ground. Paz is a great scrutinizer of the past, and nothing could be further from his thinking than utopias, even though he theoretically argues for an anarchist ideal that, in reality, it would be useless to look for in his work. His reflections on "actually existing socialism" are not made, in this book, in the name of hope or utopia. They are the discourse of power born in the cultured middle class in the name of practical common sense. It is a variant on the doublethink of Orwell's novel, which allows one to hold two opposing ideas simultaneously. We could call it *half-think*. The discourse turns out to be extraordinarily attractive and sticky: it consists of articulating a long series of commonplace sayings, half-truths, half-ideas, and half-concepts, which give the impression of being subtle insights because they are abandoned halfway, in syncopated form. The other half is not expressed, but it is insinuated. Finishing the idea would mean giving in to the evidence that these insights are banal. But a certain cultured class has discovered that silencing and hiding half of a commonplace observation is enough to give the impression of refinement. Certain French journalists are masters of this art, which more than a few intellectuals cultivate with boundless enthusiasm. They generate a truly torrential and unnecessary multiplication of entities that would do very well with a trim from Occam's famous razor.[25] By the way, readers will find a good antidote to this explosion of fractions of ideas in Umberto Eco's beautiful novel *The Name of the Rose*, where William of Occam is reimagined as a character in a logical detective story.

One explosion of this kind happens to Paz when he refers to socialism: an excessive string of half-truths and fifties concepts bursts forth from his pen. He does not understand the new debate among the Left about the nature of "actually existing socialism" in the least. It seems to him that "what is being argued about today had already led, more than a century ago, to fierce disputation."[26] Even so, what is terribly unpleasant is finding seeds of 1984 in the political discourse of Paz, when he, as an implacable judge of the history and biography of men, and in the name of a tolerance he does not practice, wishes to impose the tyranny of his judgments. In the name of what power does he allow himself to speak of the

25. A reference to the philosophical principle by which the clearest expression of an idea is always preferable, attributed to William of Occam. [Trans.]

26. Paz, 11. I had the same impression when I debated with him the ideas on socialism put forth in my book *The Imaginary Networks of Political Power*. He did not go beyond denunciations in the style of certain intellectuals forty years ago. I still think that Paz—*malgré lui*—forms part of the universe of the Left, but it hurts me to see him held in old superficial arguments, dedicated to activism *pour épater les communistes*.

"happy splashing about in the mud of an Aragon"? What horrific impulse leads him to place Ezra Pound and Louis Aragon on a balance, in order to compare and quantify the weight of their abjection?[27] See this inciting of witchhunts: "Through a moral and psychological mechanism that has yet to be described, Thorez, Togliatti, La Pasionaria and the others not only accepted the great lie but actively collaborated in perpetuating it."[28] Here, locked in the cell of half-truths that insinuate never-described psycho-moral errors, is the complex tragedy of men and women who lived on the watershed between two worlds and suffered a praiseworthy but painful inner fracture.

There is something in the nature of power that leads its servants to hate any change in the ideas, or the consciousness, of those who are considered subjects of some hegemony. Many bureaucratized minds have also inquired about the strange moral and psychological mechanisms that led Octavio Paz from being a long-standing diplomatic representative of Mexican despotism to becoming a critic of "the philanthropic ogre." Unfortunately at times Paz places himself in the same place as his censors.

In this way the monster is evoked once more: the traitor is whoever changes his ideas, whoever gives up, whoever criticizes his comrades. He must bear their hanging a shameful sign around his neck: Judas, deserter, renegade, turncoat, dissident, infidel . . . We already know that the wall separating disagreement from disloyalty is very thin, the wall separating "contradictions among the people" from "imperialist infiltration."

This monstrous sign becomes a basic cog of nondemocratic state machinery (and of authoritarian temperaments). In societies in which only one political option exists—the official party in power—disagreements run the risk of becoming signs of a supposed "internal enemy" (which, evidently, is an infiltration by the "external enemy").

Consider one example. Responding to European critics in a recent book, Cuban Minister of Culture Armando Hart correctly explains the historical reasons that led to the rise of a one-party regime in Cuba: the fusion of the July 26th Movement, the Popular Socialist Party, and the Revolutionary Directorate, and the absence of social democratic or bourgeois-democratic parties.[29] The course of history tells us why no political alternatives existed outside of those that

27. Abjection from their lengthy flirtations with extremist politics: fascism in the case of Pound, Stalinism in the case of Aragon. [Trans.]

28. Ibid.

29. Armando Hart, *Cambiar las reglas del juego: Entrevista de Luis Báez* (Havana: Editorial Letras Cubanas, 1983).

fused into the current Communist Party. But that does not mean the possibility of pluralism in the future should be closed off. The past must not swallow the future. Where can the political forces spun off by new contradictions find their place? Will they be left with the sole option of leaving by way of Mariel, into exile? The current electoral system, which excludes direct paths to candidacy and installs a pyramidal representational process, does not even guarantee the possibility of an opposition within the system (that is, as long as it's not antisocialist). Hart himself establishes the impossibility of this option:

> We could respect someone who is right-wing, and as a consequence, takes right-wing positions. We can respect that person even if we have deep contradictions with her. We can even recognize that she is an honest person, since she sincerely believes in and holds to her ideas. Such people are, to turn a phrase, *heart-felt reactionaries.* But those people who have left our country and called themselves left-wing are simply turncoats: *deserters of an idea.* They shared in a cause, they were in Cuba for a long time— some even directed cultural institutions of various kinds—and then they deserted, they betrayed their ideas and the confidence that had been placed in them. That means they are *traitors.*[30]

These hard words, which leave us stunned, reveal the full dimensions of the problem: there is no place for different socialist options; there is no recognition of the possibility that different paths to building socialism might compete democratically in an open political setting. In this way, the "contradictions among the people" evolve inevitably toward antagonistic conflicts, like the one that prompted the departure via Mariel of tens of thousands of Cubans.[31]

Here, in a few words, our very own "1984" has been sketched out. Facing this, it occurs to me to think, as if to conjure it away, of those verses of Mayakovski that say:

> Only one thing do I fear
> For you and for me
> That our souls
> Become petty
> That we raise

30. Ibid., 38.

31. A reference to the release of thousands of political prisoners to the United States through the port of Mariel. [Trans.]

To the height of communism
The banality of the blessed
And the naivete of popular songs.

Verdict: Guilty

In this essay, I have pointed out the enormous difficulties in undertaking a critique of "actually existing socialism" from a socialist position. Whoever does so—I have warned—runs the risk of being seen as an enemy. The main difficulties arise from the presence of a thought police that has escaped from the pages of Orwell's *1984* and taken up the functions of watching and censoring.

My fears were confirmed long before I expected. The essay on our "1984" did not elude the gaze of Pablo González Casanova, who published a damning verdict that appeared as an official seal stamped at the end of my text. In a few dozen words, the Ministry of Truth ruled that my article belonged to the "culture of polemical dishonesty" (Culpodis). Another article by the same author denounced the existence of "a Marxism of 'whites,' 'metropolitans,' 'social democrats,' 'Eurocommunists' and other subtly colonized terms" who want, among other things, to reduce our objectives to "a mere struggle for democracy." That recalls the phrase attributed to Cardinal Richelieu: "If you give me six lines written by the most honest of men, in one of them I will find a reason to hang him."

And in fact Pablo González Casanova, in a third turn of the screw, set out to find a motive: he wanted to continue with a trial in which, in the finest Stalinist tradition, the verdict was reached before proceedings began. In addition, and in keeping with the finest Kafkaesque tradition, the accusation was hidden in an opaque tangle of decrees. As if to confirm all this, in his denunciation Pablo González Casanova could not resist the temptation to—instead of using my name, which is not so long—refer to me simply as B. I could not avoid bringing to mind images of the famous K. who winds through the endless labyrinths of Kafka's novels.

Verdict:	Guilty
Trial:	1984
Defendant:	B.
Minister of Truth:	Pablo González Casanova
Crime:	Public exercise of Culpodis (that is: looking at the feet of Greta Garbo, in her starring role as "actually existing socialism")
Evidence:	Several ideas mutilated by the application of a dra-

	matic alienating rhetoric, with which he practiced a right-wing disillusioned Marxism (in complicity with Octavio Paz), were found in the defendant's possession.
Sentence:	B. is to be confined to cell one-zero-one.[32]

Fortunately, the circumstances that surround us prevent this trial from taking dramatic shape. On the other hand, as Pablo González Casanova's rhetoric wishes, it has turned into a melodrama. But this curious outcome should not make us forget the warning Julio Cortázar made: "The horror of 1984 can only be avoided if, paradoxically, we struggle against its seeds and its latent tendencies within the very Ormuz bloc, within a socialist process which is the polar opposite of the world Orwell imagined."

32. This is the cell Winston was confined to in *1984* and, in Spanish, *uno-cero-uno*, a pun on *Unomásuno*, another journal of the Left. [Trans.]

Between Disenchantment and Utopia

F ifty years ago, in the midst of war and confusion, one thing was clear: culture had to be defended from its fascist enemies. And some understood that
it also had to be defended from its Stalinist friends. At that dark hour, intellectuals turned on the lights, illuminating the long trenches that wound across maps
of primary certainties and disputed terrain. Although sociologists had decreed a
disenchanted modernity, locked in the iron cage of industrial society, the world
of the thirties was shaken by the spells of war and destruction. It was an en-
chanted world, or a cursed one, if you will, in which ideas easily obeyed a malign
call: find the enemy. The enemies found each other and over a few years amassed
a pyramid of forty million dead, leaving us that cold slogan some now call postmodernity. It would be better to call it dismodernity, given the disorder that governs the world—or better yet, *dismothernity*.[1]

In 1987 a group of Spanish intellectuals sponsored an International Congress of Intellectuals and
Artists called "Fifty Years After." The conference was a commemoration of the famous Congress
of Anti-Fascist Writers in Defense of Culture, which took place in Valencia in the middle of the
Spanish Civil War, and an invitation to reflect critically on the past. The congress met in Valencia in June 1987, under the presidency of Octavio Paz. The text that follows was read at that congress, at an agitated roundtable entitled "Intellectuals, Violence, and New Critical Consciousness." The next day, a local paper published the headline "The panel on violence almost came to
blows." A disagreement between Spanish writer Manuel Vázquez Montalbán and former student radical Daniel Cohn-Bendit sparked some in the public to insult two other participants,
Carlos Franqui and Marta Frayde. Spanish intellectuals Fernando Savater and Jorge Semprún
jumped up to calm down the unhappy orthodox Stalinists who were yelling, and Octavio Paz
came running to stop the disturbance, which would have produced a few black eyes if the rabid
intellectuals had not been pulled apart. I had already read my paper before spirits got exalted, but
evidently my disenchanted position had no place in that uproar.

1. See footnote 11 in the essay "The Mexican Office."

Now we do—at last—live in a disenchanted time, or so they say. Today we watch as the blood drains out of utopias wounded by reality, feeding our hunger for coherence with any of those breakable ideas that the actually existing powers toss us like pieces of stale bread. Our postmodern disenchantment is the off-spring of those times of war when it was not so hard to find a cause to fight for, and an enemy to defend yourself against. But today hope seems like a salt pillar, and our adversaries have vanished—or they are so many and so widespread we no longer notice them. Fascism and Stalinism are substances that history has di-luted but not eliminated. We could guess that the socialist and capitalist states still harbor dangerous and disturbing tendencies and that politics—to reverse the classic formula—is the extension of war by other means.

Fifty years ago, the intellectuals who came together in a congress to defend the republic of ideas against the fascist enemy correctly thought that culture was under threat. Today I would like to ask what is threatening culture in our time. As an anthropologist, my vocation is precisely the study of culture, although I understand that term in a somewhat broader way than the intellectuals who gathered in Madrid, Valencia, and Paris a half century ago. Perhaps for that very reason, it seems to me that whatever is threatening culture—today like yester-day—is hardly alien to culture itself. Obviously both fascism and Stalinism are modern versions of ancient and deep cultural tendencies. We could confirm this even if we limited ourselves to the cultural sphere in the narrowest sense: in art and philosophy, as in literature and music, we can trace the roots of the phenom-ena defined as "enemies" of culture that, as things get worse, usually attack with military and political weapons.

Having said this, I don't want to get stuck on the idea that culture devours it-self. We have known for a long time that man is wolf to man, and we have various global explanations for this tragic phenomenon. Guilt or sin oppresses us, class struggle subjects us, a reptilian complex devours us, the Thanatos instinct be-sieges us, or the power of Leviathan flattens us. Our disenchantment with these explanations comes precisely from their global nature, because they pursue us no matter where we try to escape to. That is, they operate in a similar way in cap-italism and in socialism, in industrialized countries and in the periphery, in the economy and in culture, in the individual and in society, in the spirit and in the flesh. And the disenchantment comes, I would dare to say, from a terrible excess of truths, from an implosion of verities that cluster in delirious accumulation around the core of various megadiscourses. We are facing great monopolies of co-herence that, like powerful castles, seize meaning and leave a void around it, a vast no-man's-land separating each theory from the others. To put it in other words: we live in a world where Godel's theorem has become a cultural metaphor and plays practical jokes on us that allow politico-philosophical fortresses to be formed into complexes whose internal coherence cannot be proved. Perhaps thanks to that very potential incoherence, each megasystem has a tendency to view the others as possible enemies. It is obvious that political powers are organized on a global scale into blocs whose internal coherence may be open to question, but whose outward aggression is beyond any doubt. It is less evident, on the other hand, that cultural terrain harbors blocs formed in a similar way.

As an example, I would like to point out some tendencies present in contemporary Latin American culture; we could surely find something similar in other cultural constellations. In our cultured culture—forgive the redundancy to narrow the concept—there is a strong tendency toward polarizing two blocs of intellectuals against each other. I am speaking not of two ideologies but of two cultural terrains that on occasion, nonetheless, become political bastions. Ideological influences have played an indirect, complex, and contradictory role in drawing the frontier between those who want to tell a *story* and those who prefer to offer a *reading* of events. To use Cortázar's literary mythology, I would say this is a fight to show the *cronopy* of the *famas* against those who want to impose the *famistics* of the *cronopios*.[2] Cronopy leans toward studies of a particular moment; famistics looks to decipher parallel times. Many Latin Americans think that, overall, cronopy is left-wing, and famistics is right-wing. Of course, this is a simplification. Cronopy is supposed to be closer to popular feelings, while famistics looks for the reverberations of names and great names in the patterns of history. Fortunately, there are many writers and essayists who wander or have wandered between both tendencies. Many others are only spectators of this imaginary but bloody battle. What I want to point out is that based on this mythological opposition that in some way revives the old conflict between nationalists and universalists, a dangerous phenomenon is created: the spreading of what I could provocatively call paramilitary literature. This is the kind of literature that comes straight out of the cultural fortresses with the mission not only of marking off and defending its territory but also of naming and attacking the enemy. It has its seat in universities and in literary sects, in cultural journals and in political parties, and it deepens conflicts and feeds the myth of castles of culture.

In one of those castles dwell epicurean baroque excess, magical realism, and chronic barbarism. In the other we find the civilized stoicism of gothic spirits

2. As mentioned in the preface, this mythology is derived from Julio Cortázar, *Cronopios and Famas*. A rough division, again, might place Gabriel García Márquez and Carlos Fuentes on the former side, and Jorge Luis Borges and Octavio Paz on the other. [Trans.]

and stern symbolism. Clearly what is barbarous to one is popular to the other; what one sees as the exaltation of the civilized, the other sees as a product of imperial influence. Epicureanism is rejected as vulgar hedonism, and in revenge, stoicism is deemed little more than decadent disdain for everyday tasks. The epicurean *cronista* fears the critical, learned, classicist, and academic gaze. For his part, the structuralist stoic is uncomfortable with the disdain of the (politically) committed and with the baroque feel of class struggle. From the stoics' castle, reality is seen as an arena in which forces measure their strength. The whole terrain is occupied by power; the event is reduced to power relations. Behind the opaque veil that cloaks the world, a powerful network of meanings must be uncovered. Only the cement of reality is gray and drab: deeper down or higher up lies a powerful and undying structure of myths of steel. To the epicurean cronopios, by contrast, the structural subjectivity of myths, archetypes, symbols, and heroes seems like an opaque sign of oppression. Reality, on the other hand, is magical and many colored, enchanting and poetic. The hateful subjectivity flowing from the constituted state powers, which alienates man, must be escaped to find refuge in the exoticism of a living reality full of promises.

The attraction these forces exert is undeniable. Inside they offer a comfortable simulacrum of coherence and serve up exquisite intellectual dishes, seasoned with strong political ideas: revolution, democracy, civilization, wealth, pluralism, liberalism, development, popular government, progress. The splendid banquet of history and structures cannot make us forget that we are in a land at war and that enemies are waiting for us. Do not despair: the battle can begin at any moment and we must ward off Evil!

But what if Evil doesn't exist? We are assaulted by the uncomfortable idea that the dual world is dying, about to shatter into fragments. Dialectics, the root and spark of this war, may be mortally wounded, but it does not retreat easily. Just like masters and slaves of old, friends and enemies resist leaving the stage. We are still deep in a labyrinth of loyalties and betrayals that could be summed up in the well-known medieval formula of Ramón Llull: *Befriend the friend of your enemy, and his enemy.*

But what if the enemy doesn't exist? We'll have to invent one, some will say. But by now we distrust the invention: the terrain of disenchantment has expanded. These are spaces of authentic diversity, dismissed as cultural niches, where more exiles from the great cultural wars of our times take refuge every day. We are disenchanted with the old fighting tradition. We have been made for the struggle, and many of us are the fruit of the battles that were fought here a half century ago. Thanks to them we have been condemned to permanent exile, but now—after listening for a long time to the holistic calls of the sirens—we want to find a way forward that doesn't involve gigantic demonstrations of fidelity. The virtues of man, who is essentially fragmented, tend to grow better in ruptured, broken terrain, where his individual existence finds an almost natural match in the irregular environment. A curious thing is taking place: the flight to new territories in order to evade the megasystems that monopolize meaning—and feelings—has led to a revaluation of the individual from the standpoint of traditional leftist utopias. Paradoxically, many Marxists, socialists, and anarchists are breaking with the orthodox mold to sketch the still-blurry and vague outlines of a new individualism. We are discovering that the individual is to culture what democracy is to politics: although it can be an element legitimating domination, it is also becoming a subversive and dissolving agent taking us along a shortcut toward new plural identities, local ethnicities, light ideas, free lives, and that new age that many say will come with the third millennium, when we will be able to say, in the Valencian words of poet Joan Fuster:

> Van recobrant el gust de les dreçeres
> els nostres peus amargs . . .

> [They're getting back their taste for sidewalks
> these bitter feet of ours . . .]

Nationalism, Democracy, and Socialism

I f we want to whet our appetites for a debate about the Left's place on the political map, there is nothing better than quoting old quarrels and disagreements. Just like tasting old wines, bringing back old debates will tell us whether
they have grown better or gone bitter. Since I have taken part in many of these
disputes, this essay will have an inevitably personal and committed nature.

To begin, I would like to bring up how in early 1983 Carlos Monsiváis and I had
a curious and amiable disagreement about the political programs of the Left.[1]
Monsiváis held that the Left lacked a program and worshiped the needs of the
moment. I on the other hand maintained that the Left was full of programs but
lacked the sensitivity to find its place in political moments. I still think that
what the Left needs is a new political culture, in addition to a program or a project. Recently Octavio Paz has also reproached neo-Cardenism (the PRD) for its
lack of an authentic program.

For a long time, the Left's programmatic passion blocked its decoding of the
moment and made comprehension of concrete political processes difficult.
Great changes come out of moments of rupture in the political process, not from
between the lines of programs. I bring this up again because it seems pertinent
at this moment, and because it was the preamble to another polemic that drew
the participation of several first-rank PRI members who have significant influence over today's political process. I also want to place it in the context of an-

This text was presented at the Instituto de Investigaciones Sociales of the UNAM in November
1990 and published in *La Jornada Semanal*, 20 January 1991.

1. This debate can be found in Carlos Tello, ed., *México 83: a mitad del túnel* (Mexico City:
Océano Nexos, 1983).

other old debate that—after the spectacular changes of 1989 in Central Europe—has taken on a new meaning: the dispute about the character of so-called actually existing socialism.

It seems to me that the Left's long enclosure in the programmatic catacombs prevented it from comprehending the political crisis that was coming. In this debate, I maintained:

> The Left has to be responsible in the face of the economic crisis. We have to be against the crisis, there is no reason to be happy; but what is no longer so simple is our attitude towards the political dimensions of the crisis. This is where I disagree: I think that in the political system there are elements of a crisis and very strong internal contradictions. . . . Here crisis should be welcomed, because the Left does have a concrete alternative for today. That alternative is called *political democracy*. . . . I cannot imagine how a Left alternative could grow in the short term if the authoritarian political system —the despotic hegemony of the PRI-government—does not break down and cease to operate in the anti-democratic way it traditionally has. It would be excellent for new perspectives to open up through the political crisis.[2]

Not understanding the moment meant refusing to see the symptoms of political crisis and instead seeing only permanent and apocalyptic "structural" crises or the exhaustion of global development models. It meant closing one's eyes to the true dimensions of the crisis: its volatile and fleeting character. In the face of a *momentary* crisis, one needs *alternatives*, whereas with the general idea of *structural* crisis, one usually offers a *program* or a *project*. Of course, there are some programs capable of inspiring alternatives, and there are many—the majority—that are sterile. In the debate, I claimed that the government had run into difficulties in generating alternatives: "The dominant system itself is no longer capable, apparently, of reproducing itself as such." José Carreño Carlón expressed his agreement, making adjustments for his pro-PRI view.[3]

My talk of a failure to detect symptoms of political moments is not a groundless assertion: this can be easily documented. I am going to offer a few examples from a book published in 1987, dedicated to examining the presidential succession.[4] José Carreño Carlón himself argued there that "the 1987–1988 political

2. Ibid., 60.
3. Ibid., 44–45.
4. Abraham Nuncio, ed., *La sucesión presidencial en 1988* (Mexico City: Grijalbo, 1987). Some of the essays in the book did begin with an analysis of the political crisis. For example, Porfirio

season will not essentially change the methods of transmission of presidential power." And yet it was the opposition he disdained as "the idiot of the family" that provoked an unforeseen political turn. In the same book, Enrique Semo claimed that the elections of 1988 would not offer anything new, Francisco Paoli said that a strong opposition candidate was not foreseeable, and Pablo González Casanova wrote that "in the 1988 electoral struggle, there will be no real possibility of electing any candidate but the PRI's." For Raúl Trejo, the 1988 elections would be "a kind of referendum to learn the people's confidence in their government." The possibility of a democratic change in the exercise of power—the only new element capable of provoking a political crisis—was not even considered by most of the analysts.[5] And yet in 1988 the mere specter of an electoral defeat shook the regime to its foundations.[6]

When various high-ranking regime functionaries joined in the discussion, they confirmed the ideas that saw nothing more in the 1988 elections than a continuation of the well-known six-year ritual. One of them, Manuel Camacho (at the time, secretary of planning and budget), was categorical in his reply: the state has "the *only* project capable of avoiding . . . the disintegration of the nation itself and the decomposition of political life." What is that political project? Manuel Camacho was emphatic: "strengthening our nationalism with economic and social efficiency based on a non-authoritarian rationality." A strange paradox, the singular and exclusive character of this supposedly nonauthoritarian project.[7]

Since then, reality has managed to give the lie to Camacho and all those who believed nothing new could emerge beneath the Mexican political sun. The PRI split, and the break was due precisely to the fact that one wing of the party denounced authoritarianism in the name of nationalism. The famous "efficiency" of economic management ended up with a pact of solidarity that, in its paradox

---

Muñoz Ledo claimed that this time the presidential succession would be different; Bernardo Bátiz and Ricardo Pascoe Pierce offered interesting political guesses. My own essay revolved around the thesis that the ship of state would run into serious problems in 1988.

5. Ibid., 195, 61, 227, 68, 348.

6. This was the campaign in which Cuauhtémoc Cárdenas mounted the most serious challenge to the PRI in decades—and very well could have won, except for fraudulent tampering with the results. On the party that emerged, see Bruhn, *Taking on Goliath*. On the overall ideas of future PRD leaders Cuauhtémoc Cárdenas and Porfirio Muñoz Ledo just before the elections, see Carlos Gil, ed., *Hope and Frustration: Interviews With Leaders of Mexico's Political Opposition* (Wilmington, Del.: Scholarly Resources, 1992). [Trans.]

7. Tello, *México 83*, 84–85.

of a state-imposed liberal policy, was nothing more than a belated recognition of the failure of the government's economic strategy.

In my response to Camacho, I claimed:

> The message of Miguel de la Madrid's government is clear: economic repression ("efficiency") will be necessary to get out of the crisis, but in return there will be political tolerance ("nonauthoritarian rationality"). Facing this the traditional forces of the PRI reacted with outrage, since they don't know where to turn in times of crisis. That is why Fidel Velázquez responded that the revolution was in danger. He prefers less political democracy and more corporatist populism. In this, among other things, lies the confrontation between technocrats and politicians inside the state. But if we look at things from another perspective, we cannot accept that our options lie in choosing between "political democracy" and "social democracy" as they now deceptively put it. The new technocrats have not yet become democrats, nor have the old charros ceased to be despots. There is a long way to go yet before technocrats clearly adopt a democratic approach and effect a significant advance in political reform. Even more far off seems the day on which the leadership of the official labor movement draws really close to the reformist's positions of social democracy. Nonetheless, in the face of the advance of the Right, popular pressures, and the unfolding of the political crisis, both tendencies, democratization and reform, are on the order of the day as signs of a slow and critical process of dissolution of the old authoritarian political system.[8]

Manuel Camacho classified me as "spontaneist" and answered without any evasions: "There is not yet any real alternative to the state project and it is unlikely, in political terms, to come from maximalist positions of all-or-nothing."[9] Today we see how a real alternative has emerged—they call it neo-Cardenism, and it emerged spontaneously from the PRI—but the politicians of the system dismiss it as maximalist. It is curious how it is PRI politicians—who have *all* the power—who accuse opposition parties of struggling with a maximalist perspective. That is what Camacho did in his reply:

> Bartra's aspiration is not representative democracy, where minorities can influence, engage and even govern the system when they come to have pop-

8. Ibid., 118.
9. Ibid., 121.

ular support. What he is looking for is generalized confrontation with the political system and the mixed economy. His problem is that this strategy is not viable as long as there exists a state exercising its constitutional responsibilities and generating social consensus, even in the most difficult circumstances.[10]

If there were representative democracy in the city of Mexico (and in the country), Manuel Camacho would not today be its regent (mayor). As a member of the PRI minority, he could influence or engage with decisions. But because there is no representative democracy in the Federal district, the inhabitants of this city have to put up with governors imposed by authoritarian methods that do not involve ballot boxes.[11]

But reality is tough, and the topics under discussion are still part of the burning public agenda. Today the question is posed in all its drama: Does aiming for electoral victories in the ballot box mean looking for "generalized confrontation with the political system"? If the answer is affirmative, then it is clear that the only possibility the political regime offers to opposition parties is that of remaining minorities forever. The "modernity" of the political regime lies solely, it seems, in a moving act of charity toward the opposition. "It deserves to be heard," Octavio Paz has said, "It should be given a hand." Recognize its victories in clean elections? Only if the executive branch allows it, in a few rare cases. But democratic electoral contests should not be blurred into the undefined chiaroscuro of negotiation: votes should be counted right, and at the end there is a winner and a loser. This is not maximalism; this is representative democracy.

These debates concretely reveal the Left's enormous difficulties in defining a space of its own. The establishment of a representative democracy in Mexico is one element that, to a progressively greater degree, defines the Left in the face of government authoritarianism. But it must be admitted that Mexico has also developed a strong and wide-ranging democratic Right, represented mostly by the PAN. Even within the PRI, in marginal positions, there are sectors and attitudes that wish to establish representative democracy in Mexico. And yet in the present political moment, the government is putting the brakes on electoral reforms

10. Ibid., 122.

11. Camacho was secretary of planning and budget at the time of the debate, and the appointed regent of Mexico City at the time this essay was written: he would later play an important role as the government's emissary in peace negotiations with the EZLN. When the government of Mexico City finally was elected by vote in 1997, the victor was PRD leader Cuauhtémoc Cárdenas. [Trans.]

that could change the authoritarian political system. Merely aspiring to establish the formal conditions for a change of power has been classified as "maximalist."

This confrontation could introduce us into a vicious circle whose perverse logic should be examined. We should ask ourselves if it is possible, in the short term, to win by votes significant portions of regional political power with policies radically different from the government of the institutionalized revolution. The leaders of the established system take every concession along that path made to the Left to imply the opening of "liberated zones" or "free territories" inscribed within a larger logic of confrontation. On the other hand, the Right is allowed to claim its victories (as happened in Baja California), which has opened a period of PRI-PAN alliances designed to give the established political system a breather. We found ourselves before a strange paradox: there is subtle governmental pressure for the Left opposition to keep feeding its program on the national sources of political inspiration, defined by the traditional institutionality of the Mexican Revolution, so that the PRD might be maintained as a marginal and radical appendage of the hegemonic system. From these apparently natural sources flow, deceptively and artificially, revolutionary nationalism and corporatist democracy *à la mexicana*. And so while the PRI gains time to consolidate its shift and its abandonment of the traditional nationalist themes, the Left seems to dedicate itself to taking up the burden the official party has cast off, and to entertain itself by reconstructing the ruins of the ideology of the Mexican Revolution. The temptation is great: to recompose the outline of the Left by blending nationalism and democracy. But I would question whether, in these moments, that is the adequate political recipe for cooking up a viable alternative for the Left.

Nationalism in Mexico is historically and structurally associated with the dominant authoritarian regime and political corruption. At the present moment, nationalist mediations find themselves in an advanced state of decomposition and have turned into a serious obstacle for what tends to be called the "modernization" of the state. I won't extend myself in explaining this phenomenon, which I have analyzed in detail elsewhere.[12] What seems pertinent to point out now is that the crisis the political system underwent provoked an enormous shift to the right by the PRI government. This produced the great split that gave birth to so-called neo-Cardenism and left the territory of nationalism partially

12. See my earlier essay "The Crisis of Nationalism," and my book *The Cage of Melancholy*. For a day-by-day account and "family tree" of the emergence of the neo-cardenista Left, see Bruhn, *Taking on Goliath*, 319–33.

abandoned. The Left also experienced adjustments and turns and rushed to set up shop in the unoccupied territories. But I ask myself: Is the territory of nationalism, at this moment, a promising expanding space, or an ever more hostile space that political forces are fleeing from? Is nationalist terrain the space where the fundamental problems of Mexican society today are debated, or has it turned into an old theater discarded by postmodernity? I fear that nationalism is going through a phase in which it has ceased to be a fundamental element in defining the makeup of contemporary Mexico. In reality, the crisis the Mexican political system is going through is expressed in a special way in the ruin of the values associated with revolutionary nationalism. With this, I don't want to issue nationalism a death certificate. Clearly, in our context of profound malaise and the crisis of the great ideologies, nationalism—especially in its more parochial and religious forms—can play an important role in the medium and long term, although that role will depend greatly on the course of international politics, and especially of the foreign policy of the United States.

It is not only the political crisis of the system that has drawn the Left onto nationalist territory, in a process of flowing together with the currents coming from the official party. Another essential fact should be stressed: the idea and the practice of socialism are passing through a tragic moment. We are in reality facing the collapse of everything that has been, since the October Revolution in Russia, the socialist edifice. The Mexican socialist Left had already begun a process of breakdown that, we now know, was part of a worldwide phenomenon. So under conditions Durkheim might call anomie, the Mexican Left has also had to contemplate the dramatic spectacle of the collapse of its traditional values. Because this happened at the moment that a symmetrical phenomenon happened in the PRI government, which for the first time in many years fractured seriously, the stage of the Mexican political theater underwent considerable change and began a transition period. The situation is very strange, because the new space of the Left seems like a field full of ruins and detritus, a territory covered with the rubble produced by the collapse of the edifices inhabited by socialism and by revolutionary nationalism. Since this is happening while civil society is demanding a democratic change, we could say that the new makeup of the Left is right there, in front of our noses, and we only have to reach out our hand to recognize it as our own. The sum of nationalism, democracy, and socialism would be the principal ingredient of the programmatic formula for the political space that emerged on 6 July 1988.

But things don't seem so simple to me. The use of nationalism as it has historically been implanted in postrevolutionary Mexico comes into flagrant contradiction with the idea of a representative political democracy. I don't know of any important strand of nationalist thought in Mexico that does not contain those authoritarian ingredients that set up a structural relationship between national character and the political system. The same thing happens with actually existing socialism: its antidemocratic elements are clear. On the other hand, we need to recognize that what is truly important for democratic ideas is that they become the patrimony and the practice of *all* parties and cease to be the marker of marginalized opposition groups.

After pointing out these difficulties, we can ask: Does a specific space that can give the Left a clear profile and favor its expansion as a possible governing party exist in Mexico today? To answer this question, I propose to rapidly explore a few symptomatic moments in the course of the neo-Cardenist movement.

One revealing incident, in May 1989, was the way in which the government forced the newborn neo-Cardenist party to use the registration of the PMS, the party of communists and socialists, and to renounce using the colors of the Mexican flag in its emblem. The intention of the governing group, who have done everything possible to block neo-Cardenism, was to give the newborn political force the red dress of a radicalism that does not characterize it, and block it from using the national colors monopolized by the official party. It is true, however, that these problems were heightened because various communist and socialist currents effectively did fuse with neo-Cardenism, so that the PRD was born condemned to endure a harsh period of internal conflicts. This was the price the neo-Cardenist movement recently broken off from the PRI had to pay to rapidly acquire a legal letterhead, a party apparatus, and a formal bureaucratic structure of midlevel operatives.[13]

The fact that the programmatic lines of the PRD are a more or less radical extension of the PRI's own ideology has not prevented neo-Cardenism from appearing, in the symbology of a large part of political opinion, to have a radical and socialist coloring. The programmatic discourse of the PRD undoubtedly has its conservative elements: it revolves around recovering revolutionary ideals from seventy years ago, restoring the republican project, and reestablishing federalism. It proposes halting the conscious and systematic destruction of the institutions and creations of the Mexican Revolution such as ejidos, unions, cooperatives, collective labor contracts, and state-owned firms that guarantee economic independence. In contradiction with these ideals, the PRD wants to

13. See Cuauhtémoc Cárdenas interview by Carlos Gil, *Hope and Frustration,* 159–61. On the matter of the registry, see also his speech at Jiquilpan de Juárez, 18 March 1989.

put an end to the party-state system, political repression, bossism, and corruption, which are also legitimate offspring of the regime of the Mexican Revolution.[14]

These last demands come from the critical socialist tradition and join the long series of democratic proposals the radical Left has publicly advanced since 1968. Therefore one could assert that the PRD combines contradictory ingredients: it could hardly be otherwise in a party that is the confluence of quite different political currents. But the major contradiction I am interested in pointing out is to be found not on an ideological plane but somewhere else. This is the contradiction between the programmatic line of the PRD and the new critical culture of the Mexican Left. This is the contradiction not between nationalism and socialism but between the old traditional revolutionary ideology and the new reformist democratic culture.

Perhaps more than a contradiction, we should speak of fissures or wounds. The space of the Left is fragmented and cracked and produces more than a few strange phenomena. One example of the confusions these cracks provoke is that the neo-Cardenist Left publicly defended the corrupt oil worker union leaders who were imprisoned in early 1989. This strange episode showed that when the sewer of the political system was opened up, the Left could not avoid getting bathed in dirty water. Let's examine this symptomatic moment, which, in my judgment, the neo-Cardenist Left failed to comprehend.

Acting by surprise, the government ordered the army to capture and imprison the major leaders of the oil workers' union, one of the most rotten trunks of the governing party. The operation was spectacular. But it was done in a way that was rushed and ineffective—as well as illegal, since the Constitution states that the army cannot perform extramilitary tasks in peacetime. Far worse was the quarter century of institutional illegality that allowed the monstrous growth of a corrupt labor mafia who transformed the oil workers' union into a multi-million-dollar super-subcontractor and the authoritarian club of a prideful labor aristocracy. What did this new episode in Mexican politics mean? It expressed a break produced by the internal war between the financial bureaucracy and the labor bureaucracy, between the technocrats and the so-called charro leaders. This was a dirty war between two opposing styles of doing politics and two conflicting conceptions of governmental administration. On one side is the traditional corporatist PRI style based on the populist manipulation of mass organizations.

14. See the pamphlet "Partido de la Revolución Democrática" with a text by Cuauhtémoc Cárdenas from 21 October 1988, and his "Call to the People of Mexico" from the same year.

In contrast is technocratic administration based on the manipulation of financial and budget mechanisms. For a long time both ways of governing have intertwined and combined, weaving the revolutionary fabric of a despotic state with paternalistic features. Underneath this multicolored mantle, a powerful union grew, corrupted by its parasitic relationship with Pemex, the state company that monopolizes oil drilling, processing, marketing, and sales. This state industry is also undermined by corruption and inefficiency: it is symptomatic that the last two directors of Pemex have been accused of fraud (one of them went to jail for various years, and the other ended up as governor of the state of Mexico).

Despite six years of "moral renewal" and "structural change" in the productive apparatus—two slogans from Miguel de la Madrid's administration—Mexican society continued, and continues, to be threatened by governmental corruption and economic crisis. From the beginning, the Salinas de Gortari administration opened its doors to politicians of old authoritarian roots, and even to well-known police torturers and high-level functionaries suspected of fraud, with the objective of shoring up an executive branch weakened by the electoral failure of 1988. Why did the government suddenly turn on the traditional leaders of oil workers' labor corporatism? With this agile maneuver, the PRI establishment managed to strengthen the Salinas administration and weaken the neo-Cardenist Left.

It is true that the electoral missteps of 1988 had heightened tensions within the PRI governing group, and the result was a violent opening of the breach that separated modernizing technocrats from old labor leaders. Political pressure had risen dangerously inside the PRI pot, foretelling a period of breakdown in the rules of the political game. The imprisonment of the oil workers' leaders opened an escape valve for the system's internal pressures.

But it also sparked great confusion partly because the neo-Cardenist Left took up the defense of the corrupt oil workers' leaders, who were seen as defenders of national sovereignty and labor independence.[15] Nevertheless, in a gesture typical of the Mexican system, the main oil workers' leader—José Hernández Galicia, alias La Quina—cried out from the depths of his cell his unconditional support for the president, as PRI politicians fallen into disgrace almost always have.

The defense of rotten oil workers' leaders became the Achilles heel of the Left

15. According to Cárdenas, the government's intention was to "leave a social organization as important as the oilworkers' union weakened, with a reduced capacity to react, at the moment that the government is getting ready to set the basis for restructuring the oil industry" and to provide the union "with a leadership docile and servile towards the administration, distant from na-

and of Cardenism. This misstep was the high price paid for not having freed itself of its populist and dogmatic past. Above all, it was the price paid for letting the moldy program inspired by labor nationalism overcome the rich critical culture developed by the Mexican Left. The teachings of that critical culture should not be forgotten. We have known for some time what was truly peculiar about this situation is not the confrontation between two wings of the PRI—the "moderns" and the "dinosaurs," as they are called—but the features distinguishing each side: the labor bureaucracy forms part of the political forces of the Right, while the technocracy is made up of a group notorious for its inefficiency. This singular displacement of traditional values has generated a great confusion, as is understandable.

Just as the nationalist Left failed to use La Quina's imprisonment as a moment to break with labor authoritarianism, socialists were incapable of using Fidel Castro's visit in support of the new PRI government to break with the characteristic despotism of actually existing socialism and to underscore the enormous similarities between the authoritarianism of socialist bureaucracies and the despotism of the Mexican political system. To my mind, this is a sign of the terrible difficulties the Mexican Left has in developing a new kind of reformist calling. By grabbing on to a worn-out revolutionary model, it closed off all analyses of countries ruled by communist parties that might lead to proposing profound democratic reforms to actually existing socialism. It is a shame that this happened as it did, since the deep critique of the socialist countries, a critique that went far beyond denunciation to enter into analysis, has been developed by the Left in various parts of the world since the seventies. But in Mexico, indeterminate support for authoritarian and guerrilla-flavored socialism of Castroite inspiration blinded the Left, who admitted to seeing in Afghanistan or Korea, in the U.S.S.R. or Poland, the wrongs they refused to look at in Cuba or in Nicaragua. Why did the PRD give up the critical tradition that has characterized the Mexican Left since 1968?

I think that the Left never had any hopes for important changes in the socialist bloc countries, a belief that they strangely shared with the better part of conservative or liberal right-wing views. The spirit of the Cold War and the resignation to the geopolitical status quo of a world divided into military blocs was shared by people of very different ideological colorations. Octavio Paz expressed clearly

---

tional interests." This meant assuming that the group led by Hernández Galicia was characterized by its defense of national sovereignty and its independent labor attitude. See the text of Cuauhtémoc Cárdenas's speech of 12 January 1989.

the opinion shared by so many: "I always thought that the totalitarian bureaucratic system we called 'real socialism' was condemned to disappear. But in a conflagration—and I feared its collapse would drag all of civilization down with it."[16] When I debated Octavio Paz at a roundtable in July 1980 about my critical interpretation of the socialism I liked to call tragically existing, it was clear we did not agree on an essential point. The central thrust of my argument was that democratic reform was possible in the socialist countries, while Paz thought that the totalitarian sin could be wiped clean only by confrontation.[17]

I return to those old debates because they seem illustrative. At that same roundtable in 1980, Carlos Monsiváis recommended that I "moderate my confidence" in the democratic utopia of a possible advance of the socialist state toward its own extinction by means of a Montesquieu-derived separation of powers.[18] Luis Villoro also criticized my hope in reforms to the socialist system that might open the path to democracy. I must say that they *almost* convinced me, such was the ruling despair of those times. Villoro claimed:

> It seems necessary to admit that the persistence of a totalitarian state corresponds to the interest of a class or group in power. The reform cannot come from that group. Therefore, it would have to take the form of a new class struggle that would oppose the working class to the global state.[19]

My reformist and utopian drive was moderated, but it did not disappear, as can be seen in my response to Villoro:

> I think you are right in general terms, although we cannot rule out beforehand that, under certain circumstances, profound democratic reforms could happen in certain countries, supported by revolutionary processes of a new kind consolidated in other countries.[20]

16. Octavio Paz, *Pequeña crónica de grandes días* (Mexico: Fondo de Cultura Económica, 1990), 8.

17. The roundtable to discuss my book *The Imaginary Networks of Political Power* took place in the Instituto de Investigaciones Sociales of the UNAM on 23 July 1980, with Carlos Monsiváis, Octavio Paz, and Luis Villoro. For Paz's contribution, see my article "Una discusión con Octavio Paz," *La Jornada Semanal* 71 (1990).

18. Monsiváis's comments have not been published, but a copy is in the author's possession.

19. Luis Villoro, "Roger Bartra: Estado y sociedad civil" in *En México, entre libros: Pensadores del siglo XX* (Mexico: Fondo de Cultura Económica, 1995).

20. Roger Bartra, "Marginales reales y socialismos imaginados," in *La democracia ausente* (Mexico: Oceano, 2000), 192. This essay is my broader response to these critiques.

Now we know that revolutionary process of a new kind is called perestroika or glasnost; we know that in its shadow profound democratic reforms took place in almost all of Central Europe, reforms from above—with the massive support of those below—that knocked over the authoritarian systems in 1989 and opened the way to a new world order.

Unfortunately, this kind of debate was not carried forward in Mexico, and we were left frozen in the trenches of the ideological Cold War.[21] Just as no one believed in democratic reforms to the socialist system, neither did anyone have confidence in the search for radical reforms to the Mexican political system that would put an end to corrupt dictatorial structures. Because of this freeze, the Mexican Left has been paralyzed by the profound transformations of 1989, these "velvet revolutions" that in a few months have swept actually existing socialism from the face of Europe.

Official culture has used the governing confusion of the Mexican Left to manipulate national and international public opinion, in an attempt to compare the timid reforms carried out by the Salinas de Gortari administration with the great transformations that are taking place in the U.S.S.R. and Central Europe. The fact that the PRD has not taken a defined position on the collapse of actually existing socialism has allowed the PRI government to negotiate with the socialist and democratic groups in the developed countries a change in the horrible image that the 1988 elections left in world public opinion.

It is common in the United States and in Europe to hear progressives and social democrats express a discreet and at times embarrassed support for non-democratic regimes, under the pretext that in backward countries state authoritarianism can be an adequate formula for escaping underdevelopment. Taking advantage of this, the Mexican government has for many years dedicated itself to selling cheap nationalist and Third Worldist goods on the market of the social democratic political world, enabling it to hide the authoritarian forms of the PRI government or, at least, lessening the aversion provoked by the despotism of the Mexican political system.

Some intellectuals have expressed a symptomatic idea along these lines. They start by implicitly accepting that the Mexican system is of the same nature as the Soviet system: therefore Carlos Fuentes has characterized the process led by the new administrative team as *mexistroika*. Octavio Paz compared the modernization promised by Salinas de Gortari with the reforms carried out by Gor-

21. It is symptomatic that when I tried in 1984 to continue this debate using the Cuban situation, I ran into intolerance or a wall of silence. See "Our Own Nineteen Eighty-Four" in this book.

bachev and Deng Xiaoping.[22] And he criticized the opposition—above all, the Left—for its maximalist attitudes, for sinking into the politics of all-or-nothing that the poet assumes is characteristic of Mexican history.

By contrast, I think that one of the characteristics of traditional Mexican politics has been its drabness. I do not think that all-or-nothing has been the main attitude. There has always been one alternative, not two. The sole alternative was always that singular drabness in which the political system lived. As it happened, one could not even choose between all or nothing, because that would imply the possibility of a democratic change.

The Mexican political system is a little of everything, nothing of nothing, and, when all is said and done, an aberrant and despotic stew. It has not been the "technocrats" who have brought in new airs, but the "maximalists" who have walked out of the system.

Because of the deep political crisis caused by the dirty manipulation of the 1988 elections, the Mexican government undertook enormous efforts to clean up its image in the mirror of world politics. With this objective, the PRI has renewed its political flirting with social democracy. This is about selling the image of a modern, reformist, and rejuvenated PRI threatened by the nostalgic populism of the Left and the antidemocratic conservatism of the business Right.

Yet any observer of Mexican politics can confirm that the two great pillars of the new technocratic PRI remain populist and corporatist labor and business leaders. The enormous difficulties of the governing technocratic team come precisely from the fact that the most modern political forces are abandoning the PRI and leaving it progressively more and more reduced to a hard corporatist crust that protects and at the same time imprisons the small group of conservative technocrats who surround Salinas de Gortari. The growing opposition to the PRI system is made up of modern and democratic groups of widely varying political hues that have escaped and continue to escape from the PRI and from government tutelage.

In 1990 the government made a few adjustments to pretty up the official party and the electoral law without changing the basis of the official state party regime in any substantial way. Can these events be characterized as the results of the political actions of a modern and efficient elite? They seem more like the destruction caused by a gang of dinosaurs left to their madness inside a glassworks. Perhaps the crisis of the PRI and the strength of the opposition will force those dinosaurs to carry out some reforms, but as yet it is hard to see them as the repre-

22. The catchphrase that eventually stuck was *Salinastroika*. [Trans.]

sentatives of a glasnost or perestroika à la mexicana. They are going to do every-thing possible to keep the government of the institutionalized revolution from dying out. Despite all of this, a curious flip has happened in important sectors of public opinion: Cuauhtémoc Cárdenas and the PRD are seen as an example of collapsing socialist totalitarianism, and the Televisa group and the group of or-ganic state intellectuals headed by Octavio Paz appear as crusaders for Mexican perestroika.[23]

How to explain this paradox? This is one more example of how political cul-ture and symbols count for more than all those speeches and programs. Al-though Cárdenas's speeches and the PRD's party platforms do not establish the least association with socialism (be it real, utopian, social democratic, or any other variety), evidently one cannot dwell in the space of the Left without mak-ing some connection with the ideas and practice of socialism. If the leaders of the PRD keep silent on this point—as they usually do—they not only fail to dodge the problem but, in their vagueness, generate more suspicion. The simple fact that just as Televisa organized the great show of the magazine *Vuelta* around the crisis of socialism, the top leader of the PRD was to be found in Cuba was much more revealing than the silencing that has marked neo-Cardenism's response to the collapse of so-called actually existing socialism in 1989.[24]

The great difficulties of defining, in this dark final decade of the second millen-nium, the space of the Left in Mexico should not make us forget that we are liv-ing through a process of democratic transition that was opened up precisely be-cause of the appearance of a new party, the PRD, led by Cuauhtémoc Cárdenas. What has surprised many is that it was the Left that opened the way to expanding democracy in Mexico. This unsettling event has spread confusion and unease among many Mexican intellectuals tied to the dominant political culture. What does Cuauhtémoc Cárdenas represent? Is this a massive protest against eco-nomic austerity, led by backward-looking leaders who want to return to a popu-list and patrimonialist past?

This assertion cannot withstand the factual evidence. Although the PRD is tar-nished by traditional revolutionary nationalism, it has not expanded into the terrain the PRI continues to occupy. The group of technocrats who have consoli-dated their hegemony over the PRI and the government have not freed them-

23. The Televisa group is the media empire founded by Emilio Azcárraga, a virtual private mo-nopoly. [Trans.]
24. Jorge G. Castañeda's essay on Latin America and the end of the Cold War in *Nexos* 153 (1990) reflects more his best hopes, which I shared, than the reality of the PRD.

selves from the peculiarities of the system: authoritarianism, inefficiency, and corruption. This group has had the management of the crisis in its hands since 1982, and the results have not been exactly brilliant. In addition, this same group carried out a pharaonic and populist electoral campaign that cost the government and the corporatist unions a stratospheric amount of money: the results, as we know, were not brilliant either. The PRI government continues to hold on to the traditional territory of revolutionary nationalism, and so long as it does, it is condemned to live in political crisis. The impressive—and typically populist and patrimonialist—expenditures on programs of Solidarity, combined with the policies of integration with the economies of the United States and the Pacific Rim, could produce equally stale results and contribute to widen the faults that run across the system.[25]

The PRI's failures have opened an immense new popular political space for the Center Left. This was made possible by the rightward turn of the hegemonic group in the PRI, which came along with a displacement toward the center of the PAN, the party that is trying to bring together, not without sharp internal contradictions, the *democratic Right.* It should be pointed out that the expansion of a democratic Right is another new phenomenon that many analysts prefer not to see, in order to avoid the collapse of their traditional ideological schemes.

These political slippages, owing to enormously complex causes, have contributed to the emergence of what could be called *radical reformism:* a new political territory not yet clearly defined or staked out, whose program is fed by the populist tendencies the PRI abandons daily, the social democratic aspirations of many functionaries and professionals, and the diverse leftist groups that exist in Mexico. This political space could only open up by means of a crisis of the official party and the authoritarian system. It has become the most important level for pushing along the democratic transition. I call it radical reformism more as a wager than as a certainty: this is a fertile mix of different strands who have found common ground in the radical struggle for democracy. But it is a volatile mix that could vanish if its leaders fail to understand that to consolidate a new politi-

25. With the funds obtained through privatizations, Salinas set up the massive PRONASOL— National Solidarity Program—for dispensing aid to needy communities. See Wayne Cornelius, Ann Craig, and Jonathan Fox, eds., *Transforming State-Society Relations in Mexico: The National Solidarity Strategy* (San Diego: Center for U.S.-Mexican Studies, University of California-San Diego, 1994). It was a great success for the PRI, and its head, Luis Donaldo Colosio, was "tapped" to be the successor to Salinas. Then Colosio was assassinated, and the economic portion of Salinas's program—free trade agreements with North America and Asia— sparked a massive crisis. See Castañeda, *The Mexican Shock.* [Trans.]

cal culture they should not waste their energies on obscure negotiations or on recovering ideological leftovers abandoned or betrayed by the official party.

Not all of the cards have been played. The conservative technocrats are making enormous efforts to put the brakes on the transition to a new democratic and plural system or, at least, to control it. In this task, they can still count on the support of the corrupt union bureaucracy, private and public television networks, the blessing of the most powerful businessmen in Mexico, and the government apparatus. But it is no longer possible to evade the new political reality: those opposed to the PRI are the majority, and they grow stronger every day. It is in this great space of opposition, whose guiding poles are radical reformism and the democratic Right, where the democratic transition is taking shape. Because of this, an enormous responsibility has fallen on these two groups, since their alliance is the greatest source of political energy to feed a democratic transition. Unfortunately, within both the PRD and the PAN, there are retrograde sectarian interests working in the opposite direction with the clear blessings of the PRI government. We are living in an uncertain moment at which—for the first time in more than half a century—the governing group can be forced to negotiate a peaceful democratic transition. That is the great contribution of the Left, and that is what has begun to define a space of our own.

Few things are clear on the Left's horizon, but one thing is evident: what sparked the explosion inside the political system itself were the defense of the interests of the dispossessed, popular resistance against authoritarianism, dreams of an egalitarian society, and struggles against exploitation—the great Left issues. This explosion has left PRI despotism irremediably wounded. During 1990 the danger threatening the democratic transition has been the opportunism of the right wing of the PAN, which has preferred to ally itself with the PRI and win some concessions out of the confusion, rather than pursuing an agreement with the PRD to speed up reform of the political system. Even so, as the 1991 legislative elections approach, democratic drives may take the lead in pushing the PAN toward the center of the political spectrum.

It is understandable for the PRD to cleave to the foundational myths that define its political profile. They refer back to neo-Cardenism's most important contributions: the struggle for democracy against a government that most of the population sees as illegitimate after the 1988 elections and the belief that electoral victory is now possible for a non-PRI alternative force.[26] Today the political strength of neo-Cardenism seems to be growing in the form of an inorganic party

26. See Adolfo Gilly, "Perfil del PRD," *Nexos* 152 (1990).

in which local and electoral concerns weigh more heavily than the closed, representative, and quasi-governmental structures served up by organic activists. In fact, the PRD is undergoing an intense internal struggle between two opposing conceptions of party organization. On the one hand, we find the hegemonic current, which conceives of a party of public opinion formed around its maximum leader, accepts a high dose of cult of personality, and focuses its best efforts on the 1991 national elections and, above all, the 1994 presidential contest. On the other hand, by contrast, we have the tendency that wants to build an organized party, along governmental lines, in which the positions of the party leadership are developed through a long, more or less democratic process of complicated negotiations, internal conflicts, debates, pacts, and agreements. This last current fears that the hegemonic group might win the elections and "the party might ultimately be pushed aside to open room for visions and power groups not formed earlier in and by party political struggle."[27] In the first case, we have the model of a typical civic (or "bourgeois") party of public opinion, and in the second case, we have a model derived from the communist idea of a party, which forms a sort of para-governmental watchdog structure. Curiously enough, this debate seems to pit nationalist activists against socialists and has taken on a passionate tone that matters of doctrine and program have not inspired.

One of the most delicate issues in defining the Left's profile is the relationship between its economic program and popular political culture. The demands for a democratic regime, for a halt to corruption, and for an end to fraud can be translated relatively easily into a governing program. By contrast, it is not so easy to turn the interests of poor and dispossessed sectors into a viable economic program, especially in times of crisis. The PRI government keeps the two fields carefully separated. On the one hand, it is carrying out so-called economic modernization, a policy of openly integrating Mexico into the world system that emphasizes wage austerity, efficiency, and attracting foreign capital. On the other hand, independent of this, it is channeling an immense spending handout into so-called solidarity, a collection of programs that have the evident political intention of winning the support of the most backward sectors of the population.[28] This dualism is one of the most solid structural bases of corruption in the Mexican political system.

By contrast, the PRD aspires to a unified and coherent economic policy that

27. G. Hirales, "PRD: para mirar el congreso," *Cuadernos de Nexos* 28 (1990).
28. See footnote 25 above. [Trans.]

would be an expression of popular needs and, at the same time, an efficient lever for development. The PRD is proposing raised wages, guaranteed agricultural prices, job creation, health care, social security, and housing construction. It is proposing the suspension of present payments on the external debt with the objective of opening negotiations on a new basis that would allow the government to pay off another, more important debt: the social debt to the majority.

The logic of this proposal is not just to be found in the principles of social justice that guide it. It also supposes that these new economic policies would ensure sufficient investment to reactivate the economy and bring down unemployment, thanks to the reduction in the value of the debt, the increase in taxes on speculative and financial capital, and the benefits of the resulting expansion of the internal market, driven by rising wages and employment. All of this would be done within the larger framework of a recovery of national sovereignty and a struggle against dependency that would block the close linking of the Mexican economy to international financial capital. We must, the program supposes, put an end to the recessionary policies that destabilize the national productive base, shrink the internal market, and annihilate small businesses. We must reduce public spending by eliminating corruption and excessive administrative expenditures.[29]

However, the coherence of the PRD's economic platform collides with harsh realities. The nationalist experiences of recent decades in various Third World countries show that this populist and statist governing policy has not been terribly successful, and that it has swiftly led to the imperious necessity of adjusting the national economy to international mechanisms for the circulation and accumulation of capital. There is no such thing as an independent path of capitalist development that can do without the international financial system. Not even the countries of the socialist bloc managed to keep up the pace in development and welfare, and they also marginalized themselves from the great technological leap forward of recent years.

Without going into details, I think it is necessary to point out that the political culture of the Left has accumulated a considerable stock of critical proposals about the problems of economic policy. This stock has been enriched recently by the experiences of the U.S.S.R. and the countries of Eastern Europe during their transition to a market economy. In great measure, the PRD is guided by a nationalist-tinged economic program inspired by the statolatrous Third World-

29. See the early outlines of an economic program in Cárdenas's speeches on 4 February 1989 and 18 March 1989.

ism of sixties national liberation movements, which does not match the critical visions that political culture has developed, both in the countries of the former Communist bloc and in socialist and social democratic political or labor circles.[30] This is the terrain where the contradiction becomes sharpest and clearest between the platform of the party and the shape of the multifaceted civic, democratic, critical, and popular culture beneath and all around "the party of July 6."[31] This economic platform clearly seems narrow and outworn considering the richness and complexity of the challenges faced by the Left across the world.

I hope that leftist civic culture wins out over the institutional programmatic Left, opening new spaces for thinking and creating new kinds of platforms capable of finding a place within the critical moment the Left is experiencing worldwide. The everyday political practice of the PRD leadership shows that despite all that is holding them back, they are often more influenced by critical political culture than by backward platforms, as Cárdenas's frequent trips through the United States have demonstrated.[32]

My criticisms could be seen as a sign of a spontaneist worship of the moment, of maximalism. But they aim to advance original ways to defend national sovereignty but break from revolutionary nationalism, to look for a socialist direction but break away from "actually existing" socialism, to take a pro-worker stance but disconnect from "actually existing" labor, to defend the income of the popular classes but split with populism. I think we have to throw open the doors of the parties where the Left has been institutionalized to let the refreshing winds of the new civic culture blow in, bringing worn-out platforms up to date.

30. In Mexico we have examples of nationalist programs dating back to Lázaro Cárdenas: in the sixties the Movement of National Liberation was especially notable. Later, but equally significant, was the program of the Movement of Popular Action in the eighties, whose "Theses and Program" of 1981 could be the platform for today's PRD, however dated it must seem to many of its original authors who in the meantime have opted for the "modernization" of Salinas.

31. For the date, 6 July 1988, of the elections that Cárdenas may very well have won, but that PRI fraud gave to Salinas. [Trans.]

32. Cárdenas was the first candidate to campaign seriously among Mexicans living in the United States, where he was received with great enthusiasm. [Trans.]

Is the Left Necessary?

Is the Left indispensable, or is it unnecessary? Trying to answer this question has led me back to the old controversial matter of the maturing of the conditions that supposedly are to spark revolutionary changes in society. When I addressed this question years ago, I reached the conclusion that we could not hold, as Plekhanov had for the Russian Revolution, that there were premature revolutions, since if that were the case, we would have to believe that great historical shifts could be determined by the moral decisions of leaders.[1] In that case, the vanguard could direct the process of change toward socialism based solely on its faith in the intrinsic superiority of that system, without taking into account the dangers of taking a political leap before society was ready. Commenting on my book about the collapse of socialism, Alexandra Ivanova pointed out that however uncomfortable the weight of these "moral decisions" made me, the stubborn facts show that was exactly the way it worked: the party of professional revolutionaries, following its leader, was perfectly convinced of the intrinsic superiority of the socialist system.[2] She was completely right, both about my discomfort and about those "moral decisions," and I would like to use that discomfort to think through the issue.

This essay was written for the seminar "The Future of the Left," coordinated by Jorge Alcocer at the Center of Studies for a National Project, Mexico City, 24 July 1992.

1. In *The Imaginary Networks of Political Power*, chap. 4. The thoughts that follow complement those in "Nationalism, Democracy, and Socialism"—in that essay, I concentrate on the Mexican situation, and here I look more at the general problems of the place of the Left after the disappearance of the U.S.S.R., the "socialist homeland."

2. Letter from Alexandra Ivanova, Paris, 5 April 1992.

Plekhanov had already warned, in his debates with the populists, that if the people take power before social conditions are ready, the revolution "may result in a political monstrosity, such as the ancient Chinese or Incan empires, i.e. in a Tsarist despotism renovated in a Communist lining."[3] This debate remains current not only because Plekhanov seems to have been right: the results of the October Revolution engendered numerous political monstrosities (although the reference to the ancient Incas and Chinese as examples of political teratology is by now little more than another anecdote in the old story of Eurocentrism). It is relevant because it casts doubt on the Marxist postulate that the evolution of society itself would, in due time, necessarily generate the social and political forces that would decisively shape the outcome. From this standpoint, the Left —as a metaphor for the forces that will bring change—is historically necessary. So in Mexico the necessary Left—which may or may not be the actually existing one—will bring its force to bear at the moment when history must bring an unfinished revolution to a close, or when capitalist development calls out for its grave diggers. In this way, the problem of whether the Left is necessary can be solved using Hegelian logic: freedom is the awareness of necessity.

But Plekhanov's worry opens a loophole in this nineteenth-century vision: there is the danger of a premature birth, as we watch the hatching of a monstrous Asiatic or Mongoloid Leviathan. Now the revolutionary birth is happening before its time because a group of professional revolutionaries have made the moral decision that it will be so. This is possible because they have built the instrument that makes the cesarean section possible: the party. Through the lens provided by Plekhanov, we glimpse a space in which the course of contradictions leads modern society toward a new era but leaves people with enough margin of freedom that they may force events—or not—giving those events a uniquely concrete character.

Lenin added a peculiar twist, by setting out a situation opposite to that sketched by Plekhanov:

> It would be a mistake to think that the revolutionary classes are invariably strong enough to effect a revolution whenever such a revolution has fully matured by virtue of the conditions of social and economic development. No, human society is not constituted so rationally or so "conveniently" for progressive elements. A revolution may be ripe, and yet the forces of

3. Quoted in Roy Medvedev, *Let History Judge: The Origins and Consequences of Stalinism*, 2d ed., ed. and trans. George Shriver (New York: Columbia University Press, 1989), 615.

its revolutionary creators may prove insufficient to carry it out, in which case society decays, and this process of decay sometimes drags on for decades.[4]

This phrase clearly reflects the peculiar Leninist vision according to which the rationality that enables social forces to fulfill the mission to which they have been called must be introduced from outside social forces themselves. The visual field we can see using Leninist optics considerably narrows structural determinants, opening a wide margin for the rational organization of political will in a revolutionary party.

Clearly both Plekhanov and Lenin introduced a new perspective that dominated the concerns of revolutionaries throughout the twentieth century. This perspective could be set out schematically in the following way: the vanguard can act too soon or too late, bringing on either despotism or putrefaction. If the revolution runs ahead of the clock of history, the totalitarian threat emerges. If the changes fall behind, the ghost of rot appears. Only when revolutionary intelligence is capable of applying the correct method at just the right moment will we have a harmonious historical outcome . . .

Thus the need for historical change, and consequently for the forces called to bring it on, are derived from the fact that society ripens like a fruit. It is as if the moment of ripening were already written, even though only a few people could be able to read the hieroglyphs that track the process. To maintain that at times the ripe fruit falls to the ground and rots without being tasted by anyone suggests the possibility that unnecessary or superfluous processes do take place. In this case, the Left is unnecessary: history can advance without it, but at the price of advancing along the path of decay. If on the other hand, the Left grabs the fruit when it is still green, it also commits a useless and unnecessary act, and history must inexorably strike down society with the punishment of despotism. In the first case the Left sins by its absence, and in the second case by its madness.

Today we know—or we like to think we know—that there is no such thing as a social clock marking off time with Kantian precision, with changes and reforms inscribed in its machinery. We no longer believe that modern society has created certain political subjects who are called to take the helm and set the state on a new course, be they the old proletariat, marginal groups, or the so-called new social movements. The collapse of socialism and the transition of countries ruled by Communist parties toward capitalism mark the definitive

4. Vladimir Ilyich Lenin, "The Latest in Iskra Tactics, or Mock Elections as a New Incentive to an Uprising," in *Complete Works*, vol. 9 (Moscow: Progress Publishers, 1964), 368.

end of reformist and revolutionary aspirations of sailing from the realm of necessity to the republic of freedom blown by the winds of history. Today those winds are said to have died down, and we understand that Marx was incorrect in establishing a necessary relationship between capitalist development and the socialist labor movement, the great grave digger of bourgeois society. The unfortunate truth is that Lenin was right in his argument that the vanguard—a dispensable segment of society—should organize a firm and centralized party to carry out, in the appropriate time and manner, the great changes that are necessary. From the Leninist perspective, not only is the need for transformation inscribed in events, but a vanguard party is also necessary for transformations to occur properly. Here we see two telescoped necessities: the first requires the vanguard to express itself; otherwise history remains deaf and dumb, turning into a black hole full of energy but unable to explode. Turning the implosion into an explosion is the task carried out by the party, more as an ethical necessity than as an expression of structural tendencies.

The convergence of willful political groups guided by faith in revolutionary ethics was the starting point for building a society whose basic motor was not the structure of socioeconomic tendencies but organized political will. This is the tragic paradox that saw the birth and death of twentieth-century socialism: born in the act of steely political will that released the state from the bonds of economic necessity, it died drowned by the lack of freedom and legitimacy of an economic system smothered by politics. To say it a little differently: the leap from the realm of necessity to the realm of freedom turned out to be a failed acrobatic stunt, and society dropped onto the nets of necessity. Lenin was right, and for that very reason, the socialist edifice he founded has collapsed. In this sense, twentieth-century socialism could well be considered an experiment that tried to radically change the rules of social behavior: unchained forces free of any necessary drive seized power and subjected the entire social edifice to plans derived from a political logic based on revolutionary ethics. These revolutionary ethics were supposedly based on a scientific worldview, but in reality they dated back to that originating moment, the point when the political leadership of the movement decided "the time has come" and then—prematurely, belatedly, or punctually—unleashed the changes its own strength and its opponents' weakness allowed.

The question of whether the Left is necessary has led us into this vicious circle, and I would like to emphasize that the revolutionary assumptions underlying the question make it difficult to escape. If I chose the example of the anxious search for the "revolutionary moment" typical of the Leninist groups, that is only because it allows me to condense the debate into a few metaphors. But it is not easy to escape this vicious circle from a reformist perspective, either: Eduard Bernstein's well-known proposal, so developed by Bobbio, for making political struggle autonomous from economic tendencies in order to establish socialism as an ethically desirable alternative includes in the background a benevolent variant of the Leninist thesis.[5] In the end socialists face the same dilemma, whether they are social democrats or Leninists: to base their precepts on independent ethical principles or to establish their actions as flowing in a natural and necessary way from the development of society. Of course I am being schematic here; in actual practice there were many combinations of this basic polarity. Nonetheless the socialism we have known in the twentieth century has leaned closer to the first proposal than to the second. The latter still has something of that naturalist spirit so characteristic of the nineteenth century. I think I recognize in this inclination toward willful political forms, based on revolutionary ethics, something important to understanding the tragic form socialism took on in the Soviet Union. Social scientists in the United States—including Sovietologists—were unable to foresee a peaceful transition to capitalism in socialist societies, driven by internal forces, because at root they were trapped in the same vicious circle as the Marxist-Leninists. Daniel Bell, for example, maintains that the Russian Revolution "was the wrong revolution at the wrong time in the wrong place carried out by the wrong people. And we have paid for this disastrous conscious act of 'forcing history' during most of the twentieth century."[6]

On the other hand, the liberal tradition has grown closer to the modernizing postulates of various kinds, whether of positivist, Weberian, Keynesian, or other origins. Liberal groups have come to accept more and more openly the postulates that hold that the coming of civic democracy and the market are a kind of necessary product of the course of modernizing development. Perhaps this is a matter of a belated tribute to the very origins of the bourgeois work ethic, which Weber located in Calvinist submission to the inflexible designs of divine Providence. If this is so, we could also say that twentieth-century Leninists are distant descendants of the Spanish Jesuits who so energetically defended free will against the Reformation. Even so, the expansion of modernization theories into liberal

5. See Norberto Bobbio, *Which Socialism? Marxism, Socialism, and Democracy*, trans. Roger Griffin (Minneapolis: University of Minnesota Press, 1987), 85–102.
6. Daniel Bell, "Posdata a la nueva edición de *Las contradicciones culturales del capitalismo*," *Vuelta* 181 (1991).

spaces has inspired serious resistance and debates. Two symptomatic examples could be cited: John Rawls's attempts to rescue old contractual ideas as the base for normative ethics uncontaminated by social interests, and Habermas's search for a defense of the unfinished project of modernity through the recovery of the Enlightenment by way of systems theory.[7]

I would like to jump to contemporary Mexican reality, where the tensions I am speaking of are crudely and transparently evident. As the old base of revolutionary legitimation has eroded away, Mexican government policy has more decisively adopted modernization theory. Now government policy is presented as the natural and necessary continuation of modernizing progress and this provides a scientific or pragmatic justification for authoritarian and antidemocratic political actions, as well as for economic integration with the free market of the United States. The Mexican government reflects, in a somewhat grotesque manner, one of the most crucial aspects of the body of liberal doctrine: in some strange way, it has inherited the sin of Marxism, so that liberal elites behave as if they were the indispensable banner bearers of a victorious historical necessity preordained to be fully carried out. The noisy collapse of socialism in Europe would seem like the unexpected confirmation of this triumphal march of capitalist modernization. Things in Mexico seem like a joke: the technocratic modernizing group is necessary for national progress; the Left, by contrast, is unnecessary and superfluous.

But if we look closely at the Mexican situation, we see that here as elsewhere—as Daniel Bell has pointed out—the modernizing project is under attack by two dissenting movements: fundamentalism and postmodernism.[8] As the modernizing project abandons its former ethical principles and develops pragmatic behavior, it understandably leaves the moral flank of the system undefended. And it is exactly at that point where we can see the clearest signs of the legitimacy crisis.

Before going further, I'd like to clarify what I mean by moral problems. However much the dictionaries have tried to erase the original meaning, wrapped up in seventeenth-century theology, "morals" refer to the way in which customs, habits, and rules of conduct are observed and practiced, or rejected, in different societies. Anthropologists prefer the notion of "culture," because that way we

7. John Rawls, *A Theory of Justice* (Cambridge: Belknap Press, 1971); and Jürgen Habermas, *The Structural Transformation of the Public Sphere: An Inquiry into a Category of Bourgeois Society*, trans. Thomas Burger (Cambridge: MIT Press, 1991).
8. Bell, "Posdata."

get away from the religious connotations the idea of "morals" has taken on. Yet this very mixture of meanings shows the tensions sparked by the influence of fundamentalist ideas. The crisis of modernity—with the fall of socialism as one of its most dramatic manifestations—has cleared a wide field for the growth of fundamentalist attitudes, based on rather different moral codes with metasocial ambitions. The fundamentalist critique of modernization can be made from the most varied political trenches: nationalism, environmentalism, liberation theology, Islamic theocracy, the racist New Right, Marxism-Leninism, et cetera.

In Mexico the Left has inherited and continues to shelter many attitudes of a fundamentalist bent, but in reality the Right has been fundamentalism's most important vessel. The PAN is a party that proclaims doctrinal principles of universal validity, referring to the "common good," applicable at any moment and to all aspects of social and political life. Nonetheless the PAN has accepted significant doses of pragmatism, which—combined with its firm moral attitudes— have won it more than a few political victories. In this time of transition, we should not be surprised by the great ability of the Right to form a political, cultural, and moral code of its own to face down with great effectiveness the authoritarian pragmatism of the governing party.

Things are more complicated and much more difficult for the Left, which faces the collapse of the moral and theoretical principles that guided and illustrated means of political action that were relatively independent of specific social conditions and linked together the most unlikely Leftist parties and movements. The Left includes a broad range: some reformists, others maximalists, over here Trotskyites and over there Maoists, nearby social democrats and far away Leninists, some Eurocommunists and others populists. But they were all defined by their relationship with a set of principles, whether they accepted them or rejected them. Like insects, they all orbited a single light, and their circular flight gave meaning to their differences, internal struggles, and alliances. The multiplicity of groups and positions within the Left was a function of the relative independence from political reality of these standards of behavior and rules of conduct. The tragedy of the situation we are now going through lies in that a large measure of that reality has disappeared, swiftly vanishing in the few years since 1989. This is not a question of the Left's usual difficulties in understanding the world surrounding it and reaching agreement on ways of transforming it: suddenly half of that world has vanished into thin air, and it is no more and no less than the portion occupied by actually existing socialism.

I cannot imagine a better example in politics of the postmodern condition than the situation the Left is living through now. To use Lyotard's terms, the skepticism of metadiscourses is not an ideological malaise due to a passing fashion but a condition of helplessness before the moral and material ruin of socialist mechanisms of legitimation. Various groups have tried to save themselves from this shipwreck by swimming toward what seems to be firmer land. In the midst of the storm of century's end, nationalism, populism, and even the Polish Solidarity movement have seemed like life vests.

We could look at this from another standpoint: the ruins left by the collapse of socialism are testimony to the greatest failure of modernity. The fall of socialism is the result of the most corrosive and ironic critique the Left has made of capitalist civilization. I don't want to suggest that in reality socialism as we have known it was nothing more than a strange form of capitalist modernity that failed because it was established in a weak, backward, and immature society. Nor do I believe that socialism was the slow putrefaction of a society that needed the modernization that only came with the Velvet Revolutions of 1989 and the popular uprising that ended the power of the Communist Party of the Soviet Union in August 1991. Although I would hardly deny the presence of immaturities and decay, the history of socialism is not the history of a disconnect between free political will and the clock of history. Recognizing this fact means accepting that for all its failures, socialism is one of the most modern political experiments Western culture has spawned. Of course, socialism is not capitalist development by other means; I am speaking not of a question of development but of a problem of civilization, of culture, of morals.

I would like to offer an example closer to home. As a product of the great problems of Latin America, the Cuban Revolution wanted to open an escape hatch out of underdevelopment, but it turned into a much deeper and more far-ranging alternative. The socialism of Che Guevara and Fidel Castro was shaped as much by Latin American traditions as by the imperial policies of the United States, so Cuba more than thirty years ago came to offer a civilizing cultural and moral alternative for the problems of the entire continent. Just because the governments of America were unable to recognize this does not erase the fact that the Cuban Revolution was a genuine—if unacknowledged—child of the contradictions of our continent, the westernmost part of the West. Cuba was also where the oppositions between Anglo-American and Hispano-American cultures took their most spectacular form. Just as socialism in Europe was born out of the great upheavals that shook the Old World at the beginning of the century, so the Cuban Revolution was spurred by the tensions crossing our continent at midcentury: the unbridled expansion of the United States economy, anticommunism, the underdevelopment of Latin America, dictatorships, racism, and moral and material deprivation.

Nearly forty years later, Castro's alternative is a fiasco, and the rest of Latin

America is still underdeveloped. These parallel failures are not unrelated: Cuba has become not just an example of the sterility of authoritarian socialism but also the symbol of the failure of Washington's solutions for the misery of Latin America. Despite everything, perhaps the Cuban tragedy contributed to the extinction of the dictatorships and the rise of democratic regimes in nearly all Latin American countries.

In the midst of these ruins, and these remnants of sacked former utopias, we are faced with several options I would like to group into three broad categories.

First, the Left could take hold of foundational doctrines (Marxist, populist, environmentalist, evangelical, nationalist, etc.) to proclaim the immense danger of the disappearance of a critical and transformative spirit from capitalist society. From here, a refoundation could be attempted.

Second, progressive forces could sign on to the liberal band and form a kind of left-wing watchdog group to spur on the more positive aspects of the modernizing project. This option would require a certain theoretical adjustment in a pragmatic direction.

Third, the Left could remain inside the socialist edifice in ruins and, working with the irony of the situation, try to set out the conditions for a moral critique of modernity. This alternative demands that we define it as postmodern.

Based on these three big options, I would like to return to the question that originally spurred these thoughts: is the Left necessary or dispensable? From the fundamentalist standpoint, which feels threatened that history today does not need the Left, it is necessary to recover the primeval metahistorical principles to build the strength of a self-generating political will. Precisely because the Left is dispensable and has become a species in danger of extinction, its existence must be preserved.

From the modernizing standpoint, the Left can be considered as a historical necessity, a force inseparable from capitalist development. As the inevitable counterpart of liberalism, the Left would fulfill a necessary function for the system. Precisely because it is necessary, the Left, parasite of liberalism, would have to be combated constantly to prevent its unbridled reproduction, like a plague, from destabilizing the system.

The postmodern Left has no problem with incorporating many liberal values, nor does it reject the search for the ethical foundations of political action. Liberalism and fundamentalism are parts of modern society's fragmented landscape of ruins, along with the remains of other great theoretical and political conglomerates that have illuminated twentieth-century vanguards. This Left, to borrow the charming phrase of Bourdieu, is "needed without being necessary" and accepts living in a chaotic and heterogeneous world where every day relations between social segments are governed less by economic determinations and more by a dense network of cultural and moral ties. Modern society has instituted the Left because it *needed* its presence; but the Left is not *necessary* to build capitalist society. By the way, the same thing is true of representative democracy: modernity needed it—and needs it still. But democracy is not necessary, and as we know, capitalist society can do without it.

The Left can get used to being dispensable without sheltering itself, to find historical strength and legitimacy, in the great metadiscourses that serve to consolidate its Cartesian ego. In the same way that the separation between elitist aesthetics and popular culture has been erased, so the line separating high politics from everyday morals is growing blurry, as is the frontier that divides the critique of political economy from the critique of culture and civility. The metadiscourse that legitimates the design of great national projects is losing ground to the attitudes that promote intelligent tolerance within the heart of public space and the mass media. High art and high politics are being drowned in mass culture, fashion, spectacle, sexual worries, education, crime reports, hedonism, religiosity, ethnic identities, and so on. In these new spaces, the Left is obliged to find its place, and not because history has already reserved it one.

It is a typical postmodern irony that such an old issue, already debated at the beginning of the century, still remains somewhat current. The readiness of society to accept great changes was the central theme of the famous interview that reporter James Creelman had with Porfirio Díaz in 1908. The old dictator answered the maliciously liberal questions of the U.S. interviewer with positivist solemnity, claiming that the Mexican Republic was ready for democracy, because his patriarchal policies had borne fruit in the stable development of an intelligent, submissive, and benevolent people. The time had come, don Porfirio thought, for the emergence of an opposition party.[9]

We don't know whether the revolution that exploded in 1910 was premature or immature, and we are still debating whether it was left unfinished, died in 1917, or marches on thanks to the Institutional Revolutionary Party. We have inherited from the 1910 revolution a preoccupation—Porfirian, positivist, and liberal—with the "timing" of change, with the stopwatch of politics. We have added to this heritage the Marxist and Leninist obsessions with the coming of the "objective and subjective conditions" for the revolutionary Big Bang. Now history itself has expelled us—and it hardly matters whether too soon, or too

---

9. One of the few Díaz granted during his long rule, the Creel interview fueled speculation about Díaz's succession and, in a small way, contributed to the public expression of dissent that brought on the revolution. [Trans.]

late—from programmatic certainties, cryptoscientific foundations, and revolutionary creeds. Instead it has set us down in the uncomfortable and little-known space of what I like to call "political culture," a vast and uneven terrain where the habits, standards, and customs that give legitimacy to political systems are consolidated. It was in this space that the "moral decisions" were made that gave birth to socialism in Europe. Those decisions were not only the impositions of a firm ideological will; they were also resolutions distilled and solidified on the vast terrain of political culture. On this terrain, morals—that irregular set of habits—increasingly shape the conditions under which postmodern society develops. Today we have come back to the starting point, to face new moral decisions: the difference is that now we know that history will not absolve us.

Lombardo or Revueltas?

The political culture of the Mexican Left is a vast space occupied by a rich and varied amalgam of tendencies, which over the course of a century have formed a web full of contradictions.[1] To my mind, two great historical axes run across that space and are expressed in the lives and works of two men: Vicente Lombardo Toledano and José Revueltas. With the passage of time, these two characters have ended up embodying the outer—and opposing—historical limits that mark off the space of our political culture. In this essay, I'm going to take some liberties with the complex political lives of Lombardo and Revueltas in order to move on to what they symbolize in the collective consciousness of the Mexican Left. Lombardo passed through many phases before becoming the Great Revisionist.[2] By the same token, Revueltas went through countless vicissitudes before coming to embody the figure of the Great Leftist.[3] For many, Lom-

This essay was originally published in a special 1982 issue of *Nexos* (no. 54) I edited on the Mexican Left.

1. The best general treatment of the Left in English is Barry Carr, *Marxism and Communism in Twentieth-Century Mexico* (Lincoln: University of Nebraska Press, 1992). [Trans.]

2. Vicente Lombardo Toledano (1894–1968) was an intellectual, politician, university professor, and labor leader. The son of an Italian immigrant businessman who settled in the sierra of Puebla, he was the organizer and secretary general of the Confederation of Mexican Workers, 1936–1940; organizer and president of the Conference of Latin American Workers, 1938–1963; founder and president of the Popular Party, 1948–1968; and candidate for president, 1952. He held numerous other state positions, taught at the UNAM and the Workers' University of Mexico, and was a three-time federal deputy. See Robert Milton, *Mexican Marxist: Vicente Lombardo Toledano* (Chapel Hill: University of North Carolina Press, 1966). [Trans.]

3. José Revueltas (1914–1976) was a novelist, journalist, playwright, and screenwriter. At age fifteen, he was first imprisoned, and at age sixteen, he joined the PCM: much of the remainder of

bardo was the most important Marxist and labor leader that Mexican history has given us. For many others, Revueltas was the most lucid and penetrating revolutionary the Mexican Left has generated. Each opposing group has used one of these extremes to shape their own Black Legend and to burn dizzying incense before their own idols.[4]

It is necessary to add one more element to our judgment. However bad many of us feel about it, we have to recognize that from many points of view, Lombardo and Revueltas constitute the most solid pillars on which the political culture of the Mexican Left rests. I think, for a start, that without those pillars our political culture would simply not be Mexican. That is to say, it would not be a constitutive part of national culture. If the Mexican Left is not some sad, strange, and marginal subculture, this is precisely because the lombardistas carried out the first successful effort at unifying the labor movement, and because Revueltas is a symbol of the great watershed of 1968, which opened up unsuspected political possibilities for us. Behind these two men, we can find this, and much more: sometimes, their images obscure other men who also contributed to generating a national space for the Left. I do not wish to minimize those others here: the foundations of our political culture were raised by several generations of contradictory and talented intellectuals, of persecuted peasants and workers with forgotten names, and of intuitive and persistent politicians. What they have built allows us to suspect that while Lombardo and Revueltas mark off the two extreme poles of the Mexican Left, they no longer represent viable alternatives for the revolutionary movement.

Summing Up, Paring Down

On 1 October 1968, Lombardo wrote a brief warning in the latest edition of a pamphlet of his entitled "Youth in the World and Mexico." There he attacked the young students who "claimed to be reformers of Marxism in order to defame it," and were pushing a new revolution and a new Left "down a path which is not

---

his life was spent in and out of these two institutions. He also joined and later left Lombardo's Popular Party, the Mexican Worker-Peasant Party, and the Leninist Sparticist League. For a fuller treatment in English of his writings and life, see Sam Slick, *José Revueltas* (Boston: G. K. Hall, 1983). [Trans.]

4. For an overview of the Mexican Left's relationship with the state broadly parallel to, and heavily influenced by, this essay, see Barry Carr, "The Fate of the Vanguard under a Revolutionary State." [Trans.]

that of Marxist-Leninism." The next day was the massacre of Tlatelolco.[5] Six weeks later Vicente Lombardo Toledano died, "without letting himself be dazzled"—as he wrote in the pamphlet—"by the resounding words or brilliant and audacious phrases" of the "ideologues of the new revolution." By contrast, José Revueltas *was* dazzled by the 1968 movement: the last years of his existence were illuminated by the originality of that experience, to the point that his ferociously Marxist-Leninist ideas were seriously eroded. In 1973 he wrote to his daughter Andrea that "the Leninist theory of the Party—just like the theory of the State and of the dictatorship of the proletariat—must be, in light of the experiences of this half of the twentieth century, must be and can be overcome." Revueltas died in 1976 without satisfying his obsession with writing a new prologue to his *Essay on the Headless Proletariat* openly revising his old Leninist ideas about the party.[6]

They had switched roles: the "revisionist" insisted on ending his days fragrant in orthodox holiness, and the "revolutionary" ended up throwing Marxist-Leninism out the window. This has its explanation in the ways of thinking and action of both characters. Lombardo's Marxism is a closed universe that, after his 1935 polemic with Antonio Caso, remains practically unchanged.[7] By contrast, the Marxism of Revueltas is an open universe that changes constantly. Lombardo's Marxism is held together by a long-standing obsession with formulating a global summary of truths opposed to Christian theological thought. His obsession is so great that in 1964 he writes a well-known book whose title is already symptomatic: *Summa*.[8] In ninety pages Lombardo takes his rationalism so far as to offer the new generations, who sometimes opt for "confusion or flight" in confusing times, the road that will "lead them from the cave where

5. This was the massacre of hundreds of protesting students at the Plaza of Tlatelolco by state forces, putting an end to the student movement and—for many—to any lingering state claims to embodying a popular, revolutionary project. [Trans.]

6. The first edition was José Revueltas, *Ensayo sobre el proletariado sin cabeza* (Mexico: Logos, 1962). [Trans.]

7. Antonio Caso had been one of Lombardo Toledano's teachers, and in 1935 they fought over Lombardo Toledano's attempts to impose an overall socialist orientation on teaching at the recently founded UNAM. Caso opposed this as censorship and was supported by a lively student movement. Lombardo was removed from his post, and the scheme for socialist dogma abandoned. [Trans.]

8. Vicente Lombardo Toledano, *Summa* (Mexico, 1964). In its title and ambition—if not in length—the book clearly echoes the masterwork of the medieval Catholic theologian Saint Thomas Aquinas, *Summa theologica*.

they are still suffering because of their ignorance into the splendid light of truth." In this book Lombardo declares that the universe is infinite, defines the essence of man with his Pavlovian spirituality, reveals that there are intelligent beings in other parts of the universe, explains that the real sin is the exploitation of man by man, defines private property and work, points out the path to socialist ascension, formulates an optimistic aesthetic according to which beauty is everywhere, and stresses that true love is more of an intellectual than a biological category, that the labyrinth of the modern world is due to the crisis of imperialism, that socialism is a doctrine centered on man, and that man is immortal.

Lombardo expresses the simple and happy logic of inexorable progress. By contrast, Revueltas lives troubled by his tragic awareness of a fundamental lack. That is why the great theme of Revueltas is alienation. Everything is missing something, nothing is complete: Mexican writers are often missing words, the country is missing democracy, Marxism is missing Leninism, consciousness is missing organization, and, worst of all, the proletariat is missing its head. In his own way, Revueltas imagines—or, better stated, longs for—a closed universe like Lombardo's. But every time he looks around him, he notices what is lacking; he becomes conscious of the distance between reality and his utopia of a true and organized consciousness of the proletariat, of the class that is called to build the socialist future. In his *Essay on the Headless Proletariat*, Revueltas sketches out the "collective brain" he so longed for, defining it more in terms of what it *must not be* than in terms of its positive traits. In his maddening search for the "true" party of the working class, Revueltas is drawing the outlines of the empty skull of the vanguard. What he produces is an absent and imaginary ideological world, full of ideas that slip away every time he tries to trap them.

Organizing Consciousness

For both Revueltas and Lombardo, the working class cannot exist as a revolutionary class without its political party. For Revueltas, the party is fundamentally the "organized consciousness" of the proletariat, and therefore ideologues are the political vanguard of the class. That is why the major difficulty in Mexico, for him, lies in the bourgeois-democratic ideological contamination the labor movement suffers from. The true constitution of the revolutionary party is in the organizing of the thinking head based on a set of Marxist-Leninist ideas. This willful and vanguardist conception clashed violently with the thinking of Lombardo, which tended more toward mechanistic and populist views. For the one, the prior conscious act brings everything together. For the other, political consciousness is the inevitable expression of the labor movement. The latter point of view sees fulfillment above all in a broad front bringing together all nationalist and anti-imperialist forces. Within this front, as one of its components, the Marxist-Leninist party will take shape. For Revueltas, on the other hand, the creation of the party is a conscious foundational act that defines the organization of the movement.

In the final analysis, the party is seen as the embryonic form of the state. What radically differentiates Lombardo from Revueltas is the model to base the new revolutionary party on. Lombardo sets his party inside the logic of the Mexican state; Revueltas conceives it as tied to the future dictatorship of the proletariat. For Lombardo, the Marxist-Leninist party is a logical outgrowth of the history of the Mexican Revolution. That history, for Revueltas, is the history of the bourgeois organization of all consciousness. As a consequence, the new party is created precisely to resist and annihilate the bourgeois-democratic ideology of the Mexican Revolution.

For all of his life, Lombardo saw the party as an educator of the ignorant masses. In 1924, as a leader in the CROM, Lombardo argued that "the proletarian school cannot be . . . either secular, Catholic, traditionalist, or active. It must be dogmatic, and commanding." Later on, in a thirties polemic with Caso, he expressed his support for limiting academic freedom at the National Preparatory School, since students were unable to make distinctions, so their judgments must be made for them. Lombardo was always the Teacher, and he conceived of the party in his image and likeness. It is no accident that his history is of a university intellectual who made his political career in the labor movement: he treated proletarians like a group of students gathered in his classroom.

For Revueltas, the main problem was located precisely in the very making of "political truth." He was convinced that if a general staff of ideologues managed to clearly define a true political alternative, that would be enough to start the process of reversing the alienation of the proletarian masses. His statement that "the proletariat begins to act, above all, in the head of Marx himself, in his theoretical thinking" is symptomatic. That is why he was preoccupied with the party's functioning as a team of ideologues who operated as the neurons of a "collective brain which thinks *for* and *with* the class." At root this is similar to Lombardo's framing: the difference is that Lombardo allows for the existence of an already-formed body of doctrine, while Revueltas holds that it does not exist yet. That is why Lombardo is mostly interested in spreading his own thinking, whereas Revueltas is essentially concerned with how to study and understand Mexican reality.

This last point implied that within the party there should be the greatest degree of freedom for research and debate, once it had agreed to close in on itself like a rosebud in order to study and research Mexican reality. The Leninist Spartacus League, which Revueltas himself founded, later expelled him when he ceased to accept the rigor of ideological discipline. He was caught in the sectarian Marxist-Leninist trap he had set. He never could escape this problem, except when he dreamed of a kind of Republic of Marxist Sages, a "democracy of ideologues who debate until they die, until they clearly set out a problem." That was the "cognitive democracy" he was advocating in his last years.

The Monster's Head

As Lombardo and Revueltas demonstrate, the tragedy of the thought of the Mexican Left is that it has remained trapped in statist logic, wavering between the Stalinist specter of the dictatorship of the proletariat and the despotism of the government of the Mexican Revolution. Little space was left for political democracy, which ended up being replaced by the institutionalization of the ideas-that-truly-represent-the-people, either in the democracy-of-the-eggheads model or the teacher-lighting-up-the-darkness paradigm.

Revueltas's thinking always had a real embodiment: the Mexican Communist Party (PCM). He never stopped being its ideologue, even though he became its bête noire. For his part, Lombardo was always a theorist of the Mexican revolutionary state. They were both theorists of the party and the state that "should be" but for various reasons never quite managed to emerge. In the final analysis, their political theories never amounted to more than cleaned-up versions of, respectively, the reality of the oldest party of the Left and the peculiarities of the Mexican state. One constructed the idea of a *proletarian proto-state,* and the other designed a *nationalist mega-state.* They were two imaginative projections of Mexican reality, drawn up with the help of the Marxist tool kit.

Lombardo interpreted Mexican politics based on the positions of two great axes: national forces and imperialist forces. Every event and institution could be classified according to the greater or lesser presence of those two ingredients. He even went so far as to speak of an "anti-national provocation" in the popular student movement of 1968. So with the help of the two simple yardsticks he used to measure politics—nation and empire—he defined both the Mexican state and the united front that should be the means by which the country could peacefully make the transition to socialism. In truth this front, for Lombardo, was nothing more than an extension, or a purified projection, of the state itself. The Mexican state was conceived of as a heterogeneous whole dominated by the "nationalist bourgeoisie," which was opposed—except for some vacillations—to imperialism. Lombardo's logic is not complicated: that bourgeoisie was the impulse behind expanding state capitalism, based on the nationalization and state control of natural resources and the major sectors of the economy. The state capitalism advanced by the nationalist bourgeoisie, which operated in favor of "the general interest," was in turn blocked by the forces of the pro-imperialist bourgeoisie and the direct agents of imperialism. As a result, the national liberation front should unite the working class, the peasantry, and the petty bourgeoisie with the nationalist bourgeoisie: clearly, this front should include the government, or at least its nationalist sectors. From there the possibility of a peaceful transition to socialism follows naturally, a possibility based on the continuity of the Mexican revolutionary state led—from a given moment forward—by the working class. In the end, socialism for Lombardo was the outgrowth and extension of state capitalism.

The viability of this process seemed to be confirmed by the evidence that parties truly representative of different classes did not exist in Mexico. The official party was nothing more than an electoral appendage of the government, the two heads of the bourgeoisie (the nationalist and the pro-imperialist) lacked a party, the peasantry and the middle sectors were in the same situation, and the representatives of the working class found themselves divided and enormously weakened. The only place to look for real hope was inside the state, headed by a sui generis bourgeoisie that seemed to have strangely suicidal and anticapitalist tendencies.

What is most tragic about Lombardo's option is not, as has been stubbornly held, its reformist character. Its most profoundly negative aspect is that it subordinates the struggle for socialism to the development of the state and, as a result, eliminates all the revolutionary potential of political democracy. That is to say, it subordinates society to the state. The result is that socialism is completely disconnected from democracy. And democracy is reduced to the question of whether the social and economic measures put into practice by the state are "representative" of supposed popular interests. This is the origin of the terrible leftist vice that consists of calling "democratic" any reform that would even partially tend to satisfy some popular needs, although the people themselves have no role in deciding these reforms. It is said that the means of participation only address the "form" of political reforms, when what needs to be taken into account is their "content." This vulgar and Stalinist logic leads to the famous conclusion that democracy has a purely "formal" character. In fact, what these ideas have really led to is a socialism so deformed that it cannot be recognized as such.

Lombardo's united front is conceived of as an alternative macro-state that gradually seeps into the actual government, as state capitalism mysteriously transforms itself into state socialism. Because he disdains the "form" by which the process takes place, he covers up the democratic mechanisms that allow the people to effectively govern themselves. The formal shell he throws away in order to get to the "core" of the matter contains nothing less than the one thing that is truly revolutionary about socialism: its fusion with democracy.

In Search of the Nation

Despite everything, Lombardo's interpretation points to a key problem that still has the Mexican Left scratching its head: where does the political diversity of the Mexican state come from? To be more exact, what the Left has spent decades looking for are the social bases of the nationalist and progressive aspects of government policy. The traditional answer explains the phenomenon through the existence of a fragmented bourgeoisie divided over the need to push for the bourgeois-democratic reforms every underdeveloped nation needs. It assumes the presence of a "national bourgeoisie" (or something equivalent) located in the state or its immediate surroundings, which could place considerable pressure on government policy . . . if the people support it. As a counterpoint to these ideas, Revueltas maintains that in Mexico the national unity of the bourgeoisie has already been achieved. The most brilliant pages of his *Essay on the Headless Proletariat* are dedicated to demonstrating the extraordinary and singular way in which the unification of the bourgeoisie occurred in Mexico. This is one of Revueltas's great merits: he underscores the importance of the fact that in Mexico the unity of the nation is identified with the unity of the ruling class, perhaps the only case of this in Latin America, and even more importantly, that the unity of the nation-state includes important parts of the labor and peasant movements. But Revueltas explains the nature of the phenomenon mostly through its ideological aspects: the unifying demiurge is the organized consciousness of the bourgeoisie, which takes the form of a horrendously swollen bourgeois-democratic head. In this way, Revueltas attempts to resolve the problem of the diversity of the state by means of the logic of bourgeois ideology, through the pure dialectical play of concepts. So the "progressive," "nationalist," and "popular" aspects of government policy are in fact explained as a mediating cleverness of bourgeois ideology, which manages to swallow "socialist consciousness" itself and reduce it to its own left wing. Therefore class struggle tends to appear as an unequal struggle between alienating bourgeois-democratic consciousness and true Marxist-Leninist consciousness. Ideology "takes possession of the masses" and thereby becomes a "material force." Bourgeois-democratic ideology, converted into a material force, "must put into action and satisfy the masses it has taken possession of." This is the key to the "progressive" behavior of the state: the bourgeoisie has become identified with the nation.

When Revueltas affirms that bourgeois-democratic consciousness has become hegemonic, he is not only referring to a historical process but also speaking of his personal experience. After being expelled from the PCM in 1943, for example, Revueltas ended up taking shelter in Lombardo's Popular Party and working as an editor for its paper, *El Popular.* In 1949 he published his novel *Earthly Days,* which merited a stupid rebuke from Enrique Ramírez y Ramírez, who classified Revueltas as nihilistic, antihumanist, existentialist, divisive, and anti-Soviet. Revueltas wrote a shameful self-critical letter to Lombardo and Ramírez, offering an homage to socialist realism and confessing to Sartrean deviations that only served the forces of reaction. As a consequence of this incident, Revueltas asked his publisher to take the book out of circulation: he undoubtedly felt that a strange ideology was taking possession of his consciousness with all the strength of a material force. But that strange ideology was something very different from "demo-Marxism," as he called the ideas of Lombardo and the Communists. It was pure Marxist-Leninism. That is to say, Stalinism. The ideology that deformed and alienated Mexican revolutionaries did not come exclusively from the national bourgeoisie. Mexican nationalism flowed together with the dogmatic and authoritarian tendencies coming from the tragically existing form socialism was building in the Soviet Union. The drama of Revueltas was that the fiery defense he made of Marxist-Leninist principles contained the same despotic seeds that had produced the slippery monster called the "national bourgeoisie."

The Third Way

In many ways, Lombardo and Revueltas seem like two nearly irreconcilable opposites. Lombardo was always a statesman, and Revueltas was in and out of prisons from a young age. It is true that Lombardo was always weighed down by greater responsibility; for that reason, he has been more harshly judged. Revueltas's free manner and political clumsiness brought him many problems, but they gave him a margin of freedom that propelled the flight of his uncontainable imagination.

By the time Lombardo decided—or was forced—to give up the leadership of the CTM, he had already created the conditions for a rightward turn in the most important labor federation in the country.[9] Lombardo prepared the way for Fidel Velázquez, submitted himself submissively to his old friend Ávila Camacho, and even took an active part in the political launching of Miguel Alemán.[10] He never stepped out of state bounds; he didn't even oppose Alemán's reforms to agrarian legislation, which helped to make Narciso Bassols and Victor Manuel Villaseñor leave the Popular Party.[11] For his part, the erratic zigzags of Revueltas also left their mark, but perhaps their only truly serious consequences were the enormously hostile attitudes toward all Left organizations that became widespread among intellectuals. During the sixties he managed to crystallize a hyper-ideological sectarian terrorism that ended up depoliticizing a large portion of intellectuals for many years.

The two men were also opposed in their attitudes toward the nation. On the one hand, the almost religious nationalism of Lombardo led him, for example, to open his presidential campaign invoking the fatherland in the place where he thought the remains of Cuauhtémoc were found (in Ixcateopan). "Father Cuauhtémoc, with your conduct and your sacrifice," he said—or rather he prayed —on 13 January 1952, "you have left us the eternal mandate of defending Mexico against oppression that comes from without. I promise you, in my own name and in the name of the Popular Party, believing myself to be a faithful interpreter . . ." and so on and so forth.[12] On the other hand, Revueltas was repulsed by cheap patriotism and hated more than anything else the oppression that came from within. "In its final essence," he wrote, "nationalism is the negation of man." That is why he thought that national literature should be, above all, an antinationalist literature.

If we were to carry on with this counterpoint between Lombardo and Revueltas, we would see the most important twists in the history of the Left and

9. Lombardo had organized the CTM, the central labor federation, and headed it from its 1936 founding until 1941. His successor was Fidel Velázquez, who turned the federation into a corrupt, repressive, and authoritarian arm of the state and—except for a brief interval between 1946 and 1949—remained at its helm until his death in 1999. [Trans.]

10. The latter two were the presidents who succeeded Cárdenas—Ávila Camacho (1940–1946) and Alemán (1946–1952)—and took the revolution in a far more conservative and repressive direction. [Trans.]

11. Bassols had been the author of the 1927 Agrarian Law and thus felt this to be a particularly strong betrayal. [Trans.]

12. The nephew of Moctezuma II and the last Aztec king, Cuautémoc defended Tenochtitlán against Hernán Cortés until his capture in August 1521. He is often seen as a founding father of Mexico, as in Lombardo's speech. [Trans.]

the labor movement in Mexico. From the two tangles, perhaps we could gather enough strands to weave together the tapestry of popular struggles. But that would be like sewing the mantle of Laertes, which Penelope undid every night. That task could only be carried out by a way of thinking anchored in faithfulness, awaiting the arrival of a proletarian Odysseus. Because during the last twenty years, a new alternative has been growing. With great difficulties, and still enmeshed in the dense web of a doctrinaire and dogmatic ideology, forms of action and thought have emerged whose slogan could well be "Neither Lombardo nor Revueltas!" In *all* of the groups and political parties on the Left, new voices and events emerged and took a new path. In the largest and oldest organization of the Left, the PCM, there was a twenty-year struggle between the indecision of a Hamlet/Revueltas, who questioned himself before the ghost of the proletarian skull, and the certainty of a Saint Thomas Aquinas/Lombardo, who drew the official circle of the worker's Leviathan with a finger of flame. But in the end, the PCM was able to see the moment for bringing one phase of its history to a radical close by dissolving into the Unified Socialist Party of Mexico (PSUM). This did not take place without convulsions: certain nostalgic sectors tried to restore or renew the old doctrinaire Stalinist spiderweb, terrified by the "ideological confusion" that went along with the difficult search for a new living space for the Left.[13]

That space now exists, but it does not look much like the schemes Lombardo and Revueltas drew up for us. To begin with, it is a space whose organizing axis is the struggle for democracy and whose governing principle is Marxist pluralism. This is an irreversible event: the flowing together of different theoretical currents is not directed toward their unification in a doctrinary summa or a Marxist-Leninist corpus. Unity is made on political terrain on the basis of democratic principles safeguarding the free development of minorities. That space tends to become a global alternative to the present capitalist state. Today, many realize that the battle must also be joined on governmental terrain, but that does not imply the existence of mysterious "fractions" of the bourgeoisie or the bureaucracy with whom an "alliance" would be possible. The fact that the independent Left can take advantage of certain parts of the state forms part of a war of position, not a policy of alliance. The mystery of the "progressive" facets of state policy turned out to be much more straightforward than we thought: they were due to the presence of popular forces inside the state, not the influence of

13. In 1981 the PSUM was formed; in 1987 it merged into the PMS; in 1989 significant portions of the party joined the PRD. But intense sectarian struggles have also accompanied these broadening movements and have at times crippled the operations and program of the PRD. [Trans.]

crazy fractions of the bourgeoisie. Even so, this fact, apparently so simple and obvious, has opened the door to new interpretations of the complex hegemony of the bourgeoisie and the labyrinthine forms of political consensus. We certainly can observe important signs of splits within the dominant class, but they cannot be explained using the framework set by the concepts of imperialism and nationalism.

These ideas about alliances and fronts have aged notoriously poorly. Just as we have abandoned our instrumental conception of the state, so we also must recognize that the revolutionary subject has expanded and shifted from the "fundamental core" of the working class. We can no longer think that the revolutionary alternative is built as a series of links subordinated to the "proletarian core" and the vanguard party, in which peasants, intellectuals, and the petty bourgeoisie are joined to a historic destiny determined by the "superior" instances of the class struggle.

This new space of the Left is trying to escape the rigid logic of political, military, and ideological blocs. The uselessness of raising up castles of theory full of hierarchies is demonstrated more forcefully every day. Take, for instance, the whole scaffolding of structures and superstructures that withered away Marx's original metaphor and only blocked our understanding of the close connections between everyday life, culture, politics, and economics. Subjecting each of these matters to an abstract hierarchy has greatly deformed our national reality and left us blind in the face of moments pregnant with new meanings.

Even so, I do not think the moment has come to catalog all the features of the New Left, largely—although not exclusively—concentrated in the contradictions the PSUM lived through. We still need to look back and settle our accounts with the past. We need to understand Lombardo and Revueltas, the axes marking off the narrow limits of a lost Marxist-Cartesian universe, and we need to understand them from the multidimensionality of our own times.

Marxism on the Gallows

y aim is not a trip into the past; my wish is not to review the roundtable Vicente Lombardo Toledano called in 1947.[1] What I want to do instead is bring certain aspects of the 1947 discussion to our present situation because, fortunately and unfortunately—both things at once, paradoxical business— those debates are quite current. This is unfortunate because the nearness of the forties is a measure of our backwardness. And this is fortunate because it is an indication of the place of Marxism in our national history.

There won't be space here to draw a panorama of the Left in the forties. The debates I will evoke are, up to a certain point, representative of the Left in that period: a Marxist Left stained, at least morally, with the atrocious assassination of Trotsky, a Left deeply divided, a Left unaware that it was perched on the verge of a sharp confrontation with the government.[2] A Left squarely in the middle of

During nearly two weeks in January 1947, a wide range of representatives from across the spectrum of the Mexican Left met for a marathon roundtable entitled "Objectives and Tactics of the Proletariat and the Revolutionary Sector during the Current Phase of the Historical Evolution of the Country." Coming less than a decade after the assassination of Trotsky and repeated internal purges had deeply split the Mexican Left, this meeting was a crucial moment of unity and reflection for the Left. In October 1983, along with other scholars and protagonists from that period, I took part in a seminar organized by the Center for the Study of the Workers and Socialist Movement called "The 1947 Roundtable and the Situation of the Left in the Mid-Forties." This essay was my contribution to the seminar.

1. On the importance of the roundtable, see Barry Carr, *Marxism and Communism in Twentieth-Century Mexico*, 156–64. The complete minutes of the proceedings have been published as *Mesa redonda de los marxistas mexicanos* (Mexico: Centro de Estudios Vicente Lombardo Toledano, 1982). All citations are from this text.

2. Trotsky was assassinated in Mexico in 1940, and the Mexican Communist Party was deeply

a period of modernization and economic growth, but waiting for the final crisis of capitalism. In sum, a Left that was digging its own grave. It is worthwhile to remember this, since the present-day Left sometimes seems devoted to that same task. It seems devoted to placing itself at the foot of the gallows.

Socialism Delayed

In drawing conclusions after several days of debates between Marxists, Lombardo Toledano let slip a phrase that marks the direction of leftist thinking at the end of the forties and also points to the enormous distance—almost an abyss—that separates us from that time: "Let's not aim for socialism in our country tomorrow."[3] In the eighties we expressed one of our major principles with the opposite formula: *We demand socialism now.* The thing is, many of us have very different ideas of what socialism should be in Mexico, and we know that building its democratic foundations begins *before* the revolutionary change and the seizure of power. We also know that the theoretical design of stages of transition has served for very little, other than as a filter for blurring national reality. We know that if socialism has a future, it has to be built from the present.

The phrase "let's not aim for socialism in our country tomorrow" revealed the peculiar situation the Marxists of that time had gotten themselves into. They had locked themselves voluntarily into the political and theoretical space of the 1910 Mexican Revolution and, as a consequence, accepted as a matter of course that any movement of the Mexican Left was by necessity inscribed within the lines of the bourgeois-democratic revolution. Their yesterday, today, and tomorrow were marked off by the parameters of what was called a bourgeois-democratic revolution *on the march.* According to Lombardo, it was the government of Lázaro Cárdenas that began rapid development toward the bourgeois-democratic regime. Miguel Alemán, "the cub of the revolution," was his heir. Dionisio Encina of the PCM supported these ideas with his heavy and dry language; his worries were focused on the brakes the Right was placing on the revo-

---

implicated in this act. Shortly before the assassination, Hernán Laborde and Valentín Campa had been removed from party leadership—they were later expelled from the party—owing to, among other things, their unwillingness to go along with the killing. Dionisio Encina took over as general secretary from Laborde and kept the post for nearly twenty years, through a long period of political disarray and organizational decline. [Trans.]

3. *Mesa redonda,* 591.

lution. It seemed evident to all that the Mexican Revolution was still on the march; the problem was managing to place the proletariat at the head of this bourgeois-democratic process. We should not find this odd. The enormous influence of the revolution, and of Cárdenas's deep reforms, was still strongly felt in 1947. Even today we can still recognize in the core of the Left this same preoccupation—although expressed in different terms—with stretching further the space of the Mexican Revolution.

The idea that the future of the Mexican Revolution on the march must be socialism was an affront to all the reigning schemes of Marxist dogma. That is why Lombardo—who was one of those who followed Stalinist dogma most closely— was so grateful for Dimitrov's notion that certain countries could reach socialism without passing through the stage of the dictatorship of the proletariat. Here was a formula, fallen from the heavens and blessed by Moscow, that allowed Lombardo to shore up his positions about national unity. Curiously enough, the contemporary heirs of Lombardo have been the most ferocious defenders of the dictatorship of the proletariat as an unavoidable first stage in the process of building socialism. For Communists at the time, Dimitrov's formula also seemed to fall from above, but seemed more like a cold shower. Despite admitting that he was not familiar with the writings of Dimitrov, Dionisio Encina was quick to cite Marx, Engels, Lenin, and Stalin in support of the idea that the class struggle would necessarily lead to the dictatorship of the proletariat. Later on, Blas Manrique, also a member of the PCM, cited Dimitrov at length to demonstrate that in his declaration he did not "necessarily renounce the dictatorship of the proletariat." In conclusion, like every dogmatic used to receiving rigid orders, he was especially interested in demonstrating that such a renunciation was possible in Eastern Europe, but was not obligatory. And so, in the name of flexibility—according to which each country would find its own way to socialism— he justified dogmatism . . . and even more curiously, thanks to that very dogmatism, he found a way to come to a rough agreement with Lombardo's ideas about national unity.[4]

These juggling acts, worthy of the Vatican's finest theologians, did not prevent important disagreements from spreading, even though they were camouflaged beneath obscure and cryptic terminology. Consider one example which seems comical from a distance although it was of course debated with great solemnity at the time: the dispute about how to define the character of the administration of Miguel Alemán. At the roundtable at the Fine Arts Palace, every variation on

4. Ibid., 210, 340.

Lombardo's definition was debated vehemently, as if the direction of the government depended on it. His definition came from his strategy of national unity, which implied renouncing—for now—the exclusive objectives of the proletariat, in order to establish an alliance with the so-called progressive bourgeoisie. Therefore, Lombardo defined Alemán's regime as a government of the petty and progressive bourgeoisie. In a mocking tone, Siquieros pointed out that the Left had voted for a government of national unity, and now that turned out to be a government of the progressive bourgeoisie. Dionisio Encina confirmed that the government of Alemán, whose candidacy had been supported by the PCM, was "a force for national unity," even though that unity should not be formed "around the government in a simple and straightforward way." The Alemán period should be classified, in the words of Encina, "as a government of the progressive bourgeoisie, not a government of national unity, even though the government as a representative of the progressive bourgeoisie was a force for national unity." For his part, Valentín Campa also accepted the progressive character of the Alemán regime. But he stressed the importance of its reactionary and antipopular elements and attacked the theory that justified the changes to Article 27 of the Constitution (about the protection of agrarian smallholding) on the assumption that those changes would promote the emergence of "progressive capitalist landowners."[5]

Lombardo was right on one point: his idea that "the composition of the government, considered as a whole, is nothing more than a projection of the correlation of forces that exist outside." But he was utterly wrong in his judgment of that correlation of forces. He usually assessed that projection in an extremely mechanical way that primarily offered post facto theoretical justification for whatever alliances he had reached—in this case with the "cub of the Revolution."

The Progressive Bourgeoisie

These days the Left's support for the government of Miguel Alemán seems bizarre, and the debates about its progressive dimensions seem ridiculous.[6] But we should realize that these false judgments about the first administrations after Cárdenas played a role in sinking the Left into a marginality that lasted more

5. Ibid., 181, 223, 226, 106.
6. This administration marked the beginning of a long period of persecution for the party and a turn to aggressively pro-business strategies for the nation. See Carr, *Marxism and Communism*. [Trans.]

than twenty years. For that reason, it is important for us to go a little deeper into the theoretical roots nourishing those false judgments, since such vices might very well still survive today.

Around the roundtable at the Fine Arts Palace, everyone agreed that Mexico had to industrialize. Everyone also thought that industrialization could take place only within the framework of capitalist development, since the country was not ready yet—they thought—for the transition to socialism. This was a case of an obviously mechanical application of certain classical Marxist tenets that should themselves be opened to question, namely, the naturalist conception of historical progress based on a unilinear economic determinism.

In the face of this situation of "immature" capitalist economic development, Valentín Campa and Hernán Laborde proposed an alternative of struggle directly inspired by Leninist principles, according to which state capitalism is precisely the waiting room for socialism. Campa argued that what he called "bourgeois-democratic industrialization" should be encouraged, adding that given a choice between alternative forms, "only by following the line of state capitalism can we seriously speak of industrialization." This idea was rejected with great verbal violence by José Revueltas, who at that point was more Lombardo than Lombardo. Revueltas accused Campa of being the "authorized advocate of sectarian opportunism and of left-deviationism." Revueltas's argument was very confused, and he limited himself to supposing that the goal of state capitalism ignored the existence of other social classes in Mexico (in fact, he wanted to defend the status of the so-called progressive bourgeoisie).[7]

Hernán Laborde set out most clearly the alternatives in this debate over the nation, as the various options for development within a capitalist context have later been called:

> Are we opposed to capitalist development? No. We are not opposed to that development, but there are two possible paths to capitalist development in our country, in the present situation, there are two possible paths of bourgeois-democratic development: one which strengthens financial capital, especially imperialist financial capital . . . basing itself . . . on commercial capital, part of industrial capital, and landowners. . . . Following that path for developing the economic system of our country, the national bourgeoisie will inevitably intensify the oppression and misery of our people. The other possible path to capitalist development is the one which progressively suppresses the rule of foreign capital nationalizing the key

7. *Mesa redonda*, 108–9, 374.

sectors of the economy, which weakens the influence of native financial capital as well, by means of the intervention of the state in the economy and the progressive, although partial, introduction of state capitalism, not suddenly, not from one day to the next, but in a progressive way, according to the country's circumstances and the international situation. This is also the path which nationalizes the banks and reforms finances and the credit system in a democratic direction.[8]

This was the position of those who, according to the followers of Lombardo, were suffering from leftist deviationism. For his part, Laborde classified José Revueltas as a "neo-Menshevik."

Lombardo answered the proposals of Campa and Laborde in his final intervention. Based on a rather dubious reading of a text by Engels, Lombardo held that nationalizations are only progressive—and inevitable—when the overly fast growth of the means of production or communication outstrips the control of private corporations, when there is an incompatibility between the modern development of the means of production and the capitalist form of property. Lombardo asked:

> Can we say that capitalist development in our country allows us to claim that private enterprises, and not just a few, but those which make up the industrial economy of the country, that they have reached such a level of development that they overwhelm all possibilities of what might be called "normal" capitalist growth?[9]

Lombardo gave a clear answer: no. Then he offered a statement that is a veritable model of political blindness. Lombardo said mockingly:

> As for state capitalism, our comrades [Campa and Laborde] argue that we should move in that direction, and that we should go little by little. From a purely verbal standpoint, the problem seems easy; from the standpoint of political possibilities the problem is very different. Say tomorrow we nationalize all the stocks that belong to Yankee businesses. Sure, nothing happens in the actual historical situation we are living in. The next day, we expropriate the electrical businesses, the ones belonging to the Yankee trust and the British trust. Sure, nothing happens. A little while later, we expropriate the telephone company. Nothing happens then either. Little by little

8. Ibid., 400.
9. Ibid., 589.

we're moving towards state capitalism, gradually. I think that proclaiming this course as a systematic way to industrialize the country is simply day-dreaming.[10]

What is especially curious is that over the following decades, the Mexican state carried out, by and large, precisely the policy that Lombardo condemned as imaginary. Nationalization and the broadening reach of state capitalism have in fact been a powerful lever for advancing industrialization and controlling economic crises. In reality, Lombardo was just defending his alliance with Miguel Alemán, who represented—according to Lombardo—a progressive bourgeoisie that had to be protected against every possible nationalization. In reality, Campa and Laborde were far more coherent with Lombardo's model of national unity than Lombardo himself.

But Campa and Laborde failed to understand two things. First, the path of state capitalism is not necessarily anti-imperialist in character; on the contrary, it is just another modality of modern integration into the global capitalist system. Second, this "bourgeois-democratic" path of state capitalism develops despotic and authoritarian tendencies that are undoubtedly bourgeois, but hardly democratic. These two facts, whose meaning and importance were forcefully revealed after the Second World War, allow us to consider the original Leninist tenets from another viewpoint. Understandably, this also has a direct relationship with the idea of socialism we have been developing in recent years, especially after 1968. Lenin wrote in September 1917 that "monopoly state capitalism is the complete material preparation for socialism, the waiting room for socialism, a step on the stairway of history with *no intermediary steps between it and the step called socialism.*"[11]

In fact, in the same text, Lenin offers a conception of socialism that is a direct consequence of this definition: if socialism is the next step after monopoly state capitalism, then in reality "socialism is merely state-capitalist monopoly *which is made to serve the interests of the whole people.*"[12]

Lenin's reasoning is the following: once the growth of monopoly produces that top-heaviness of the state, it is the state that determines the character of society. If the state is in the hands of the people, then we have a step toward socialism under the form of revolutionary democracy. If the state is in the hands of the

10. Ibid.

11. Vladimir Ilyich Lenin, "The Impending Catastrophe and How to Combat It," in *Complete Works* (Moscow: Progress Publishers, 1964), 25:358. Italics mine.

12. Ibid.

capitalists, then we have an imperialist republic, that is, a reactionary bureaucratic state. I think recent history has demonstrated the falsity of these ideas: just switching the general staff who occupy the state apparatus is not enough to overturn the socioeconomic structure of imperialist republics—as is clear from socialist experiences in Greece, Portugal, France, or Spain.

On the other hand, in the countries that have developed a kind of economy some Marxists dub "monopoly state capitalism," state and business structures have grown that could only with great difficulty be compatible with our ideal of democratic socialism. On the contrary, gigantic monopolies are one of the most powerful factors in the appearance of new repressive and authoritarian tendencies, and one of the most solid foundations for building a split and segmented society according to discriminatory and elitist patterns. So only in a narrow economic sense could one sustain Lenin's thesis that "if a huge capitalist undertaking becomes a monopoly, it means that it serves the whole nation."[13]

The Proletariat in Diapers

The Marxists at the 1947 roundtable did not manage to escape the theoretical trap implied by the assumption that the interests of the working class should be identified with the demands for building the step on the staircase of history thought to immediately precede socialism. Both the lombardists and the Communists argued vehemently about what character the step that joined the underdeveloped present to the socialist future should have. Everyone was sure that once the intermediate stage was reached, socialism would be the inevitable next step or, at least, would be within arm's reach. Nonetheless historical experience has demonstrated, in my judgment, that socialism was an option closer to the Mexican society in the thirties than in the following decades. Before 1940, socialism made up an important part of Mexican political life and, for all its deformations and naïveté, was a visible option. On the other hand, industrialization and the expansion of capital into the countryside managed to drive socialism off the political horizon and out of daily political practice for three decades. This was undoubtedly helped along by Marxists' difficulties in accepting that conjunctures favorable to socialism ("revolutionary moments," as they were called) were not tied to any specific phase of capitalist development but shaped by the complex confluence of a great diversity of factors of all kinds, ranging from psychological and political to economic and social.

13. Ibid.

Hernán Laborde, who noted this problem, did not completely shackle the destiny of the working class to the teleology of a history inevitably linked in phases. That is why he passionately attacked those who believed that the Mexican proletariat was still powerless to lead the revolutionary process, because it was small, weak, and semirural, in short because it was—as Laborde put it—an "underage" proletariat, a poor "nursing baby" that had to be carried around and nursed for a few years more by the forces for national unity. His criticisms were formally aimed at Carrillo, Revueltas, and Torres, but their obvious target was Lombardo, even though Lombardo had pointed out that the proletariat should lead the bourgeois-democratic revolution (without, however, clarifying when or how). The debate was all the more difficult because then as now, lombardists disguised themselves in the garb of orthodoxy and radicalism. At that time it could already be guessed that ten years after the conflictual Sixth Congress of the CTM, the Marxists—lombardists and Communists alike—were being pushed to the fringes of the labor movement. That marginalization was a product of Lombardo's practice of treating the working class like a "nursing baby" firmly grasping the governmental teat and also of the Communists' sectarianism, as Campa and Laborde recognized.

Lombardo's actions were based on two ideas: (1) that the demands of national unity indicated the need to create a great revolutionary front under the auspices of a broad popular party, not defined by its Marxist, leftist, or worker character, and (2) that this party would take the place of the Party of the Mexican Revolution (PRM), which, according to Lombardo, had expired, and whose place could not be taken by the PRI, which was only a belated effort to revive the PRM for the limited electoral purpose of closing off the path of an agent of foreign imperialism (with this he was referring, I suppose, to Ezequiel Padilla).[14]

These ideas guided Lombardo's gradual abandonment of his struggles with labor to turn to constituting the imaginary popular front that ended up as a sad marginal party symbolically facing down the all-powerful PRI, which Lombardo had declared nonexistent. He had underestimated the political potential of the organized working class. That potential was channeled toward the state, and since then it has not ceased to grow, even within the government's limits. From there it has contributed to the expansion of state capitalism, which has been of little help in incubating a socialist alternative. On the contrary, the official labor movement has promoted the consolidation of the most authoritarian and corrupt features of the Mexican political system.

14. Padilla was an opposition candidate in 1946. [Trans.]

The proposal of building a great revolutionary front was shared by all. This was the idea of alliances as a series of concentric circles spreading out from the vanguard of the workers, thought of as the only class that can build socialism and wants to. This idea tacitly recognized that the "true" partisans of socialism were a minority who had to use various tactical arts to form broad popular, nationalist, and anti-imperialist fronts made up of allied social sectors who at the moment of socialist construction would have to be subjected to the dictatorship of the proletariat. Based on these tenets, the Left accepted that it was impossible for most of the people to acquire a socialist consciousness before taking power, and that it was only by using the state as a mass educating instrument that a socialist majority could be achieved. Hence the idea of seizing the state first, and later becoming the majority. Lombardo Toledano introduced a modification into this scheme: he aimed to use the educating power of the revolutionary Mexican state before the change to socialism, but to do so he counted on nothing more than the strength of his speeches and the given word of President Miguel Alemán. Failure was inevitable.

In the face of this old idea of class alliances as concentric circles, today a process of expanding the revolutionary subject is taking place, in practice and in theory. The notion of the Left reflects this idea of a growing political space that extends itself as a movement for generating a new *majority* hegemony. The socialist state will not be the authoritarian educator of a society largely resistant to socialism. In reality, it is the state that must be educated by society. The expansion of a leftist space refers to an objective social process that is placing the nonworker masses in conditions of becoming conscious revolutionary subjects, not just second- or third-class allies. This space of the Left should have one or, better yet, several mass parties set up as electoral and political organizations capable of drawing together the majority into a revolutionary social process. That is to say, aimed *directly* for building socialism. Obviously this is not simply a question of winning some elections, a matter that—as we all know—is not at all simple. But the task is more complex still, since electoral power needs to be reinforced in such a way as to allow socialist beliefs to reproduce by democratic means with the same naturalness with which we breathe the air that surrounds us.

Suffering Souls

Any concern for basing the development of parties and fronts on a representative political democracy was totally alien to the participants in the Fine Arts Palace roundtable, even though all of them accepted as a necessity the coming of a regime they called "bourgeois-democratic." Nonetheless they completely accepted the idea that the Left should support and promote reforms to the system. For the forties Marxists, democracy as an idea was limited to a series of social and economic reforms. The idea of establishing mechanisms for representing the people as a set of citizens had been replaced by the idea of representing them as social classes.

Reforms were understood by the lombardists as an inevitable and providential historical course carrying the proletariat toward an unquestioned shining future, and by the Communists as tactical advances to achieve the final phase of capitalism, the sure trampoline for taking the revolutionary leap into the waters of socialism. What mattered was therefore the (teleological) "historic significance" of the reforms. Neither group clearly understood that socialists should support a reform not only because it was linked to a "phase" or "step" but primarily because it benefited the working class and the people in an objective and immediate way. Reforms should be proposed and struggled for to the degree that they form part of socialism, that is, that they contribute to the well-being of the majority. They are reforms because their implementation does not openly and violently contradict the reproduction of the ruling system, not because they are inscribed in a capitalist model or a project for transition. They are reforms because they are directly inscribed in a socialist dynamic, not as something transitional or traditional but as something that should be part of a socialist society. The independence and autonomy of parties, unions, and social organizations with respect to the state will be indispensable to the socialist society we want. Self-management and decentralization will be required by the socialist nation of tomorrow. Peace, not permanent war, will be part of a socialism free of international power blocs. That is why we must struggle starting today to bring peace, liberty, and democracy to humanity, independence and autonomy to political movements, self-management and decentralization to society. That is what it means, to my mind, to be a "reformist" today. It means making revolution every single day, turning it into an everyday event.

I have insisted on underscoring the enormous differences that separate us from the roundtable Marxists of 1947, and I have simultaneously suggested how close their debates seem. Close and distant at the same time, Marxism now seems in perspective to have stood at a watershed in its history in the forties. It still enjoyed the great vitality the popular movement had given it in the previous decade, but found itself already on the downward slope toward a long internal exile. The roundtable at the Fine Arts Palace briefly shook up, with its fresh gust of unity, a sleepy Left already entering into a period of hibernation. Yet the sleep of the Mexican Left was not peaceful at all: not only did it suffer the harshness of repression, corruption, underdevelopment, and the one-party state, but its own nightmares were full of curses, sectarianism, dogmatism, expulsions, and divisions. More than twenty years would have to pass before the various currents of the Left began a fruitful process of convergence and unity. Today the important organizations of the Left are enjoying and suffering such convergences: the days in which those parties showed off their monolithic purity have ended. Those groups and activists whose hearts do not bear the traces of the three great currents of the Left—leftism, reformism, and communism—are those who are always ready to toss the first stone at their comrades. But most of us accept our "impurity" and recognize that we are influenced by all these currents. The three currents were present at the Fine Arts Palace roundtable in 1947. From those experiences and later debates, we can conclude that a New Left will emerge strongly only if it recognizes itself as a fruit of the confluence and diversity of different currents, although it must, at the same time, point out the obstacles and contradictions that each current brings along with it.

I would like to offer three brief examples of this. Leftism, whose origins are to be found beyond any doubt in anarchism, took on a populist naïveté and a youthful freshness that allowed it to have a certain sensitivity toward new social movements. But the long periods of immersion in the hard Marxism of the Stalinist period, and later in Maoist sectarianism or Trotskyite doctrinairism, covered leftist spontaneity over with a dogmatic Marxist shell. So leftism, which gained new strength in 1968, lives a contradictory life: by day it wears a rigid Marxist-Leninist corset, but by night it strips naked and goes out drinking with the marginals and the heterodox.

Of reformism, on the other hand, we know that it is as old as the Mexican Revolution, in whose ashes it still finds heat and hope. Mexican reformism has always revolved around the state, and its most developed classical form was lombardism. It has nurtured a certain sensibility for detecting changes in the correlation of political forces that change the balance of state power, and a denunciatory capacity for discovering conspiracies against the nation. But it also put on a dogmatic straitjacket, in this case Soviet-made Marxist-Leninism. The contradictory result has been something like a social democratic party that supports the dictatorship of the proletariat. That is, in contrast to what happened in Europe, Mexican social democratic tendencies are rather resistant to representative political democracy.

For its part, the communist current is also living through singular contradictions, the most obvious of which is perhaps the opposition between its Stalinist past and the democratic tendency that rejects actually existing socialism as a model. We must say that the new elements of the democratic tendency come largely from reformism and leftism. The communist tradition is entering into a new phase based on nothing more than the confirmation of the importance of democratic reforms and the spirit that animated the struggles of 1968 all over the world.

These various currents can flow together in two ways: the first is through evoking their respective doctrinary traditions, whether those are of recent or ancient origin. There is room there for agreement, since there will always be some formula of Marx or Lenin that can be shared. In this way, taking a mortal leap over decades of confrontations and discrepancies, the past can unify us. But the past unifies us only symbolically.

The second way in which the currents of the Left can draw together consists in taking the opposite path, of unity through difference: accepting the insufficient character and historical incongruencies of each current, and accepting as well the need for joint work and for polemics, within a context of diversity.

The first way of coming together will not lead us to anything more than restoring old patterns of leftist behavior, patterns that have already proved themselves sterile. That restoration would be a return to the 1947 roundtable, to try to find the ghosts and bêtes noires we have each dreamed wandering the hallways of the Fine Arts Palace. In those hallways, during this imaginary but not impossible restoration, we would run into the ghost of the tolerant and sharp revisionism of Laborde, and the radical specter of Lombardo, hand in hand with the renewing spirit of Revueltas, master of the political zigzag. We would also come across the nationalist and pragmatic soul of Bassols and the frightening apparition of the dogmatism of Encina.

We could go on invoking the suffering souls of a restored Marxism. But that would mean exalting all that was lifeless in the Marxists who met years ago at the Fine Arts Palace. Those who need ghosts, let them choose theirs; let them retell their true account and bring back the inquisitors. I prefer to speak of what those souls made flower, to debate their living ideas, to end here before more ghosts appear and to dedicate these reflections, as a tribute, to one of the participants in that 1947 roundtable, Valentín Campa, who managed to change so much and at the same time keep a socialist hope alive.

Great Changes, Modest Proposals

We are living a paradox. If we consider the spectacular changes that have occurred across the world since 1989, the part of the planet we inhabit —the north of the American continent—seems, by contrast, to be one of the most quiet, stable, and boring regions of the earth. Here ideologies have hardly been knocked down; if anything, they've been built up. The actually existing socialism we have next door (Cuba) lives on in its most orthodox and dictatorial form. And when we use the prefix "neo" to speak of Washington's liberalism, it is more out of courtesy than as a reflection of any truly new move. United States policy has not undergone any great change: the bloody war against Iraq, the foolish blockade of Cuba, and the public airing of the sexual problems of elected officials continue in the finest Cold War tradition. As far as Mexico goes, we can't say that history has come to a sudden end here, either. Better stated, history seems hardly to have begun walking again since the gaze of the official Medusa turned it to a gallery of stone statues. Viewed from the standpoint of the great changes of our time, Mexico seems like a country frozen in the backwardness of its authoritarian political system, uncertainly struggling to keep afloat an impoverished and inefficient economy. What are NAFTA and the technocratic makeovers of the Constitution but melancholy and harmless scratchings at the face of the Saturn that is devouring us in an era that has radically changed the direction of history?

But what do I mean when I speak of the "great changes" of our time? I mean

This essay was prepared for a "Winter Colloquium" on the theme of the "Great Changes of Our Time" held by the National Autonomous University of Mexico (UNAM) and the National Council for Culture and the Arts (CNCA) in February 1992.

the collapse of the socialist experiment, and the resulting end of the Cold War and its blocs. We must ask: Why did these changes happen? What forces toppled socialism, ate away that immense military-bureaucratic complex that never ceased, ironically, to proclaim the imminent end of capitalism? Much remains to be researched and thought through, but we do know one thing: actually existing socialism was not brought down by Pentagon hawks, neoliberals, the CIA, NATO, or the Rambos and Kremlinologists of the Cold War. Socialism collapsed for internal reasons. It collapsed thanks to, among other things, the critiques of those old moles dismissively called "revisionists," "renegades," "reformists," "neometaphysicists," "Eurocommunists," "crypto-reactionaries," "postmodernists," and "critically minded imperial spokesmen" who fought for democracy against the form of tragically existing exploitation that actually existing socialism turned out to be. With their hopes and weaknesses, those critical groups crystallized around a tragic political figure who succumbed to the very contradictions he had helped to bring to the surface: Mikhail Gorbachev. By surprise and against all predictions, the Communist regime was able to change—from within and from above—and to spark the democratic transformation of the former Soviet Union and the Eastern European countries shaken by their own velvet revolutions. This is not the end of the democratic Left; this is a liberation from Leninist and Stalinist chains.

From this standpoint, I cannot share the attitude of those who, with the Berlin Wall fallen, are now raising a new wailing wall around the Third World. I am convinced we must give up the endless fundamentalist jeremiads that mourn inconsolably over the arrival of all kinds of plagues that, in any case, a wailing wall will not hold back. The collapse of the Second World has not left the Third in worse shape than before. And it has confronted us with a naked reality. Now we have no choice but to accept that the Third World, in theory and in practice, was a space bipolarity created to dispose of the refuse of decolonization and the Cold War and to hide the failures of modernization. Socialism had to fall for those of us in countries like Mexico to realize that we had always been part of the First World, and we should look there for alternatives.

But in our region of the world, we are still living immersed in the old days. The Left continues to defend Castro's dictatorship, and the Right puts its hopes in the market and the world of money, as if nothing had changed. It is important that the Left break with actually existing socialism and demand free elections and an end to the dictatorship in Cuba.

A large part of the liberal Right—especially in the United States—supports in Mexico what it refuses to tolerate in Cuba: the dictatorship of a governing party that does not base its exercise of power on free and clean elections. In this case the scenario is similar to various Far Eastern countries, including China: the United States accepts authoritarianism as long as the regime encourages an economic transition toward modernity. In Latin America we know this old formula all too well.

The Mexican government rules the country according to old premises. The solutions for the ills of Mexico—misery, inefficiency, despotism, corruption—are not to be found exclusively, or even primarily, in economic policy. This is one of the lessons we can take from the great commotions the planet is living through. The capitalist world is heterogeneous and offers many different alternatives and possibilities for reform. We can now understand that the most solid basis for so-called development is not found solely in the economy. It is found, above all, in a culture able to appropriately shape civil society to perform efficiently and creatively at work and at play, under conditions that ensure a minimum of social welfare and high levels of justice and equality. I have said it many times and never tire of repeating it: Mexico faces an intricate problem of civilization, not just a problem of development. In other words, our country is living through a deep cultural malaise, not simply an economic crisis.

The nationalist and revolutionary culture that has dominated Mexico for decades established solid networks of legitimation that ensured the continuity of the Mexican political system. Those cultural networks not only excluded democratic forms but also encouraged the worship of a melancholy Mexicanness that became the natural complement of official corruption and the what-the-hell shortsightedness of workers and businessmen. To put it bluntly: a society cannot escape backwardness if its hegemonic culture revolves around the prideful stupidity of María Félix and the labyrinthine submission of Cantinflas. When re-created and amplified by the para-governmental mass media, these and other stereotypes of national identity undoubtedly produced wide-ranging legitimacy effects for the system. But these were perverse effects that extended the life of an outdated system whose dying days, if they last too long, could poison an entire society. One need not look far to find such perverse effects within refined intellectual culture itself.

The Mexican government is smaller than the country, and not only because it did not receive enough votes in 1988 to obtain democratic legitimacy. The government is smaller than the country because its narrow technocratic and economistic vision allows it to see problems only in terms of money and markets. But it cannot appreciate that in this new culture, in this new civility, democracy can no longer be disconnected from legitimacy. What we need now is a democratic legitimacy that bars public powers from looking to win from the co-optation and manipulation of peasants, unions, and intellectuals the legitimacy they did not win at the polls.

The foundation of a democratic civility could mean a great change for our country. Who will drive this change, and how will it happen? One or two decades ago, the answer would have been obvious: the so-called new social movements would drive the great transformation from below, with the support of nationalist and populist social programs. Today we can no longer say the same thing: recent experiences show that we have entered a time in which the sparks for change are often to be found in the most unexpected reaches of the political apparatus itself, in the very state institutions that were originally designed to maintain the status quo. Transformations of the state are not simply a product of neoliberal policies; they are the fruit of critical tensions that, as happened in the period leading up to the 1988 elections, can bring surprises (and, of course, awaken social movements or create new parties). The very smallness of the Mexican government could be the source of great changes.

Unfortunately, a great part of the Left is still looking backward, searching for change at ground level, down below, where traditional doctrine placed the people. But in reality, our civil society has risen up and is ready to take off. The government itself traces out low-flying solutions with its programs for co-opting solidarity and application of predictable economic policies. The crisis of socialism and social democratic and populist alternatives does not leave us much room for choice from the standpoint of economic development, if we think of it in narrow terms. But if we can have a global cultural vision, if we can think about the crisis not as a problem of markets and investments but as a deep condition of Western civilization, then I think that we can glimpse many alternatives and great variations in tone behind the neoliberalism that, at times, seems to be the only option left standing.

Now, to conclude, I offer a modest proposal, in the words of Swift, who besides traveling with Gulliver also did politics. This proposal is not an original idea; I have plagiarized it shamelessly. If I am right in my idea that the cracks of our state pyramid are concealing people and forces who could unleash the "great changes" we have not yet seen, I would like to try my luck: maybe they are listening or reading right now. To be able to dream of "great changes" at all, I would like to suggest a minuscule adjustment to our political system: firmly remove the government from the electoral process. What I mean is: bar the government from spending vast sums, from using the mass media, and from organizing its employees on behalf of the governing party, and let the orchestration of elections—and, above all, the counting of votes—be done by an independent institution watched over by all political parties. Of course, this simple reform would require a devilishly complicated agreement between all political forces, an agreement with a high civic, and civilizing, content.

But if my modest proposal seems excessive and impractical, I ask you to forgive me and take up instead the one Swift made more than 250 years ago: let the rich eat the children of the poor.

POSTSCRIPT

The Dictatorship Was Not Perfect

Around noon on Sunday, 2 July 2000, before I had headed out to vote, a rumor reached me of an internal poll from the PRI itself that put Vicente Fox ahead in voter choice. "This must be some government trick," I thought, "to spur a final effort out of its armies of vote chasers." A little while later, I was interviewed for a radio program, and I told them I hadn't decided yet whom I was voting for, that I was thinking it over, but that I would go to the polls before long. Journalist Miguel Ángel Granados Chapa was on the program, and he asked me, mystified, why I was waiting so long to decide. "It's a way of criticizing politicians who haven't done their job well," I told him. "It's an ironic punishment for the parties: a high percentage of undecided votes creates a healthy democratic uncertainty." We now know that most of the undecided voted against the PRI, and for change. Later on, I joined the poet Hugo Gutiérrez Vega, a leftist ex-PAN member, on a television program hosted by Mayté Noriega: by that time we knew the PRI had lost the elections, and we celebrated it enthusiastically.

At the Moment

For many years now, the authoritarian system had ceased to function adequately. Political crisis began eating away at the government in 1988, but by 1994 authoritarian power found itself enormously weakened, deathly wounded. Even so, there had been so much talk of the extraordinary vitality of the institutionalized revolutionary regime, and so much stress on the force of the "perfect dictatorship"—in Mario Vargas Llosa's curious description—that we ended up bitterly skeptical. Many of us were convinced that the PRI would win the elections again—by a very narrow margin—and the transition would lead sooner or later to a new political crisis. I was afraid—and fortunately, I was wrong—that the democratic transition would have to come to an end owing to the fragmentation of a system that was no longer capable of governing. That seemed to be our tragic fate: to be governed by a completely outmoded, inefficient, and worthless system that, despite its abject perfection, would at some point break apart, dragging us into dangerous situations. We would have to wait until some faction of the leadership—like the post-Franquists in Spain or post-Communists in Russia—openly accepted the need to negotiate the transition.

But the dictatorship was not perfect, and it was brought down by surprisingly simple means: it was enough for citizens to express their vote peacefully, in clean and democratic elections. What was going on? Powerful forces within the government, supported by President Ernesto Zedillo, had neutralized a substantial portion of the official and extraofficial fraud machines. The growth of new democratic processes within the government was not evident, because they were hidden behind the drab and opaque mask of the supposed weakness of the executive branch. Few recognized the evidence: the weakness of the presidency strengthened democracy and generated a great unease among the most authoritarian traditional tendencies, the so-called dinosaurs. One of the representatives of the authoritarian restoration, Manuel Bartlett, came to this realization too late. He declared on 4 July: "The president has lost his leadership ability, he has ceased to be the moral leader of the PRI." In reality, the president had abandoned that "leadership ability" some time back, which led the PRI to its perdition. To avoid any dangerous meddling, the president was quick to recognize the victory of Vicente Fox before the PRI did.

The Mexican authoritarian system is collapsing in a surprising way. The extraordinary event has amazed many all over the world, who cannot escape their marvel at contemplating Mexico's easy and peaceful transition to democracy. In Mexico many analysts and intellectuals are stupefied, not knowing whether they should celebrate or deplore the electoral results. Not many sense that the twentieth century has just come to an end in Mexico, that we are already in another country, in an unknown territory full of unforeseen alternatives. Progressive intellectuals think they are seeing a strange victory of conservatives who would continue the *cristero* tradition and join up with the neoliberal Salinism inspired by Reagan and Thatcher under the leadership of an incongruous charlatan. One old PRI historian, Vicente Fuentes Díaz, protested angrily to President Zedillo: "Let's not forget that sixty years ago, General Cárdenas stopped the right wing headed up by Almazán from taking over the government." To be sure, the 1940 elections were the first successful instance of patriotic fraud in the name of the institutionalized revolution. Lázaro Cárdenas himself justified authoritarian power. When confronting Calles in 1935, he wrote in his notes that Mexican conservatives were opposed to "the social program of the revolution" and aimed for a democracy along the lines of capitalist states, "that is, freedom for their interests and impositions of their criteria."[1] General Cárdenas carefully applied this doctrine in 1940. Today many suffer the defeat of the PRI as if it were the victorious return of the ghost of Juan Andrew Almazán, who might have won the 1940 elections, even though he officially received only 15,000 votes (versus 2.5 million for Ávila Camacho). Perhaps PRD candidate Cuauhtémoc Cárdenas saw that ghost on the night of 2 July and therefore refused to congratulate Vicente Fox. He justified himself by saying that "what is happening is a disgrace for the country."

This is a disgrace because, supposedly, Mexican society has not only been subjected to marketing manipulations but also shifted toward conservatism. This is wrong. Vicente Fox, his party, and his alliance are a political expression of the Center Right, with strongly pragmatic and modern overtones. The mass of votes he has received reflects an even wider range of support, because it includes an enormous sector of the citizenry that in an act of simple common sense has chosen to end the "perfect dictatorship." The ingredients that are conservative, properly speaking, have been marginalized both by the overwhelming pragmatism of the "friends of Fox" and by a society sick of corruption and fraud. Even so, I fear that some of the hard-line, reactionary, and conservative sectors— present in the PAN, the Catholic Church, and business groups—might read events the same way as the hard-line Left or the retrograde PRI and take the victory of Vicente Fox as an invitation for conservatives to take over the state apparatus.

Whether the Fox administration manages to keep its shifting balance between the Center and the Right depends on many, and quite complicated, factors. Key among them are the critical processes both the PRI and the PRD are going through. Will the official party fall apart? Will the party of the Left split?

The economic and financial interests that traditionally allowed themselves to be represented by the PRI will predictably make an opportune turn to support the new government. Part of the technocracy will do the same. The PRI will be shored up by right-wing unions, the organizations of the most backward peasantry, the corrupt remains of a widespread reactionary bureacracy, and the restorationist groups driven by certain regional powers. There also remain, of course, the political leadership that headed the last months of the regime (directed by

1. Lázaro Cárdenas, *Obras*, 1:334.

President Zedillo) and the millions of heterogeneous voters who opted for continuity. It is not certain that under these conditions the PRI will manage to metamorphose into a modern party and escape the restorationist temptation that would lead it to suicide. The danger is that party members might fail to recycle the PRI and then, instead of depositing the remains of their party in the garbage can of history in a civilized way, leave its rotting corpse in the middle of society, causing alarming contamination and many provocations.

The PRD, whose foundation was closely linked to hopes of bringing down the authoritarian regime, is living through the democratic transition as if it were attending its own funeral. In a certain sense, this is true: the mixture of hard-line, sectarian, nationalist, and populist positions that governed those who guided the campaign of Cuahtémoc Cárdenas has failed completely. The PRD and its confusing allies unsuccessfully presented voters with a slightly leftist version of old revolutionary nationalism, the outdated culture that has inspired the official party for decades. But the official party, in its attempts at renewal, might invade the Center Left territory occupied by the PRD in order to recover its former domains. And then the worst could happen: an alliance between the PRI and the PRD, which would be more about restoration than opposition.

The option the Left has always had—the social democratic path—remains attractive, although a little worn-out. The PRD could give it a try, but it will not advance toward making a modern and dynamic party without abandoning its aspirations to swallow social movements—which often produce indigestion— and without ceasing its permanent internal agitation.

During recent years, the country has been governed by a Right wearing nationalist, revolutionary, carrancista, corrupt, and terrribly authoritarian clothing. Now we will be governed by a pragmatic and democratic Right full of many unknowns, which does not itself know what profile it will take on. The mystery will clear itself up as the rain of words gives way to actions. What alliances will Fox manage for his government of a "plural and inclusive transition"? Some fear he may make important concessions to the Far Right. Perhaps the Fox administration will slowly become a sweetened, light, clerical, and cleaned-up version of the technocratic PRI.

Without a doubt there will be many jolts, but little by little they will be accompanied by the typical postpartum depression of democracy. Equality, the great promise of democracy that we now have in view, close enough to see its charms but too far away to enjoy them, will not be reached, and we will discover that outside the authoritarian cage we are still bothered by the famous but strange democratic melancholy Tocqueville spoke of.

On Reflection

Let us try to imagine, just as Niklas Luhmann would have liked, whether the new and democratic Mexican political system will be able to function and reproduce itself without deriving its legitimacy from the society surrounding it, except though the functioning of its own electoral mechanisms, and whether it will be able to solidify its internal cohesion without invoking external normative structures. This would be a self-legitimated and autonomous system based on the government's rationality, formality, and capacity for generating the political conditions for well-being. Under such assumptions, the political system would no longer require mediations or, as a result, extrasystemic sources of legitimacy. In order to remain in the thermodynamic area of open systems, government activity would be structured so as to manage not only to rule over the surrounding social environment but also to reduce its complexity, even as the complexity of political action increased. Chaotic order—entropy—in society, and systemic order in government.

This is undoubtedly the dream of many technocrats and administrators, who would love to have enough freedom of action to try to launch political activity aloft on its own wings, on the basis of quality and rationality, without any need to resort to ideological structures or social mediations. Within this dream, if there were any lack of rationality or efficiency, the system itself would cure its own wounds with administrative measures.

This systemic utopia allows us to rapidly identify several key points. To begin with, governance must be based on a new culture replacing PRI revolutionary nationalism. There has been talk of a management culture whose symbolic structure should be able to articulate the identity of the political system. There is no doubt that, across the world, such a governmental culture has been built up by many different experiences and enriched by the transfer of habits and practices from the business world. I don't want to linger over technical details, but to pose the question: is management culture alone enough to give a democratic political system legitimacy? I don't think so, not even in the unlikely case that such a culture might bring economic well-being to broad segments of the most impoverished population. By itself, the economy does not produce legitimacy.

If management culture were hegemonic, then after the PRI loss, Mexican culture would no longer need any other external source of legitimacy. Efficiency alone would be sufficient to guarantee continuity. But it is obvious and known to all that this is not so. The mechanisms of governance in Mexico are far too inefficient and far too contaminated by corruption, paternalism, and corporatism to function solely according to the logic of a new management (and marketing) culture. Curiously enough, it was the left opposition (the PRD) who first began talk of how a group of politicians led by Vicente Fox had won the 2000 elections thanks to their skill in manipulating political advertising and tricking millions of voters. In this view, the new government would now attempt to translate its management proficiency into public administration.

This is a simplistic explanation that does not allow us to understand that the defeat of the PRI was part of a larger complex process of democratic transition. I would distinguish between short and long cycles of transition.[2] The short cycle began with the political crisis of 1988, extended to the great tensions of 1994, and ended with the elections of 2000. During this period, a political transition to a democratic system took place. But the deeper causes of this transition, which imply a great cultural crisis, are inscribed in a longer cycle begun in 1968 that has not yet come to a close. This longer cycle involves the crisis of nationalist political mediations and the slow growth of a new political culture. It is precisely in this long-term cycle where we can find signs of new means of legitimacy. Some indications can be seen in the changes and adjustments encouraged by the system in crisis itself. For example, when facing the crisis of nationalism, the PRI government opted to push forward the Free Trade Agreement and globalization, then later, facing credibility problems, promoted a political reform that established an autonomous and trustworthy electoral process. With these measures the PRI government accelerated its end, although its objective was the exact opposite: to lengthen its permanence in power. The Left opposition read these situations poorly: they found it necessary to return to original—Cardenista and even Zapatista—sources of revolutionary nationalism and developed a populist distrust of electoral democracy. The modernizing sector of the PRI also had an incorrect reading: they believed the technocratic sectors of the government, baptized in the new culture of management and efficiency, had gained enough legitimacy to win the 2000 elections. They were wrong, and their candidate lost.

That outcome should also be a warning sign to the new Fox officials: while their business abilities, their technocratic bent, and their managerial inspiration will undoubtedly be useful in the everyday tasks of administration, they will not be enough to guarantee a new legitimacy. The new democratic regime

2. I first expressed this idea in a debate with Jorge G. Castañeda (today the foreign minister of the Fox administration) and University of Chicago professor Claudio Lomnitz. The debate was organized by the magazine *Fractal* and published in 1999 as issue 12 under the strange title "The Transition, That Bald Metaphor."

will have to extend its roots into the same long-term processes that drove the authoritarian system to collapse. What we do not know is whether the government of Vicente Fox will be capable of promoting that deep process of change, or will be contented with a skillful and decorous administration that will, at best, stave off the bankruptcy of the country. The recent history of other Latin American countries—Argentina, Bolivia, Ecuador, Peru, Venezuela—tells us we are not safe from the dangers of a shipwreck. In that case, the angel of history would thank the Fox administration for having become an efficient funeral director entrusted with burying the authoritarian system, but would not view him as a great reformer who had opened the door to a new political civility and an advanced political culture. There are some unsettling signs that the Fox government could turn against the deep course of the transition, thereby contributing to slow down a cycle that is already slow enough on its own. In any case, I don't think it would be possible—or beneficial—to mix together the mechanisms that the Fox government can use to maintain and even expand popular support and the processes of promoting a new civil and democratic culture. But opposition between the government and the emergent new civil culture would be dramatic and disastrous.

Whatever the advertising resources of the new government, one hopes that the governing group understands that a reform of the Mexican state is necessary. Both so-called globalization and democratic electoral reform (and their consequences, NAFTA and the defeat of the PRI) have shown that Mexico is headed down a road leading toward decentralizing, federalizing, and parliamentarizing power. This process brings us face to face with a problem: current political trends have shattered all paradigms. The borders and axes that defined and classified state activity have been broken or bent out of shape.[3] One of the most spectacular manifestations of this is the fact that the functions of the three branches (executive, legislative, and judicial) have been greatly distorted and overwhelmed by the functions of a fourth branch that respects no borders: the legitimating power that guarantees governability.

State power is not legitimated solely by an efficient executive, a representative legislature, and a vigilant judicial system. It is principally legitimated by cultural, educational, moral, and informative processes that make up networks of communicating vessels that do not respect traditional borders: neither those

3. The final part of this essay summarizes the arguments and proposals I presented to the Commission for Study of State Reform, headed by Porfirio Muñoz Ledo, whose conclusions were apparently accepted by Vicente Fox in November 2000 when he was just about to assume the presidency.

dividing the three branches, nor those of a territorial nature (electoral, state, national, etc.), nor those separating hierarchical orders. These networks tend to establish new, different, and relatively autonomous forms of citizen power.

These networks are extraterritorial, metademocratic, transnational, global, and even postnational. At first glance, these cultural networks encompass an extremely heterogeneous group of things: mass media (press, radio, TV, Internet); schools and universities; ethnic, religious, and sexual groups; publishers and hospitals; nongovernmental organizations; churches, sects, and marginal groups with diverse aims—from paranormal activities to paramilitary actions, from vegetarian pacifists to dogmatic terrorists.

We are speaking of a new space of power shaped more by cultural and symbolic flows than by the exchange of material goods: a legitimate space, a generator of legitimacy, but one regulated barely and poorly, driven by an emerging economy based more on the production and circulation of ideas than that of objects, and more on software than on hardware.

Considering that within the current division of power, the decentralization, federalization, or parliamentization of the Mexican state leaves major national and general problems unresolved, it will become more and more necessary to constitutionally establish the existence of administrative areas with a high degree of autonomy outside the three branches of government, as well as outside municipal, state, and federal authorities. These autonomous administrative areas could be constituted as councils, commissions, or institutes entrusted with governing on a national scale spaces such as culture, higher education, indigenous autonomy, churches, the media, the electoral process, and even certain portions of tax collection. Forming these areas means bringing some parts of state power closer to civil society: in a certain way, this is a "statization" of civil society, but it is also a "civilization" of state administration.

However these reforms of state agencies take place, they will add up over time, in a course of change that will gradually insert Mexico into a global network of democratic countries with expanding economies. Evidently, I am making a connection between the regulated management of areas of autonomy, on the one hand, and, on the other, Mexico's deep insertion in so-called globalization, as the neocapitalist economy, propelled by a great technological revolution, expands on a global scale from North America and the European Union. I am perfectly aware that the insertion of backward countries with authoritarian legacies into this process is extremely difficult. But it is not impossible. The experience of countries like Spain, Greece, or Portugal can enlighten us to both the difficulties and advantages of this entry in neocapitalist globalism. If we add the experience of certain Asian countries, such as South Korea or Indonesia, to our reflections, our enthusiasm will undoubtedly be chilled. Even so, given the geographic coordinates defining Mexico, I do not see any better option at the moment. In addition, it seems to me that this is a predictable process inscribed into the longer cycle of transition I mentioned earlier. The problem for the most advanced sectors is exacting a high level of contributions, in money and in reforms, from the accumulation and circulation of wealth, in order to generalize well-being. But I won't dwell on that problem here.

The expansion of areas of autonomous and democratic administration tends to be connected to another phenomenon: the gradual emergence of a postnational condition. The erosion of nationalism and its crisis as a legitimating mechanism is not an invitation to promote a new nationalism as a replacement. Instead, it is a sign that we are beginning an era in which the resources of governability are not to be found in the ideological exaltation of national values. That this situation should alarm the democratic Left is understandable: to some degree we are witnessing the collapse of old progressive paradigms and the rise of renewed threats. But the Left has met these new processes with a conservative and narrow-minded attitude: it only sees the threats of privatization and dependency in global networks, failing to understand that other aspects of the process need to be promoted, such as the broadening of democratic autonomies and the struggle against corruption—of business, bureaucracy, or drug trafficking and organized crime.

The old Left still reacts conservatively to these changes, adopting so-called globalophobe attitudes instead of critically analyzing the process to determine what aspects could promote a general rise in everyone's living standards and quality of life. We are facing a complex and dramatic situation: we have confirmed that capitalist development does not necessarily lead to the material impoverishment of the population—as many believed, and some still do—but does, however, open up new spaces that contribute to the cultural and spiritual impoverishment of society.

This is a thorny and complicated problem. Cultural impoverishment is not, as we thought in the sixties, a worldwide lowering to a uniform standard, adapting the population to a single market in accordance with models produced by highly industrialized consumer societies. The largest threats do not come from the global circulation of merchandise, ideas, values, and cultural symbols, but from the other process that accompanies globalization as its shadow: the strengthening of local powers that in many cases restore parochial cultural traditions saturated with religious customs and ethnic fanaticisms, with the interests of corporatist bodies or small tyrants. I am not speaking merely of the regional powers that arise from decentralization or federalization but also of those forces taking advantage of the deregulation and autonomy of what I have been calling the fourth branch of government—the cultural branch, especially the mass media, education, and religious institutions—to promote not the globalizing symbols of neoliberalism and the world market, but instead a strange mixture of rancid conservative values with the clumsy aggressiveness of the nouveau riche. We are daily offered a cocktail of globalization and parochialism by many declarations of the church hierarchy as well as by numerous radio and TV programs. An extreme but revealing example is the culture of drug trafficking, a combination of parochial Catholicism with a cruel and reckless appetite for riches, of ranchera kitsch with transnational business. Another example occurs when certain parochial customs are transformed into legally sanctioned laws of municipalities or states. Doing this runs the risk of consecrating fundamentalist, sexist, discriminatory, religious, corporatist, or authoritarian forms of government. The example of Guanajuato last year was dramatic: when the uses and customs concerning the taboo against abortion, based on religious beliefs, were transformed into legal obligations by a small state, they created a spectacular nationwide confrontation. Local problems became national, and that is why the governor had to veto the legal principles the congressmen of Guanajato had voted for.

I have emphasized cultural problems not only because my anthropological vocation leads me to but also because I am convinced that the future of democracy in Mexico is closely tied to how political culture extends new legitimacies. I have also pointed out some reforms that could govern the new cultural processes. But in closing, I would like to face another question: what cultural processes will really take place in the coming years? Since I am not so optimistic as to believe that the new government will decisively push for a broad set of reforms, nor to believe that there are not powerful forces in Mexican society that will attempt to block changes even before they can be formally proposed, I find myself obliged to assume we will be facing a period of political turbulence. There may be surprises, but there are signs that turbulence itself will provide certain stabilizing elements that could strengthen the cohesion of democratic forces and increase the effectiveness of the democratic system. These are—symptomatically—elements from outside the system generated by the tensions placed on old structures and ancient ideologies and by the trend toward the savage accumulation of capital. These elements outside the system make up what could be called a fringe of hyperactive marginality, composed of segments of the rotting PRI, virtual guerrillas and real ones, organized crime and drug cartels, urban and suburban protest movements, and various paramilitary or terrorist groups. This isn't something we've never seen before. In reality, ever since 1994, with the Zapatista uprising and the spectacular political assassinations, Mexican society has been beginning to experience the typical processes of cohesion and contraction that give a certain legitimacy to government activity, if they don't overflow critical thresholds.

In my opinion, we can see some fragility in this peculiar spectacular dialectic between hyperactive marginality and the corresponding cohesion of the forces attempting to stabilize democratic norms around the new government. It is true that this process implies the legalization (or at least the legitimation) of a great range of political, ethnic, sexual, and religious groups—an enriching event. Yet it also enshrines customs associated with violence, corruption, and illegal forms of protest that should be prevented from expanding. These customs are like drugs: their use can create dependency, which only strengthens the forms for producing consensus out of fear rather than civic conviction. At the same time, this process blocks the consolidation of a democratic and republican system of modern political parties, and without this consolidation it is almost impossible to think of a new democratic legitimacy, whose plurality can open the doors to social imagination and political creativity.

Now, in the first year of the millennium, we are fully immersed in this process. The march of the EZLN was the first act of the grand political play. The spectacle continued in a second act, during which senators and congressmen debated the project of reforms of indigenous rights and culture, and approved amendments to the constitution. The legislators decided not to tie the exercise of autonomy by indigenous peoples to a specific territory, thereby avoiding the implementation of a Mexican variation on the Indian reservations of the United States. With this they avoided one of the more conservative dimensions of the San Andrés Accords, but they drew the ire of the EZLN.[4] The situation is unstable. The way that the process goes forward will give us a sign of the course that democracy will follow in Mexico. I have the hope that the next acts will dissipate both the temptations of provincialism and guerrilla war for the Left and the influence of business and parochial habits on the Fox administration, allowing political actors to look beyond the conservation of their own interests and the opportunistic use of momentary advantages. I hope that marginal and sectarian conspiracies will flow together into the great democratic convocation that so many citizens are committed to.

4. On this, see my essay "Derechos indígenas: imaginería política e imaginería legislativa," *Letras Libres*, 29 May 2001.

Glossary

axolotl. A mythical Mexican salamander that I jokingly use in my book *The Cage of Melancholy* as an emblem of national identity.

cabildo. A Spanish form of town government by a council of notables.

cacique. A leader or chieftain within a given community or region.

CANACINTRA. Cámara Nacional de Industrias de la Tranformación/National Chamber of Manufacturing Industries.

carranclan. A carrancista; specifically, the conservatives within the PRI.

caudillo. A strong leader on a regional or national level.

CCE. Consejo Coordenador Empresarial/Coordinating Council of Businessmen, a joint lobbying group incorporating representatives of major business associations.

Celestina. The main character of an early Spanish novel, who amused herself by arranging and meddling with the romantic affairs of others; more broadly, a romantic intermediary.

charrazo. The authoritarian legal coup by which a corrupt union boss is put in office.

charro. Literally, a Mexican cowboy; figuratively, a corrupt union boss.

CMHN. Consejo Mexicano de Hombres de Negocios/Mexican Businessmen's Council, an elite lobbying group with only thirty members.

cobanáhuacs. Leader of the Yaqui people.

COCOPA. Comisión de Concordia y Pacificación/Commission for Concord and Pacification, a nongovernmental organization, supported by the EZLN, which negotiated a peace agreement with the government that became the basis of new laws on indigenous rights considered by the Mexican Congress.

COPARMEX. Confederación Patronal de la República Mexicana/Employers' Confederation of the Mexican Republic, a broad-based business organization.

corregidor. A Spanish colonial magistrate.

cronopio. A mythical being invented by Julio Cortázar; roughly speaking, cronopios are intuitive, effusive, spontaneous, expansive, temperamental, and disorganized. See also *fama*.

dismothernity. A play on the disorder of modernity.

ejido. A parcel of land collectively held by a community; securing and developing ejidos have been a central concern and rhetorical claim of agrarian reform in Mexico, especially since the Cárdenas administration (1934–1940).

EZLN. Ejército Zapatista de Liberación Nacional/Zapatista Army of National Liberation, an indigenous guerrilla group based in Chiapas whose armed uprising began on 1 January 1994
and played a significant role in weakening the PRI, driving forward the democratic transition, and bringing indigenous concerns to the center of political debate.

fama. A mythical being invented by Julio Cortázar, characterized as rigorous, restrained,
prudent, scientific, dispassionate, and ordered. See also *cronopio*.

fiador. An indigenous politico-religious authority.

fotonovela. A kind of comic book illustrated by photographs rather than drawings that was
extremely popular in mid-century Mexico.

ladino. A Spanish speaker, especially a Spanish-speaking Indian or mestizo who serves as a
cultural or political broker between indigenous communities and the state.

licenciado. A university graduate; this title takes on great symbolic and honorific power in a
country still characterized by significant illiteracy and limited access to higher education.
The term also refers to the educated, cultured advisers of political strongmen.

malinchista. One who betrays the fatherland out of love for the foreign, as La Malinche,
Cortés's indigenous lover and interpreter, supposedly did.

maquiladora. An in-bond manufacturing plant, usually foreign-owned and generally located
near the northern border, where final assembly and other labor-intensive tasks are per-
formed. Notorious for terrible wages, working conditions, and environmental consequences.

matria. The "motherland" or local region to which many Mexicans are loyal, according to historian Luis González and a sector of the Right. This hometown loyalty is often contrasted
to loyalty to the patria—the fatherland or nation.

mestizaje. Generally, a process of racial, and by extension cultural, mixture; specifically, the
way this process has been seen as emblematic of the broader integrationist, assimilationist
cultural project of the Mexican state.

mestizo. Generally, a person of mixed race; specifically, an enduring metaphor of mixed,
impure, unstable Mexican identity.

Mexistroika. Carlos Fuentes's early term for reforms under the Salinas administration (1989–
1994).

neopanismo. The New Mexican Right, as reflected in the more pro-business orientation of the
PAN.

pachucos. A forties term for flashy, stylish, rebellious urban Mexican American men.

PAN. Partido Acción Nacional/National Action Party. The Catholic party that has long been
the "loyal" right-wing opposition to the PRI and won the presidency in 2000.

PCM. Partido Comunista Mexicano/Mexican Communist Party.

pelado. A migrant to the city, frequently represented as lost, rootless, hybrid, both disconnected
from national reality and cursed by indigenous heritage.

piarol. An indigenous politico-religious authority.

PRD. Partido de la Revolución Democrática/Democratic Revolutionary Party. The left-wing
opposition party founded by dissident elements of the PRI and much of the Mexican Left
after the disputed 1988 elections.

PRI. Partido Revolucionario Institucional/Institutional Revolutionary Party. Heir to the various parties that ruled after the revolution, and the ruling party of Mexico from its foundation in 1946 to its defeat in the 2000 elections.

PSUM. Partido Socialista Unificado de México/Unified Socialist Party of Mexico. The "plural" leftist party formed by the PCM and others in the eighties.

rezandero. An indigenous politico-religious authority.

sinarquismo. A radical clerical popular right-wing movement in rural Mexico between the late thirties and the mid-forties.

sinarquistas. Followers of sinarquismo.

telenovelas. Mexican soap operas.

Tlaihtoani. An indigenous leader.

Bibliography

Aguilar Camín, Héctor, and Lorenzo Meyer. *In the Shadow of the Mexican Revolution: Contemporary Mexican History, 1910–1989.* Trans. Luis Alberto Fierro. Austin: University of Texas Press, 1993.

Aguirre Beltrán, Gonzalo, and Ricardo Pozas A. "Instituciones indígenas en el México actual." In *Métodos y resultados de la política indigenista en México*, ed. Alfonso Caso. Mexico: Instituto Nacional Indigenista, 1954.

Almond, Gabriel, and Sidney Verba. *The Civic Culture.* Boston: Little, Brown, 1965.

——, eds. *The Civic Culture Revisited.* Boston: Little, Brown, 1980.

Appiah, Anthony. "The Multiculturalist Misunderstanding." *New York Review of Books* (October 1997).

Bartolomé, Miguel Angel. "El antropólogo y sus indios imaginarios." *Ojarasca* (October 1997).

Bartra, Roger. *Agrarian Structure and Political Power in Mexico.* Trans. Steven Ault. Baltimore: Johns Hopkins University Press, 1993.

——. *The Artificial Savage: Modern Myths of the Wild Man.* Trans. Christopher Follett. Ann Arbor: University of Michigan Press, 1997.

——. *The Cage of Melancholy: Identity and Metamorphosis in the Mexican Character.* Trans. Christopher J. Hall. New Brunswick: Rutgers University Press, 1992.

——. "Changes in Political Culture: The Crisis of Nationalism." In *Mexico's Alternative Political Futures*, ed. Wayne Cornelius, Judith Gentleman, and Peter H. Smith. San Diego: University of California Press, 1989.

——. *La democracia ausente.* Mexico: Oceano, 2000.

——. "Una discusión con Octavio Paz." *La Jornada Semanal* 71 (1990).

——. *The Imaginary Networks of Political Power.* Trans. Claire Joysmith. New Brunswick: Rutgers University Press, 1992.

——. "Kitsch tropical y elecciones." *La Jornada Semanal* 267 (July 1994).

——. "Mexican Heart of Darkness." In *El Corazón Sangrante = The Bleeding Heart*, ed. Elizabeth Sussman. Boston: Institute of Contemporary Art and University of Washington Press, 1991.

——. "La tentación fundamentalista y el síndrome de Jezabel." *Enfoque* (supplement to *Reforma*) (June 1996).

———. "Violencias indígenas." *La Jornada Semanal* 130 (1997).

———. *Wild Men in the Looking Glass: The Mythic Origins of European Otherness.* Trans. Carl T. Berrisford. Ann Arbor: University of Michigan Press, 1994.

Bell, Daniel. "Posdata a la nueva edición de *Las contradicciones culturales del capitalismo.*" *Vuelta* 181 (December 1991).

Boas, George, and Arthur O. Lovejoy. *A Documentary History of Primitivism and Related Ideas.* Baltimore: Johns Hopkins University Press, 1935.

Bobbio, Norberto. *Which Socialism? Marxism, Socialism, and Democracy.* Trans. Roger Griffin. Minneapolis: University of Minnesota Press, 1987.

Bobbio, Norberto, Nicola Matteucci, and Gianfranco Pasquino, eds. *Diccionario de política.* Mexico: Siglo Veintiuno, 1991.

Boone, Elizabeth Hill. *Stories in Red and Black: Pictorial Histories of the Aztecs and Mixtecs.* Austin: University of Texas Press, 2000.

Bruhn, Kathleen. *Taking on Goliath: The Emergence of a New Left Party and the Struggle for Democracy in Mexico.* University Park: Pennsylvania State University Press, 1997.

Camp, Roderic Ai. *Entrepreneurs and Politics in Twentieth-Century Mexico.* New York: Oxford University Press, 1989.

Cárdenas, Lázaro. *Obras, I: Apuntes 1913–1940.* Mexico: UNAM, 1972.

Carr, Barry. "The Fate of the Vanguard under a Revolutionary State: Marxism's Contribution to the Construction of the Great Arch." In *Everyday Forms of State Formation: Revolution and the Negotiation of Rule in Modern Mexico,* ed. Gilbert M. Joseph and Daniel Nugent. Durham: Duke University Press, 1994.

———. *Marxism and Communism in Twentieth-Century Mexico.* Lincoln: University of Nebraska Press, 1992.

Castañeda, Jorge G. *The Mexican Shock: Its Meaning for the United States.* New York: New Press, 1995.

———. *Perpetuating Power: How Mexican Presidents Were Chosen.* Trans. Padraic Arthur Smithies. New York: New Press, 2000.

Centeno, Miguel Angel. *Democracy within Reason: Technocratic Revolution in Mexico.* University Park: Pennsylvania State University Press, 1994.

Chaianov, Aleksandr Vasil'evich. *A. V. Chayanov on the Theory of Peasant Economy.* Ed. and trans. Basile Kerblay, Daniel Thorner, and Robert E. F. Smith. Madison: University of Wisconsin Press, 1986.

Clastres, Pierre. *Society against the State.* New York: Urizen Books, 1977.

Cornelius, Wayne, Ann Craig, and Jonathan Fox, eds. *Transforming State-Society Relations in Mexico: The National Solidarity Strategy.* San Diego: Center for U.S.-Mexican Studies, University of California–San Diego, 1994.

Cornelius, Wayne, Judith Gentleman, and Peter H. Smith, eds. *Mexico's Alternative Political Futures.* San Diego: Center for U.S.-Mexican Studies, University of California–San Diego, 1989.

Cortázar, Julio. *Cronopios and Famas.* Trans. Paul Blackburn. New York: Pantheon Books, 1969.

———. "El destino del nombre era . . . *1984.*" *Sábado* (*Unomásuno* supplement) 314 (November 1983).

Craig, Ann, and Wayne Cornelius. "Political Culture in Mexico: Continuities and Revisionist

Interpretations." In *The Civic Culture Revisited*, ed. Gabriel Almond and Verba Sidney. Boston: Little, Brown, 1980.

de la Fuente, Julio. *Relaciones interétnicas*. Mexico: Instituto Nacional Indigenista, 1965.

Dumézil, Georges. *The Destiny of the Warrior*. Chicago: University of Chicago Press, 1970.

Edelman, Gerald. *Bright Air, Brilliant Fire: On the Matter of the Mind*. New York: Basic Books, 1992.

Fabila, Alfonso. *Las tribus Yaquis de Sonora, su cultura y anhelada autodeterminación: Primer Congreso Indigenista Interamericano*. Mexico: Departamento de Asuntos Indígenas, 1940.

Franco, Jean. *Critical Passions: Selected Essays*. Durham: Duke University Press, 1999.

Fry, Roger. *Vision and Design*. London: Chatto and Windus, 1920.

Galeano, Eduardo. *Open Veins of Latin America: Five Centuries of the Pillage of a Continent*. Trans. Cedric Belfrage. New York: Monthly Review Press, 1973.

García de León, Antonio. "Chiapas, estado de ánimo." *Fractal* 8 (1998).

———. "Identidades." *La Jornada Semanal* 133 (September 1997).

Gibson, Charles. *The Aztecs under Spanish Rule: A History of the Indians of the Valley of Mexico, 1519–1810*. Stanford: Stanford University Press, 1964.

Gil, Carlos, ed. *Hope and Frustration: Interview with Leaders of Mexico's Political Opposition*. Wilmington, Del.: Scholarly Resources, 1992.

Gilly, Adolfo. *The Mexican Revolution*. Trans. Patrick Camiller. London: Verso, 1983.

Girard, René. *Violence and the Sacred*. Baltimore: Johns Hopkins University Press, 1977.

Gómez-Peña, Guillermo. *Warrior for Gringostroika: Essays, Performance Texts, and Poetry*. St. Paul, Minn.: Graywolf Press, 1993.

González Casanova, Pablo. *Estudio de la técnica social*. Mexico: UNAM, 1958.

———. *La nueva metafísica y el socialismo*. Mexico: Siglo XXI, 1982.

———. "La penetración metafísica en el marxismo europeo." *Sábado (Unomásuno* supplement) 270 (January 1983).

González, Luis. "Suave matria." *Nexos* 108 (1987): 51–59.

González y González, Luis. *San José de Gracia: Mexican Village in Transition*. Trans. John Upton. Austin: University of Texas Press, 1974.

Gorkin, Julián. *Caníbales políticos*. Mexico, 1941.

Habermas, Jürgen. *The Postnational Constellation: Political Essays*. Trans. and ed. Max Pensky. Cambridge: MIT Press, 2001.

———. *The Structural Transformation of the Public Sphere: An Inquiry into a Category of Bourgeois Society*. Trans. Thomas Burger. Cambridge: MIT Press, 1991.

Hamilton, Nora. *The Limits of State Autonomy: Post-revolutionary Mexico*. Princeton: Princeton University Press, 1982.

Hart, Armando. *Cambiar las reglas del juego: Entrevista de Luis Báez*. Havana: Editorial Letras Cubanas, 1983.

Harvey, Neil. *The Chiapas Rebellion: The Struggle for Land and Democracy*. Durham: Duke University Press, 1998.

Hernández Medina, Alberto, ed. *¿Cómo somos los Mexicanos?* Mexico: CREA, 1987.

Hernández Navarro, Luis. "¿Violencias indígenas o derechos pendientes?" *La Jornada* (September 1997).

———. "Zapatismo: La esperanza de lo incierto." *Fractal* 8 (1998).

Hirschman, Albert O. *Journeys toward Progress: Studies of Economic Policy-Making in Latin America*. New York: Greenwood Press, 1963.

Huntington, Samuel P. "The United States." In *The Crisis of Democracy: Report on the Governability of Democracies to the Trilateral Commission*, ed. Michel J. Crozier, Samuel P. Huntington, and Joji Watanuki. New York: New York University Press, 1975.

Jameson, Fredric. *Postmodernism, or, The Cultural Logic of Late Capitalism*. Durham: Duke University Press, 1991.

Joseph, Gilbert M., and Daniel Nugent, eds. *Everyday Forms of State Formation: Revolution and the Negotiation of Rule in Modern Mexico*. Durham: Duke University Press, 1994.

Keeley, Lawrence. *War before Civilization: The Myth of the Peaceful Savage*. Oxford: Oxford University Press, 1996.

Knight, Alan. "Cardenismo: Juggernaut or Jalopy?" *Journal of Latin American Studies* 26 (February 1994): 73–107.

———. *The Mexican Revolution*. Lincoln: University of Nebraska Press, 1986.

Kohn, Hans. *American Nationalism*. New York: Macmillan, 1957.

Kundera, Milan. *The Unbearable Lightness of Being*. Trans. Michael Henry Heim. New York: Harper and Row, 1984.

Kuper, Adam. *The Invention of Primitive Society: Transformations of an Illusion*. London: Routledge, 1988.

Lazarsfeld, Paul F. "Problems in Methodology." In *Sociology Today*, ed. R. K. Broom, L. Cottrell, and L. S. Merton. New York: Basic Books, 1959.

Le Bot, Yvon. "La autonomía según los Zapatistas." *Masiosare* (supplement to *La Jornada*) (March 1998).

Lenin, Vladimir Ilyich. "The Impending Catastrophe and How to Combat It." In *Complete Works*. Moscow: Progress Publishers, 1964.

———. "The Latest in Iskra Tactics, or Mock Elections as a New Incentive to an Uprising." In *Complete Works*. Moscow: Progress Publishers, 1964.

Lévinas, Emmanuel. *Entre Nous: On Thinking-of-the-Other*. Trans. Michael B. Harshav and Barbara Smith. New York: Columbia University Press, 1998.

Lipovetsky, Gilles. *L'ère du vide: Essais sur l'individualisme contemporain*. Paris: Gallimard, 1983.

Lombardo Toledano, Vicente. *Summa*. México: Universidad Obrera de México "Vicente Lombardo Toledano," 1975.

López, Luis Enrique. "Ruinas étnicas o nación inexistente." *El Angel* (supplement to *Reforma*) 240 (August 1998).

Lustig, Nora. *Mexico, the Remaking of an Economy*. 2d ed. Washington, D.C.: Brookings Institution, 1998.

Lyotard, Jean-François. *The Postmodern Condition*. Minneapolis: University of Minnesota Press, 1984.

Mabry, Donald. *Mexico's Accion Nacional: A Catholic Alternative to Revolution*. Syracuse, N.Y.: Syracuse University Press, 1973.

Medvedev, Roy. *Let History Judge: The Origins and Consequences of Stalinism*. Ed. and trans. George Shriver. New York: Columbia University Press, 1989.

Melville, Herman. *Moby-Dick, or The Whale*. New York: Penguin, 1992.

Mesa redonda de los marxistas mexicanos. Mexico: Centro de Estudios Vicente Lombardo Toledano, 1982.

Meyer, Michael C., and William H. Beezley, eds. *The Oxford History of Mexico.* New York: Oxford University Press, 2000.

Middlebrook, Kevin. *The Paradox of Revolution: Labor, the State, and Authoritarianism in Mexico.* Baltimore: Johns Hopkins University Press, 1995.

Milton, Robert. *Mexican Marxist: Vicente Lombardo Toledano.* Chapel Hill: University of North Carolina Press, 1966.

Miranda, José, and Silvio Zavala. "Instituciones indígenas en la colonia." In *Métodos y resultados de la política indigenista en México,* ed. Alfonso Caso. Mexico: Instituto Nacional Indigenista, 1954.

Monsiváis, Carlos. "1968–1978: Notas sobre cultura y sociedad en México." *Cuadernos Políticos* 17 (1978).

——. "Muerte y resurrección del nacionalismo mexicano." *Nexos* 109 (1987): 13–22.

Muñoz, Maurilio. *Mixteca Nahua-Tlapaneca.* Memoria del Instituto Nacional Indigenista 9. Mexico: Instituto Nacional Indigenista, 1963.

Nuncio, Abraham, ed. *La sucesión presidencial en 1988.* Mexico: Grijalbo, 1987.

Olalquiaga, Celeste. *The Artificial Kingdom: A Treasury of the Kitsch Experience.* New York: Pantheon, 1998.

——. *Megalopolis: Contemporary Cultural Sensibilities.* Minneapolis: University of Minnesota Press, 1992.

Osorio Marbán, Miguel. *El partido de la revolución mexicana.* Mexico: Impresora del Centro, 1970.

Paz, Octavio. *One Earth, Four or Five Worlds: Reflections on Contemporary History.* Trans. Helen R. Lane. San Diego: Harcourt Brace Jovanovich, 1985.

——. "The Will for Form." In *Mexico: Splendors of Thirty Centuries.* New York: Metropolitan Museum, 1990.

Ploncard d'Assac, Jacques. *Rousseau, Marx y Lenin.* Paris: Editorial Tradición, 1978.

Pullen, J. J. *Patriotism in America.* New York: American Heritage Press, 1973.

Ravicz, Roberto. *Organización social de los mixtecos.* Mexico: Instituto Nacional Indigenista, 1965.

Rawls, John. *A Theory of Justice.* Cambridge: Belknap Press, 1971.

Revueltas, José. *Ensayo sobre el proletariado sin cabeza.* Mexico: Logos, 1962.

——. *The Stone Knife.* New York: Reynal, 1947.

Ricoeur, Paul. "Structure et herméneutique." *Esprit,* no. 322 (1963): 596–628.

Rubinstein, Anne. "Mass Media and Popular Culture in the Postrevolutionary Era." In *The Oxford History of Mexico,* ed. Michael C. Meyer and William H. Beezley. New York: Oxford University Press, 2000.

Ruíz, Ramón Eduardo. *The Great Rebellion: Mexico, 1905–1924.* New York: W. W. Norton, 1980.

Salinas de Gortari, Carlos. *Political Participation, Public Investment, and Support for the System.* Research Report Series no. 35. La Jolla, Calif.: Center for U.S.-Mexican Studies, University of California–San Diego, 1982.

Schmucler, Héctor. "Carta a Julio Cortázar." *Sábado* (supplement to *Unomásuno*) (December 1983).

Sherman, John. *The Mexican Right: The End of Revolutionary Reform.* Westport, Conn.: Praeger, 1997.

Slick, Sam. *José Revueltas.* Boston: G. K. Hall, 1983.

Smith, Peter H. *Labyrinths of Power: Political Recruitment in Twentieth-Century Mexico.* Princeton: Princeton University Press, 1979.

——. *Mexico, Neighbor in Transition.* Headline Series no. 267. New York: Foreign Policy Association, 1984.

Smith, Robert Freeman. *The United States and Revolutionary Nationalism in Mexico, 1916–1932.* Chicago: University of Chicago Press, 1972.

Soria, Georges. *Guerra y revolución en España.* Barcelona: Grijalbo, 1978.

Steiner, George. *In Bluebeard's Castle.* New Haven: Yale University Press, 1971.

Stent, Gunther S. *The Coming of the Golden Age: A View of the End of Progress.* New York: American Museum of Natural History, 1969.

Subcomandante Marcos. *Our Word Is Our Weapon: Selected Writings.* Ed. Juana Ponce de León. New York: Seven Stories Press, 2001.

——. *Shadows of Tender Fury: The Letters and Communiqués of Subcomandante Marcos and the Zapatista Army of National Liberation.* Trans. Frank López, Leslie Bardacke, and the Watsonville Human Rights Committee. New York: Monthly Review Press, 1995.

Tannenbaum, Frank. *Mexico: The Struggle for Peace and Bread.* New York: Alfred A. Knopf, 1956.

Tello, Carlos, ed. *México 83: A mitad del túnel.* Mexico: Océano Nexos, 1983.

Turner, Frederick C. *The Dynamic of Mexican Nationalism.* Chapel Hill: University of North Carolina Press, 1968.

Van Alstyne, R. W. *Genesis of American Nationalism.* Waltham, Mass.: Blaisdell, 1970.

Verbisky, Eva. "Análisis comparativo de cinco comunidades de los altos de Chiapas." In *Los mayas del sur y sus relaciones con los Nahuas Meridionales: VIII mesa redonda de la Sociedad Mexicana de Antropología.* San Cristóbal de las Casas, Mexico: Sociedad Mexicana de Antropología, 1961.

Villiers de L'Isle-Adam, Auguste. *Cruel Tales.* New York: Oxford University Press, 1985.

Villoro, Luis. *En México, entre libros: Pensadores del siglo XX.* Mexico: Fondo de Cultura Económica, 1995.

von Sauer, Franz. *The Alienated "Loyal" Opposition: Mexico's Partido Acción Nacional.* Albuquerque: University of New Mexico Press, 1974.

Weyl, Hermann. "Symmetry." In *The World of Mathematics,* ed. James Roy Newman. New York: Simon and Schuster, 1956.

Williams, Adriana. *Covarrubias.* Ed. Doris Ober. Austin: University of Texas Press, 1994.

Womack, John, Jr., ed. and trans. *Rebellion in Chiapas: An Historical Reader.* New York: New Press, 1999.

Zamiatin, Evgenii Ivanovich. *We.* Trans. Clarence Brown. New York: Penguin Books, 1993.

Zolov, Eric. *Refried Elvis: The Rise of the Mexican Counterculture.* Berkeley: University of California Press, 1999.

Index

fraud, 118–23, 224–25; election of 1940, 70, 224–25; election of 1988, 173

Fuentes, Carlos, viii, 66–67, 157 n.2

fundamentalism, 22–43, 160–80, 185–89, 231–32. *See also* Left; nationalism, Mexican

García Márquez, Gabriel, viii, 157 n.2

gender, 61–64, 130, 133–36, 232. *See also* matriotism

González, Luis, 116–18, 123

González Casanova, Pablo, 139n, 142–43, 153–54, 162

Gorbachev, Mikhail, 172–73, 217

Gramsci, Antonio, 71–72, 127–28

Guadalupe, Virgin of: right-wing politics and, 92, 94, 96 n.12, 123, 131. *See also* Catholic Church; Partido Acción Nacional (PAN); Right

Guevara, Ernesto "Che," 147

Habermas, Jürgen, 63–64, 185

heart of darkness, 16–17, 20

hermeneutics, 51–58

Hernández Galicia, José (La Quina), 169

ideology: collapse of, 9, 62; nationalism as, 8, 19

Imaginery Networks of Political Power, The, 22, 24, 43

indigenous peoples, vii–ix, 5–8, 12, 15–43, 49–50, 96, 130, 134

Jaramillo, Rúben, 91, 142

Jezebel syndrome, 22, 24, 43

Jung, Carl, 57

labor movement, 68–69, 71–72, 75–76, 87–88, 109, 112, 129, 163, 168–70, 179

Laborde, Hernán, 207–12

Left, the: democracy and, ix, 21–26, 62, 77, 102–3, 107–11, 160–80, 186–90, 196–99, 209–10, 219, 225–28, 230; divisions within, 139–54, 160–80, 186–215; electoral results, 120; historical necessity of, ix, 180–90; internal repression and, 139–54; nationalism and, 62, 86–89, 160–80, 228; New, 141–42, 158–59, 201–2; political culture of, 139–

215; rise of fundamentalism within, viii, 21–22, 166, 228; statolatry and, 62, 71, 86–89, 126–27, 160–80, 194–97, 203–14; Zapatista uprising and, 21–26. *See also* Communism; Lombardo Toledano, Vicente; nationalism; Partido de la Revolución Democrática (PRD); Revueltas, José; socialism

legitimation: by bureaucracy, 6; by myth, 6, 44–58, 61–65, 104–7; postdemocratic forms of, 23, 29–38, 49–50, 227–28, 232–33. *See also* crisis; fraud; Jezebel syndrome; nationalism

Lenin, Vladimir Ilyich, 181–83, 186, 189, 205, 209–10, 217

Levinas, Emmanuel, 56

Lévi-Strauss, Claude, 53, 56 n.7, 57

liberalism: and the Right, 9, 92–95. *See also* modernity; technocracy

licenciado, 4, 133–36

Lombardo Toledano, Vicente, 191–202; biography of, 202 n.1; labor movement and, 71, 191–92, 199–200, 210–12; nationalism and, 196–98, 200; negation of political democracy, 197; Partido Popular and, 71, 211, 199–200; reaction to 1968 student movement, 192–93, 196; statolatry of, 81, 83, 196–97, 203–14; support for PRI, 71, 196–98, 199–202, 204–6, 210–12; theoretical production of, 192–98, 204–6, 210–12; and vanguard party, 194–96. *See also* Left; nationalism, Mexican; Partido Revolucionario Institucional (PRI)

López Portillo, José, 79–89

Malinche, 61–64, 134

Mao Tse-tung, 145–46, 214

Marcos, Subcomandate, 17, 19, 38

Mariátegui, José Carlos, 68

Marx, Karl, 16, 47, 66, 68

Marxist Roundtable of 1947, 203–15

matriotism: conservative variant of patriotism, 115–19

mestizaje, 11–12, 23, 49, 129; "Cosmic Race," 134. *See also* dualism; indigenous peoples; Orientalism; primitivism

Mexican Businessmen's Council, 75

Mexican character. *See* nationalism, Mexican

Roger Bartra is a professor at the Universidad Nacional Autónoma de Mexico. He is the author of many books, including *The Artificial Savage: Modern Myths of the Wild Man* (1997), *Wild Men in the Looking Glass: The Mythic Origins of European Otherness* (1994), *Oficio Mexicano* (Mexico, 1993), *The Imaginary Networks of Political Power* (1992), *La jaula de la melancolia: Identidad y metamorfosis del Mexicano* (Mexico, 1987; English edition, 1992), *La democracia ausente* (Mexico, 1986), and *El reto de la izquierda* (Mexico, 1982).

Library of Congress Cataloging-in-Publication Data
Bartra, Roger.
Blood, ink, and culture : miseries and splendors of the post-Mexican condition / by Roger Bartra ; translated by Mark Alan Healey.
Includes bibliographical references and index.
ISBN 0-8223-2908-5 (cloth : alk. paper)
ISBN 0-8223-2923-9 (pbk. : alk. paper)
1. Mexico—Civilization. 2. Nationalism—Mexico. 3. Right and left (Political science) 4. Mexico—Relations—United States. 5. United States—Relations—Mexico. I. Title.
F1210 .B23 2002   972—dc21   2001007925